FAMILY SECRETS

FAMILY SECRETS

Crossing the Colour Line

CATHERINE SLANEY

Foreword by Dr. Daniel G. Hill III

NATURAL HERITAGE BOOKS
TORONTO

Published by Natural Heritage / Natural History Inc.
P. O. Box 95, Station O, Toronto, Ontario M4A 2M8
www.naturalheritagebooks.com

Cover visuals, *clockwise from top left*: Julia Margaret Hubbard,
Donald Anderson, Marion Abbott (Young), Dr. A.R. Abbott and Gus Abbott.
Cover visuals are courtesy of the Abbott family.
All visuals not credited in the text are courtesy of the author.

Cover and text design by Blanche Hamill, Norton Hamill Design
Edited by Jane Gibson

Printed and bound in Canada by Hignell Printing Limted

The text in this book was set in a typeface named Granjon.

National Library of Canada Cataloguing in Publication

Slaney, Catherine, 1951–
Family secrets : crossing the colour line / Catherine Slaney.

Includes bibliographical references and index.
ISBN 1-896219-82-9

1. Abbott, Anderson Ruffin, 1832–1913. 2. Black Canadians—History.
3. Black Canadians—Biography. 4. Physicians—Canada—Biography.
5. Abbott family. 6. Slaney, Catherine, 1951–.
7. Racially mixed people—Canada—Biography. I. Title.

FC3097.9.B6Z6 2003   971'.00496'00922   C2002-904396-4
F1059.5.T689N458 2003

ONTARIO ARTS COUNCIL
CONSEIL DES ARTS DE L'ONTARIO

THE CANADA COUNCIL | LE CONSEIL DES ARTS
FOR THE ARTS | DU CANADA
SINCE 1957 | DEPUIS 1957

Natural Heritage / Natural History Inc. acknowledges the financial support of
the Canada Council for the Arts and the Ontario Arts Council for our publishing
program. We acknowledge the support of the Government of Ontario through
the Ontario Media Development Corporation's Ontario Book Initiative. We also
acknowledge the financial support of the Government of Canada through the
Book Publishing Industry Development Program (BPIDP) and
the Association for the Export of Canadian Books.

CONTENTS

ACKNOWLEDGEMENTS

THERE ARE MANY PEOPLE who supported this project over the last twelve years and I could never begin to thank them enough for their belief in the merits of this book.

A very special thank you is due to Dr. Daniel G. Hill and his son Lawrence Hill, who both took the time to walk me through the arduous research and documentation process of this project. Countless other librarians and archivists were most patient and helpful all over Canada and the United States, but I especially want to thank Christine Mosser of the Toronto Reference Library for her great assistance from the very beginning. There were many other archivists and historians who lent a hand or an ear over the years, such as Shannon and Bryan Prince from the Raleigh Township Centennial Museum, Gwen Robinson of the Heritage Room, WISH Centre in Chatham, and Dalyce Newby who authored a biography of Anderson Ruffin Abbott and uncovered so many minute details pertaining to his life.

James W. St. G. Walker, Professor of History at the University of Waterloo, has boldly supported this project from beginning to end, with his optimistic encouragement during the initial stages of my quest and with his final reading of the manuscript upon its completion. Rosemary Sadlier, President of the Ontario Black History Society and a talented author and historian in her own right, also stood by throughout the duration of my endeavour, and I thank you both for caring so much.

My entire family will treasure forever the special gift that Dinah Christie and Tom Kneebone gave us with the musical play *Doc Ruffin*, as they so artfully brought our forebears to life. It was a fantastic excuse for a long-overdue family reunion and we were all thoroughly entranced by the lure of the greasepaint. During that period we were immensely impressed with the many individuals from the Civil War Re-enactment groups that so graciously came forward to honour and commemorate the memory of Anderson Ruffin Abbott at the Toronto Textile Museum's exhibition of

Lincoln's shawl and Smile Theatre's gala performance of *Doc Ruffin*. Special thanks to Ray Huff for the printing of the poster of Anderson Abbott, to Paul Culliton for his valuable research on Canadians in the American Civil War and Oliver Claffey, Brian Brady and the Boys of Company 'C' for their musical accompaniments to these portentous events.

Of course, my love and eternal thanks must go to my husband, Ken, my children, David, Christine, Scott, Ashley and Tyler. To my parents, Marion and Howard Young and to all my relatives, especially to those who drew so much from personal memories like my uncle, Bob Abbott and my cousins, Gus Abbott and Wynn Stubenvoll. To all of my cousins, I can only say, thank you for taking me into your hearts. It has been a great privilege to find you and know you.

Finally, it goes without saying that *Family Secrets* would never have come to fruition if my editor Jane Gibson and her husband, publisher Barry Penhale, had not seen the promise of a remarkable story now within the covers of this book. Thank you for believing in my quest.

FOREWORD

IN 1978, MY WIFE Donna and I co-founded the Ontario Black History Society for a number of reasons. We wanted to highlight and celebrate the history of Blacks in Canada. We knew that there was a wealth of personal, professional and social histories involving Blacks in this country. And we knew that much of this history ran the risk of being lost to subsequent generations, because it was unwritten and unrecorded.

The African tradition of passing along family and community histories from generation to generation served Blacks in North America for hundreds of years. We were stolen out of Africa, shackled and transported in the most barbaric conditions to the New World, where we were enslaved and deprived of the faintest shreds of human rights for the better part of three centuries. Nevertheless, we have survived—and done so admirably. Despite the fact that throughout slavery we were legally barred from learning to read and write, we have managed to retain and celebrate our humanity and our history, including the sad but ultimately uplifting tale of survival against all odds.

How have Black people managed to preserve their own history? The oral tradition of storytelling, unique social institutions such as the Black church and Black advocacy organizations and artists—musicians, painters, writers, dancers and others—have all helped save our history to date. But how, as we move into a new millennium, are we to remember our histories, so that we never have to relive them? How are we to grow increasingly conscious of who we are, where we've come from, what struggles our ancestors have made—in short, our history in all its subtleties?

The challenge in documenting and analyzing Black history in Canada was revealed to me in the 1950s, as I began to research my University of Toronto Ph.D. thesis on Negroes in Toronto. For the most part, Black Canadian history did not exist, on paper, at that time. It is true that since then, Canadians have witnessed the growth of a body of academic and literary works devoted to the Black experience here. Nonetheless, there remain profound and revealing family and professional histories that disappear forever from sight—and from our collective consciousness—as those of us within the community age and die. It was to resist and vanquish the extinction of Black history that my wife Donna and I co-founded the Ontario Black History Society. One of our most pressing concerns was to document and tape-record oral histories among the elderly in the Black community. Indeed, oral history became a key *raison d'être* of the OBHS in its early years.

The need is no less urgent today and I commend Catherine Slaney for the many thousands of hours of work she has invested in researching and writing about the history of the Abbott family in Canada and the United States. In *Family Secrets*, Ms. Slaney walks the reader through her own discovery that her ancestors were Black. I find it deeply satisfying to know that my own interest in the Abbott family history helped encourage the reflection, research and family reunification inherent in this book.

Daniel G. Hill III, Ph.D.
Toronto, Ontario

INTRODUCTION

*To trace what you can recognize in yourself back to them; to find the
connection of spirit and heart you share with them, who are, after all,
your United Front.*[1]

FOR SEVERAL YEARS I have perused the evolution, the dissolution and
the resolution of my extended family over the course of the last two
centuries. As a white woman writing about my Black ancestors, I have
gradually pieced together a very remarkable story. In the year 1837,
when many American Blacks were suffering from the barbaric repercussions of slavery, unfair Black Codes and a lack of suffrage, some
Canadian Blacks[2] were becoming prominent, wealthy and considerably progressive in the upper echelons of society. It appeared as if they
had inexplicably begun to part the tides of discrimination and segregation, while they managed to attain a solid position within what was
to become an elite circle of "old-line Black families"[3] in Toronto. Unlike
many other Black communities[4] across Upper Canada,[5] most of the
members of this group were not destitute or poor and many of them
were self-employed.

By 1837 there were at least fifty families of refugees settled in Toronto,
many of whom were from Virginia, where formerly they had been
engaged primarily in service occupations (such as waiters, barbers, cooks
and house servants). Most had brought sufficient means to purchase
homes; later, after they had become more established, they built churches
and organized benevolent and fraternal organizations.[6] One of these
families was the Abbott family. Anderson Ruffin Abbott, reminiscing
about the social and political conditions that prevailed during these times,
cautions us to consider the circumstances:

It must be understood also that these people were not voluntary immigrants seeking a home of their choice among a people whose habits, temperament, social life were akin to their own and whose character had not been formed under the same molding influence. They did not come in response to a friendly invitation or under the patronage of fraternal societies of their own countrymen. They were not in quest of wealth or pelf (money). They were not given a choice in the matter. They were exiles, and forced to seek a refuge in some asylum where they might be permitted to live and enjoy unrestricted those rights and privileges which pertain to every human being. Happily, they had brought with them those habits of industry and frugality, those strong social instincts of southern hospitality, and by these means the members of the little colony were drawn closer together and were able to organize societies and build churches, in which all their social religious and political activity centered. Up to the year 1850, their associations with their fellow citizens were on the whole satisfactory. Some apprehension was felt at first that these involuntary immigrants would become dependent upon the community, but up to 1850 nothing of the kind had transpired to disturb the peace or arouse jealousy, suspicion or ill-will between the classes. A spirit of tolerance and amicable adjustment to the new conditions were apparent on all sides.[7]

As I proceeded with my investigation, I discovered that over a period of two generations a curious shift transpired within the Abbott clan when some of their offspring began to marry into the white race. While the early Town of York[8] accommodated a surge of new immigrants from the United States and Europe, some miscegenation,[9] or mixing of the races naturally occurred. Later, when the New World was plagued with social, economic and political upheavals, some light-skinned Blacks chose to "pass"[10] as white, when it best served their prospects or the interests of their families.

Although tales of family and individual accomplishments have been handed down through the generations, the fact that some of my antecedents were "Black" was imperceptibly deleted from the stories told to my own mother. Since so many of my "dark" cousins lived in the United States and most of the "light" ones lived in Canada, it was a simple task to discreetly omit the fact. My mother was the last child born to Gordon and Ann Abbott and, since her father was the youngest in his family, she found herself to be an entire generation younger than the rest of her first cousins. Thus, as the "baby" of the clan, it was easy for her parents to skim over the colour question and allow her to assume a "white" identity.

As the years ticked by, some of the "white" Canadian Abbott descendants gradually drifted away from their "Black" American cousins. Of course, this was likely due to a variety of factors that would include distance between branches of the family, age differences between the cousins and the inevitable generation gap. So as the "white" side gradually lost touch with the "Black" side, the once-strong family ties began to dissolve and all that remained to tell the story was a pile of dusty old papers stacked in the Toronto Archives.[11]

When I first became aware of my Black antecedents, I was very bewildered. I had heard much about my mother's father and how wonderful and gracious a man he had been and yet suddenly, I was faced with this ruse. Why had he hidden his racial ancestry from my mother? Had he acted alone in this endeavour or had the rest of the family gone along with him? Whatever the reasons, I wanted to believe that it stemmed from a profound love and consideration for his daughter, but I was curious as to why he had felt such a need to protect her. What kind of life had led my grandfather to think the way he did? Was it just the times—those years between 1920 and 1950 when the Depression and World War II were a part of his daily life? Had he sensed some terrible consequences if she were to become aware of such knowledge? If he had lived past 1950, would he have changed his mind and how might he have responded to the current public revelation?

As I pursued my investigation, nagging questions lingered in my mind. I was perplexed. I had always been taught that colour didn't matter and that everyone should be considered equal. Certainly growing up in Toronto in the 1950s,[12] as middle-class white children within mainstream society, my siblings and I had never been aware of any personal instances of racial discrimination. In fact, the question of race simply had never been an issue.[13] From what cruel indiscretions and ignorance had our privileged lifestyle shielded us?[14] After all those years, even though I am now aware of the circumstances my grandparents faced, I, for some unfathomable reason, found myself harbouring certain feelings of guilt, embarrassment, unworthiness and even shame. Avery Gordon, a sociologist, proposes the concept of a "haunting" as "recognition that a profound social phenomenon is persistently addressing itself to you, distracting and disturbing your daily life, often messing it up and leaving in its wake an uneasy feeling."[15] It was as if an irreversible transformation had taken root within my being, as I engaged in this effort to wrestle with both my inherited 'Blackness' and 'whiteness' and the questionable legitimacy of the privileges and assumptions I had previously taken for granted.

As I began to dig into the question of racial passing, I was confronted with a number of conflicting explanations. Some researchers proposed that it was practised as a form of individual resistance to racial discrimination; some suggested that it was merely a form of opportunism or selling out; some went further to describe it as an underground tactic that challenged oppression by subverting the line between the oppressor and the oppressed and, in this case, between those who were Black and those who were white.[16]

References found in early 20th century fictional literature[17] validate such attitudes during that period, and appear to indicate that those who participated in the act of passing did so surreptitiously with deliberate secrecy, often denying contact with their extended family members in the process. Reading these stories I am inclined to believe that my grandparents were forced to live out similar experiences. Today, the word "passing" continues to evoke some of those ambivalent feelings that I felt when I first heard about it, as I am beginning to realize that, in a sense, I am a product of this practice. Imber-Black notes that "skin color may underpin painful family secrets, including scapegoating family members whose skin color is most different from the rest, [and] 'passing for white,' while living a double life, or cutting oneself off totally from one's family."[18]

The entire revelation awakened in me a strong yearning to know more about my family down through the ages. I had not originally intended to search for my roots, but it became a necessary step in opening the shutters of ignorance and fear. I realized that the process of self-exploration in a racial and cultural context, through an historical lens, was an important step in my personal evolution. In conversations with other family members, we were able to review some of the experiences of our ancestors and subsequently reflect on the repercussions that presently affect our own lives and those of our children. According to Imber-Black, many family narratives comprise "tangled webs of relationships [and] an embeddedness in a wider culture that shaped their beliefs about secrecy and openness."[19]

With these considerations in mind, I set off on a journey that would eventually culminate in a family collaboration to "re-story" our collective history and resurrect our common racial and cultural heritage in a most profound way.

FAMILY SECRETS

In loving memory of Robert Abbott, Augustus Abbott,
Eleanore Osborne and Meredith Lewis, who had
to pass on before we were finished our quest

CHAPTER 1

ON A QUEST

We all touch upon each other's lives in ways we can't begin to imagine.[1]

IT WAS A BRIGHT, sunny Labour Day in 1975 and the whole family was helping my parents move from the city, into their new home—a century farm situated in the rolling hills of Erin township. The property had been neglected for many years and the two barns were consequently in much the same shape as they may well have been fifty years before. The large family room that served as a side entrance, mudroom and kitchen had previously housed a few sheep during the annual lambing seasons. The rough and tumble shed, precariously clinging to the sagging shoulders of the cooking section of the kitchen creaked and groaned with the addition of each item being placed in its temporary confinement, until a more suitable place could be found. Pick-up trucks, cars, trailers and moving vans were wedged carefully into convenient positions in the barnyard for the extrication of furniture and boxes. Cavorting children and a wide selection of dogs and cats joined the throng of close friends and welcoming new neighbours who dropped by throughout the day.

The event was to mark the beginning of a new life for my parents. Prior to this they had spent the last twenty-five years in the suburbs of Toronto, whilst paying off their mortgage and raising their five children. By now all but the youngest were off to university, or like myself, married and involved in other personal ventures. It was a good time to start over, and Mom and Dad had finally decided to trade in the city life for new horizons in the rural landscape.

Wynderin Farm was located on the top of a prominent hill, commonly referred to as the highest point in the neighbourhood, and had enjoyed several monikers over the last century. During the First World War, a

Wyderin Farm in the Township of Erin, Wellington County, 1976. Renovations were a perpetual occupation in the early years.

government tower was erected atop the hill to send marconigrams[2] across the country and thus it earned the name Tower Farm. Later, when sheep farmers took it over, according to what my dad was told, it was known as the Dummy Barbour Farm,[3] after the two brothers who had simultaneously suffered a childhood illness that left them both deaf and mute. One day, while up in the granary, Dad showed me the boards displaying the notes they had written to each other during their daily chores.

As their new life evolved, my dad, like all the local farmers, would trundle off to the weekly auction sales in his brand new pick-up truck every Saturday morning. Late in the afternoons, we would spot him wending his way up the laneway, his pick-up loaded to the gills with various odds and sods that were essential to any self-respecting farming hobbyist. Occasionally some sorry, four-legged creature would precariously crown the collection of treasures, having been passed over by the more astute and experienced buyers. Gradually an impressive selection of horses and ponies filled the two barns to capacity as he turned to the business of breeding horses. To complement this hobby, he gathered a fascinating array of cutters, sleighs, wagons and buggies, all at rock-bottom prices (my dad, being of full Scottish descent) and all in need of some kind of critical repair, along with numerous spare wheels, axles, harness pieces and other questionable items. However, in the initial throes of moving day, we had little inkling of the endless hours of labour, love and

4

hard-earned money that we would invest into this new venture.[4]

On that day, one more significant event occurred when my Uncle Bob (Abbott) arrived to help with the move. It seemed he had something on his mind, which he needed to discuss with my mother right away. With great trepidation and certain foreboding, he took her aside to reveal the deep, dark family secret. Now one might wonder why at that moment, he suddenly felt the need to shed such a burden, as he had known about the secret for most of his life. It was not until much later that we were able to fully appreciate his real sense of angst over the public disclosure. It turned out that Dr.

Dad (Howard Young) and his tractor, 1990.

Daniel G. Hill,[5] a well-known sociologist and authority on Canadian Blacks, while researching the history of some of the Black families in Ontario had discovered the "Abbott Collection," now housed in the Baldwin Room of the Toronto Reference Library. The time of atonement was nigh! Apparently their father was the son of Dr. Anderson Ruffin Abbott, who just happened to be the first Canadian Black doctor![6] This was the first my mother had heard about the "colour" of her relations and she was quite excited to share the news with my dad, despite my uncle's reticence. Bemused, my mother laughed and gently kidded him saying, "I think it's a little late for him to change his mind now!"

Although the rest of us were surprised upon hearing the news, we thought it interesting and simply accepted it as part of our heritage. My mother remembers feeling a little miffed at the time, wondering why her parents had been so secretive and had not entrusted her with the knowledge of the truth. However, it is difficult to explain why other people do certain things and, since she was only twenty years old when her father died, she believes he would have told her, had he lived longer.

Shortly after that fateful day in 1975, Dr. Hill and his wife Donna came to meet the family and speak about our ancestors. He informed us that, in 1963, Fred Hubbard, Anderson Abbott's son-in-law (and therefore my great-uncle), had deposited numerous volumes of handwritten

Tally-ho! From left to right: me, my dad, my sister Laura Young, and my son Scott Slaney, 1992.

notes and scrapbooks in the Baldwin Room at the Toronto Reference Library in the name of his late mother, Grace Hubbard (nee Abbott). These were papers left behind by Dr. Abbott. Dr. Hill strongly encouraged us to read them and explore our family history more thoroughly. Fascinating as this new revelation was, we did not pursue it at that time, for we were all very busy with young children, new homes, careers, university and, of course, the new horse farm. Any further genealogical search was simply not a priority. As a young mother in my twenties, I was fully occupied, raising a pack of foster children along with my own hefty brood of five and teaching full-time at a local community college. In my spare time, I ran a dog grooming business, trained horses and judged horse shows. Archival research just did not fit into my agenda.

It would take another fifteen years before there was a slight lull in my schedule and, on impulse, one December evening, in 1990, I met my sister at the Toronto Reference Library to survey some of that famous Abbott Collection. In the space of an hour before closing time, we poured over photographs, a diary, legal documents and volumes upon volumes of handwritten notes, whose pages had been carefully preserved on silk backing by the library archivists. In one box, we found hundreds of newspaper clippings of the late 19th and early 20th centuries, all scrupulously pasted into scrapbooks. The enormity of the prospect of reading this material was staggering and I left, ecstatic but overwhelmed. It was an amazing discovery and I found it incredible to think that all this had been sitting here for so many years and none of us had ever displayed the slightest interest.

Ultimately, I decided that the only way to discover what lay within those handwritten pages was to obtain copies that I could take home and study. I had to wonder how anyone could assess the value of the information in those papers when they were stashed away in such disarray. How wonderful, I thought, if I could compile a collection of his writings so that others could access them, even if they were only valuable to historians and researchers. After some investigation into the practicalities of using micro-film, photography or photocopying, the library undertook the task of photocopying the documents on acid-free paper and mailing them to my home where I could sit at my pleasure and sift through the pages.

When the first shipment finally arrived, I plunged with enthusiasm into the exercise of painstakingly transcribing every little note and variance. This proved to be an enormously long and tedious task. One of the main problems was that the handwriting was practically illegible, for often his notes were scribbled over previously used ledgers or bits of scrap paper. Sometimes the script was scrawled, criss-crossing on top of other notes or scrunched into the ragged corners of the pages, or squeezed along the narrowest of margins. All of this, coupled with the consequences of time on the papers and the inadequate images produced from the photocopying made the papers almost incomprehensible. To add to my problems, the vocabulary and turn of phrase, typical of the 19th century proved to be one of the toughest challenges.[7] Operating with an average competence of the English language, I often found myself sifting through an enormous selection of possible words before striking success. Accurately interpreting the letters and the gist of the phrases and then grammatically tying the words together involved no small feat. Night after night, sometimes until the wee hours of the morning, I would hunch over the keyboard, chipping away at my jigsaw puzzle.

As the stack of transcribed pages mounted, I became terribly disap-pointed, for they began to reveal only portions of speeches, editorials, journal entries and lectures. By this time, I had conceived the notion that perhaps I might be able to create a small biography of my great-grand-father, but the papers shed little more than the slightest hint of personal details about his family or his professional life as a doctor. Most of the writings focused on the general news of the day, whether local, national or international, and they tended to reflect a variety of issues regarding racial and social relations of the time. It was quite fascinating to read about such history from the perspective of a Black man of that era and it was even more curious to consider that it was coming from the heart and mind of my own great-grandfather. Nevertheless, I had to face it.

My mom, Marion Abbott, married my dad, Howard Young, on July 8, 1950, at St. Clement's Church in Toronto.

This was not the "big picture" I had been seeking for, in actuality, I had collected only a small portion of the material necessary for pulling the whole saga together.

My next approach involved a detailed analysis of the scrapbooks in which Dr. Abbott had carefully compiled newspaper clippings of his own articles, along with those of others, all pertaining to his multifaceted interests.[8] Still in good spirits, I valiantly attacked the new and even larger stack of printed pages as I surmised that with the assistance of a computer, I might efficiently transcribe and document a rather unique glimpse of Canadian history. But as the weeks and months dragged on, I became completely bogged down, typing incessantly about events and people that triggered little interest for me, as I thought many of the articles were exceedingly boring and tediously detailed. I began to find other things to do with those evenings. Even sleeping was more exciting than this! Finally, I gave up altogether, for it just seemed pointless. By this time, I wasn't even sure what to do with all this stuff anyway.

Yet I remained more than a little curious about the family and the real live people to be found. I decided that perhaps it would be better to probe the relatives. My mother had only a few remaining cousins left alive, as her mother and father and even one of her two brothers, Don, had died soon after she was married in 1950. Her brother, Bob, had already made it perfectly clear that he did not want to explore the story any further. He had chosen not to tell his own children and was quite appalled when they learned about their Black ancestry from a television documentary based on Dr. Hill's work. Before the show was even over, the television was clicked off and their enthusiastic inquiries were brusquely whisked aside, choking off any further discussion indefinitely. Although my uncle had been aware of his Black family ancestry, he had followed the example set by his own parents and had kept silent, even with his own children. Frankly, it would seem he had little to tell. This

A photograph of Marie Seon, Jay's mother, with her friend Etta Isobel Lightfoot (1889–1909) taken about 1905. Isobel is the daughter of Levi Lightfoot and Elizabeth Hannah Casey Lightfoot (sister to Mary Ann Casey Abbott, wife of Anderson Abbott).

absence of ancestral knowledge may also have resulted in hurt feelings and a blow to his pride, for it must have provoked in him a sense of exclusion. For many years afterwards, he would stiffly explain that his own parents had not discussed their racial history with their children when he was growing up and, although he had harboured his own suspicions, he had respected their wishes. "I never asked about it—it was just a sense I had."[9] During a conversation with my Uncle Bob and Auntie Jay, I discovered that my aunt's family, the Seons, had originated in Barbados and that, although her father was of white, Scottish stock, her mother was not.[10] Since both the Seons and the Abbotts had by this time gradually assimilated into the mainstream population of Toronto, they naturally expressed alarm when their children became romantically inclined and the prospect of "dark" grandchildren loomed in the forecast.[11] A great deal of family angst was endured by all, but the Second World War was underway and my uncle had already enlisted in the Armed Forces. Despite vehement objections on the part of her family, particularly her father, Peter Sorley, they went ahead with the wedding. Although her parents did not attend the ceremony, her father immediately afterwards revoked his objections and resolved to become a most loving grandfather to their eight children.

Uncle Bob (Abbott) and Auntie Jay Sorley on their wedding day in 1944. *Courtesy of the Abbott family.*

Indeed, I can attest to the fact that a dark complexion did manifest in most of the children, but the odd set of blue eyes and blonde hair showed up in some of them too. One of the darker ones did experience some discrimination in elementary school, when she was ostracized by a particular teacher, for she recalls spending much of her time in the corner for no apparent reason. When her parents inquired about the situation, the teacher intimated that she was not prepared to teach "nigger" children. After a number of secretive meetings and lots of fuss, the school discreetly handled the situation and no more was said about the incident.

My Auntie Jay explained how important it was that she kept her children so exceptionally well-dressed and groomed. I can remember how much fun it was when we spent time together, for my own mother went out of her way to ensure that I was groomed accordingly and, along with my five female cousins, I was outfitted in the most adorable dresses, coats and bonnet, with my hair always curled fastidiously into a variety of fashionable sausage rolls. Our shoes were always freshly polished and our white socks bleached and neatly rolled at our ankles. We were immaculate, because that's just the way it had to be. No one would ever be given a chance to comment on our dark complexions and questionable "race" when we so perfectly fit into the parameters of acceptability. When I think about it now, I realize that although my aunt had her own reasons, my mother was still completely unaware of the situation.

However, with respect to the research, at this stage I was not prepared to approach my aunt and uncle and reopen those old wounds. Instead I decided to try my luck with my mother's one remaining (or so I thought) American first cousin, Gus, who was the only son of her father's brother, Wilson.[12] My mother was more than a generation removed from Gus in age and thus I was confident that he would be old enough to be able to recall those years and fill in some of the missing blanks. Alas, it was not to be, for to my surprise I encountered a powerful reluctance on his part to

10

delve into the "family closet." His mother, Florence Nightingale,[13] had died when he was a young child and he had been raised by her parents who were white.[14] They and his father, had chosen to shelter him from any knowledge of his father's racial ancestry, and it was not until after his father's death that Gus learned about his Black heritage. Consequently, he considered such family business to be private and he refused to contribute to the research at that time. His response echoed my uncle's voice, reflecting the influence of his upbringing. "My Father was very evasive about his family and I soon learned it was wisest to ask very few questions."[15]

With my curiosity immensely piqued and my immediate sources of information depleted, I sought out a more distant cousin, Lorraine Hubbard, whose father Fred was Black and whose mother Irene was white.[16] She had assisted Dr. Hill when he was collecting research for his book and, in fact, they had co-founded the Ontario Black History Society together. With her distinctive wisdom and experience she was able to give me some good, solid counsel and encouragement, and subsequently provided me with a few more names and telephone numbers. Dr. Hill was also a great catalyst in terms of providing enthusiastic support for the project and he offered to put himself and his name at my disposal to help penetrate those walls of denial. Soon, as the quest evolved, I began

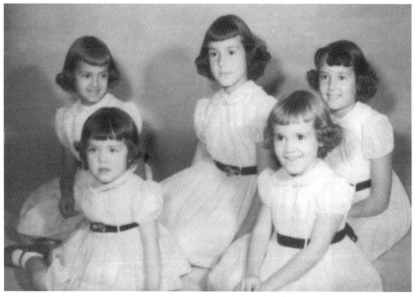

Bob and Jay's daughters in 1955. *Left to right, back row*: Linda, Barbara and Janice. *Front row*: Virginia and Patricia.

seeking out even more distant relatives, writing innumerable letters, contacting dozens of genealogical societies, sifting through archives and accumulating reams of background material. In the process of uncovering a little history, I had come to see and appreciate the life of my family ancestors from a new perspective. Thus, I went from simply uncovering a family secret to documenting a little bit of Canadian history.

When I began the project, there was no doubt in my mind that the family "secret" arose out of the desire of parents to protect their children from the insidious effects of racial discrimination during the time of the Depression and War—a time when many were more concerned about immediate survival than about fairness and equality. But such presumptions may have been premature. As I dug deeper, I began to realize that the effects of racism could be far more extensive than I had initially thought. Why had this prominent Black family chosen to hide behind the sanctity of their light skin? Why had they relinquished their roles as leaders and advocates for freedom and justice for all races and classes of people to become typical of the white mainstream? Had racism really been that prevalent and powerful in our "true north strong and free?" Was it still? Despite my trepidation, I had to go on.

Originally, this was going to be a story that would trace the life and times of my great-grandfather, Anderson Ruffin Abbott, and, it was hoped, in the process reveal some family roots. Over the years, it became increasingly apparent to me that the real story lay in the cover-up and gradual disclosure of our family secret. Maybe the Abbotts were not typical, but I suspect that there are many other mixed-race families that have harboured similar secrets, in the belief that it was the right thing to do. I was not prepared to settle for that premise, for when I considered the "big picture of life," I could not help but see that such secrets simply served to snatch away the very essence of our heritages.

CHAPTER 2

IN THE BEGINNING

It is one of the most conspicuous evils of caste and oppression, that they inevitably tend to make cowards and serviles of their victims, men ever ready to bend the knee to pride and power that thrift may follow fawning, willing to betray the cause of the many to serve the ends of the few; men who never hesitate to sell a friend when they think they can thereby purchase an enemy.[1]

MY IMPRESSIONS OF MY esteemed great-great-grandparents are somewhat obscure as they are based on sketchy records and documents that reveal only their bare statistics and a few of their accomplishments. My great-great-grandmother, Ellen Toyer Abbott, appears to have been a hard-working, but sweet gentle soul, who followed a strict adherence to Christian virtues and self-discipline. As a coloured woman, she was rather unique for the period in that she could read and write and, consequently, she would have appreciated the importance of securing a good education for her children. Sadly, very little written documentation that might provide us with a glimpse into Ellen's personal life has been discovered. Her obituary, recorded by her son Anderson, indicates that she maintained a very strong Christian faith, and after a year-long struggle with heart disease, went to her reward with great joy and anticipation, having "exemplified in her life the graces of womanhood in all her relations of wife, mother and friends, and all the virtue and piety which adorns the character of a devout follower of the meek and lowly Jesus."[2]

In contrast, we find more regarding the deeds of the men of those times. My great-great-grandfather, Wilson Ruffin Abbott, appears to have been a very ambitious man, for he energetically sought his fortune in every project that he undertook. He lived by the firm conviction that all men deserved a just reward for an honest day's work. He harboured high expectations of both himself and others, and his strong sense of integrity and righteousness must have made him an ideal role model for many

13

new immigrants, of any race, to Canada in the 1830s. Wilson arose out of a life that was plagued with unfairness, injustice, discrimination and cruelty and yet, in the end, he secured for himself and his family, a position of social prominence and significant wealth. He was the true embodiment of a pioneering entrepreneur.

Wilson Ruffin Abbott was the eldest of five children, born in Richmond, Virginia, on the 6th of November in 1801. Throughout his life, he claimed that his father was white and of Scottish-Irish stock and that his mother was a free, coloured woman. This is all that he has shared with us about them and, so far, any proof of his free birth has defied detection. Wilson never did produce manumission papers or any official record to prove that he was legally a free man, and this may have accounted for his abhorrence of the demands for such proof when the contentious Black Codes[3] were enforced.

However, my mother does recall hearing rumours from her parents that suggested that the Abbotts were descended from an "FFV" family, which implied that they were one of the "First Families of Virginia." Such families were considered the first white settlers in Virginia and I suppose it was meant as a reference to their "white" infusion and British roots![4] During the early 1800s, in the City of Richmond, Virginia, Wilson would have encountered a true cultural mosaic, for it was home to a vibrant population of people encompassing free Blacks, enslaved Blacks and new immigrants. The city's central location in the State of Virginia, on the banks of the James River, made it extremely vital as an economic trade centre.

In any case, Wilson adamantly maintained that he was born of free parents and vehemently resisted any attempt to label him a product of slavery. However, even if Wilson's parents had considered themselves married, their union would not have been legally sanctioned at the time. In fact, if a white man purchased the freedom of a slave and then married her, the law would have designated him as an unmarried slave owner and the children would have inherited their mother's status of slave. Even if Wilson's father was white, Wilson would not have been recognized as an American citizen and would have no voting privileges. However, his father might have granted him some consideration. We see that Wilson had enjoyed an apprenticeship as a carpenter, thus learning a skilled trade. Maybe he was emancipated by his master or indentured, eventually buying his own freedom.

Yet we must consider the possibility that he simply escaped from slavery and from then on, claimed to be free.[5] When he was fifteen years old, Wilson left Richmond to seek his fortune, and made his way to Alabama where he found employment in the hotel business in return for his room and board. As the perpetual adventurer, his free spirit eventually led him to a mariner's life and he settled into work as a steward on a Mississippi River steamship. One day, while traversing the dockside, a cord of wood fell on him and he suffered a serious neck injury. Ellen Toyer, a "coloured" woman from Baltimore, who had accompanied two young girls travelling from Boston, was permitted to nurse him back to health. She may have been a governess or chaperone or perhaps even a slave, however, what we do know about her suggests that she was well-read and possessed a strong Christian background. Although she may have been free at the time, the Abbott records subtly indicate that Wilson purchased her freedom

Wilson Ruffin Abbott (1801–1876) brought his family to Toronto in the mid-1830s. *Courtesy of the Abbott family.*

shortly after their meeting. In later years, he performed the same generous act for both of Ellen's sisters, Jane and Mary, as well as for many other indentured individuals who were able to repay such charity in a dignified manner by working off their "purchase price" through wages earned in honest employment.

Wilson Ruffin Abbott and Ellen Toyer were married in 1830 and settled down in Mobile, Alabama, where Wilson had already established himself over a period of years. There they operated a general provisions store that may well have catered to both a white and Black population. During this period, there was a large community of free Blacks living in the area,[6] along with a mixture of both white slave owners and Black slaves. Their community prospered and Wilson purchased a number of valuable properties, lodging his family in a lovely residence located on one of the rivers that flow into Mobile Bay.

As fate would have it, just a year later, the Nat Turner Insurrection in Virginia crushed any dreams of Southern comforts for the Black community, as the white population recoiled in horror and fear with the realization that this outbreak could occur in their community. Nat Turner, a bold and enraged fugitive slave, had incited a group of other slaves to participate in a gory uprising, murdering their masters, including more than fifty-five men, women and children. Many states reacted, compelled by their terrified citizens, by instituting or reinforcing the infamous Black Codes—a most insidious and contentious challenge to the question of human rights faced by early Americans, regardless of their race. These codes were legal edits that required free Negroes to post a monetary bond with two white men of good standing and to wear an armband at all times verifying that the bond had been posted.

Indeed, in Alabama, the Mobile Commercial Registry had already compelled all free people of colour, including the free Negroes and mulattos residing in that city to post a bond and carry identification. Not one to willingly submit to this type of discrimination, Wilson, in his 28th year, was forced, nevertheless, to comply with the ordinance on April 14th, 1830.[7] But this band-aid solution did not resolve the underlying social insecurities and some of Mobile's white residents devised their own plan of action. Wilson's store was targeted. The fact that Wilson had proven himself to be a successful businessman who earned more than enough to support his own family and, furthermore, to purchase properties, provided substantial grounds for resentment among the white population. Indeed, the whole idea of property ownership (and people ownership) is closely linked to relations of legitimization, authority and power. Elizabeth Fox-Genovese writing in 1988, notes that "the white community would be more likely to view property held by [Black] men...as a potential threat to white dominence."[8]

By this time, Wilson had lived in Mobile for nine years and had acquired a significant number of valuable properties through real estate transactions. He had freed numerous slaves by indenturing them; he had established a successful mercantile business and, for all intents and purposes, had ventured dangerously close to the social status of white folk. As fear of racial uprisings increased, certain radical white men stepped into the fray. Feelings of alarm and trepidation had probably been present throughout the community for some time and so when word spread that specific attacks would take place, Wilson's normally complacent friends and neighbours turned a blind eye. It was in this atmosphere, that a friend of Wilson's anonymously slipped a desperate warning to the family, thus allowing Wilson to expediently redeem his ready cash and dispense Ellen and their infant son safely on a New Orleans steamer. Meanwhile, Wilson remained behind to surreptitiously witness this anonymous informer partaking in the ransacking and burning of his store.

16

Many years later Wilson would attempt, with the aid of lawyers,[9] to reclaim some compensation for the loss of his property but to no avail.

No further record of the family could be found over the next three years. They did attempt to settle in New York City, but there they encountered tremendous racial turbulence, as thousands of Irish fleeing the potato famine in Ireland, competed for the limited jobs and opportunities with other new immigrants. It is amazing that the family survived those times as it could not have been easy to convince everyone that they were legitimately free and simply not runaway slaves. They must have relied heavily on their savings, as business ventures and employment opportunities would have been extremely scarce, especially if the family had no papers to substantiate their freedom during this period of so much unrest.

CHAPTER 3

THE CANADIAN
ALTERNATIVE

*Moreover, the presence of fugitive slaves in Canada assumed a symbolic
importance for the entire anti-slavery movement. Some anti-slavery
activists maintained that if Blacks prospered in Canada, it would show
that they were ready for freedom, while others claimed that if Blacks
failed, it would prove the pro-slavery contention that they could not
compete with whites and that liberation would be a mistake.[1]*

THE ABBOTTS CONTINUED TO seek a safe haven in which to raise
their family, develop a future and enjoy their cherished freedom. In 1835,
Wilson and Ellen relocated to Upper Canada and settled in the Town of
York, on the shores of Lake Ontario. No doubt they were encouraged
by the 1834 Proclamation Act, which abolished slavery within the colonies
of the British Empire. Up until that time, they must have been living
with a growing concern for the welfare and freedom of their children in
the United States. What better assurance of a more secure life than to
relocate to a British colony?

Yet slavery and indentured service had been an institution in Canada
since at least 1790, when early British and French settlers brought their
slaves with them.[2] A number of slaves were household servants for the
local officials in early York. In some instances, local indigenous people were
enslaved, called panis, but often they too engaged in the capture of slaves,
occasionally buying or kidnapping Black slaves from the Americans.

Colonel John Graves Simcoe, the first Lieutenant Governor of Upper
Canada strongly advocated the abolition of slavery and, in 1793, he was
instrumental in repealing earlier laws that allowed the legal importation of slaves. This same legislation also declared that the children of
Negro slaves would be considered free once they reached the age of

twenty-five years, and any offspring of these children would be born free. However, the legality and ultimate success of the Act, passed by the first parliament of the Province of Upper Canada in 1793, was dubious. In reality, up until 1841, the Judicial Committee of the Privy Council in England maintained that British colonial laws were deemed supreme and slavery was not officially abolished in the British colonies until 1834. Although the 1793 law did not free the slaves, it did prohibit the importation of any more and ensured the rapid extinction of slavery in Upper Canada.

The War of 1812 highlighted the animosity between Americans and Canadians. Accordingly, most Black Loyalists hoped that their commitment to the British side would reaffirm their affiliation and would remove them that much further from the prospect of American slavery, which they perceived as a calamity that might spread clear across the continent. Their concerns, however, would fester during the ensuing decades of American threats of invasion. The Fugitive Slave Laws[3] and Black Codes further served to aggravate these sentiments. Propitiously, the British grasped this opportunity to weaken the American position and offered freedom to any escaped slaves entering British territory, thereby laying the foundation for a future Canadian ideology of freedom and equality that would bear repeated challenges over the course of the next century.

By the 1830s hundreds of free Blacks, as well as escaping slaves, had already migrated to Canada, coming up through Detroit and Windsor to settle in the agricultural areas of Buxton, Dresden, Amherstburg and

Parliament Buildings, Front Street (Toronto) 1841. Artist William James Thomson (1858–1921), after a lithograph in Sir Richard H. Bonnycastle, *The Canadas in 1841*, 1841, vol. 1, frontispiece. *Toronto Public Library (TRL): T12032.*

Chatham. Others had entered through the Niagara Peninsula and established themselves in more urban centres such as Niagara Falls, St. Catharines, London, Bronte,[4] Dundas, Hamilton and Toronto. Sailing ships and freighters landed a stoic group of Black fugitives on the shores of Lake Huron,[5] who eventually established successful permanent colonies in Owen Sound, Collingwood and Priceville.[6]

Despite concern about the growing exodus of Blacks from the United States, the Canadian provinces did not submit to a Black Code. But as the Black population increased in certain pockets of what was to become Ontario, some white residents began to express their consternation. In 1843, when two Chatham Black militia companies mustered in response to the threat of an American invasion, the white residents forced them to disband.[7]

On March 6, 1834, the Town of York became the City of Toronto. Its population had, by then, mushroomed to a total of 9,300, including about 500 Blacks.[8] When the Abbotts arrived in 1835, the racial climate seemed favourable. In later years, Anderson Abbott asserted that, in his opinion, this state of affairs remained fairly consistent, even during his own lifetime:

> ...I do not claim that there is no race prejudice in Canada. In Toronto, at least it is innocuous. There are no indications of it in our churches, schools, societies, hotels and places of public resort. I can therefore confidently commend our city to Afro-American tourists as an eligible objective point where they can enjoy life without being subjected to all sorts of humiliating experiences.
>
> ...Afro-Americans in Toronto are just entitled to the respectful treatment they receive for several reasons. They are and always have been loyal, peaceful and law-abiding. By providence and industry they have secured homes and educated their children, who are employed as tradesmen, mechanics, laborers; some are in the service of government and a few are following professional pursuits, besides the usual quota of waiters, barbers, restaurant and boarding-house keepers. There is not a saloon in the city kept by an Afro-American. Our young men are not in the habit of frequenting barrooms or gambling dens; our young women are not indolent and empty-headed. In fact our young people are too much concerned with the serious affairs of life; too many opportunities within their reach, too many incentives to make use of them, to permit them to indulge in frivolities.[9]

As a light-skinned, Black family who were law-abiding, self-sufficient and behaving like respectable, temperate Christians, the Abbotts met with little social or economic opposition. In family, religious and social matters, they kept to their own kind, but in the commercial and political sectors they became admirable pioneers among all races of people. Wilson developed a real talent for numbers and, as a result of Ellen's diligent training, he became a proficient reader. An astute businessman, he initially installed his family in quarters above his tobacco shop located on King Street East, where the present-day Canada Life building now stands.[10] When the shop failed to be profitable, Wilson quickly turned his hand to real estate and, by the time of his death in 1875, he had accumulated a small fortune and seventy-five properties, including forty-two houses, five lots and a warehouse, located in the centres of Toronto, Buxton, Chatham, Hamilton and Owen Sound.[11] Unfortunately, long before the present-day descendants could realize the potential of this real estate, several economic depressions had taken their toll and the meagre proceeds from the sale of the properties had long since been dispersed.

A unique racial and political climate, different from that prevailing in the United States, was developing in Upper Canada. Most of the power and wealth still resided in the hands of those individuals appointed by the British Crown and affiliated with the Anglican Church. While early 19th century Upper Canada saw many different Reform movements, the Legislative Council, with its over-ruling power, managed to veto 58 constitutional bills introduced by the Legislative Assembly in 1828, thus pitting the powerful and wealthy Anglican upper class against the poor, common people. This was a time of extreme political strife as Robert Baldwin promoted his new philosophy of Responsible Government while William Lyon Mackenzie, a Reformer, actively vied for more radical political change. Although Canada was beginning to pull away from British authority, many Canadians were uncomfortable with what they perceived as Mackenzie's close alignment with the Americans. The new Black colonists certainly had no desire to endanger their freedom by becoming objects of an American conquest.

Having finally achieved financial security and personal freedom, Wilson Abbott had good reason to defend his new home and lifestyle. In 1837, he eagerly joined Captain Fuller's Company of Volunteers, to fend off William Lyon Mackenzie and his rebels.[12] Years later, as the political climate changed, Wilson would switch gears and enthusiastically rally support for the future Reform Party. However, as a recent immigrant, he joined his fellow coloured comrades and enlisted in the militia:

21

Nearly a thousand volunteers for service…Blacks were an important part of the British forces. In all, five companies of Black soldiers (still under white officers!) took part."[13]

One stormy night Wilson found himself summoned to Chippewa, on the Niagara River, to assist in an effort to drive the rebels from Navy Island. During this fray, his militia attacked the American supply boat, the *Caroline*, ultimately sending it over Niagara Falls. Many years later, while referring to his father in a speech, Anderson Abbott demonstrated his pride in the way Wilson stood up for his rights:

I am also proud of being a descendant of one of the patriots of 1837. My father has often narrated to me the stories of the stirring events that transpired during that troublous period. How he, with other hastily summoned volunteers, marched out of Toronto one morning and attacked the rebels at Montgomery's Tavern, defeated and dispersed them, taking many prisoners.[14]

The American Steam Packet Caroline *Descending the Great Falls at Niagara, December 29th, 1837.* A lithograph by the firm of J. Grieve after a sketch by W.R. Callington of Boston. The *Caroline* after having been set on fire by the British. In the distance is Navy Island. *Toronto Public Library (TRL): T15275.*

22

The records do not tell us much about Ellen Toyer. However, noted on the inside cover of her diary is an address for Walter Toyer[15] at 160 Fayette Street in Baltimore. As a married woman, far from her homeland, she must have suffered some difficult times, for although they had eight children, only one daughter and two sons survived to adulthood.[16] Their first son, who was given the name of Wilson, was born in the United States in 1832, but he appears to have died shortly after the family left Mobile. Another boy, Walter Ruffin, born in 1833, also in the United States, died after only three days. Their third child, Martha Elizabeth, appeared soon after the couple settled in Canada, but she too succumbed at the early age of nine

A portrait of Amelia Abbott, Wilson's sister, who married John Watkins. *Abbott Collection, Toronto Public Library (TRL): S-90.*

months. Finally, in 1837, Anderson Ruffin was born, and two years later was followed by another daughter, Mary Ellen. She lived for only one year.

In 1842, Amelia Etta[17] arrived, and survived to become a well-educated patron of the arts, living a rather privileged lifestyle. She married John Watkins, a "coloured" man who was a Toronto clerk by profession, possibly even a legal clerk. They had one son, John Lloyd Watkins, who died as a relatively young man at the age of 22 years. Their daughter Helene Amelia became an accomplished pianist and soprano soloist. Frequently, she would perform in churches and at public concerts. Helene Amelia proved to be a special source of inspiration for her Uncle Anderson, and it was he who gave the wedding speech at her marriage to Bruce Yancy of Minneapolis. On this occasion, he expressed a growing concern for the future of the Black families in Ontario. Observing that "the flower of our youth is leaving us yearly,"[18] he notes the threat of racial assimilation, urging young people to seek to strengthen their presence in the community lest they be gradually diluted into the masses. Since Helene married an American and then seemingly dropped out of sight, it would seem that his pleas went unheeded.

Finally, in 1844, Eliza Jane was born, but she too died at an early age. The handwritten list in Ellen's diary indicates the birth of two more children, Josephine Elizabeth Miller, born in 1842, and Wilson Ruffin Abbott Miller, who was born and died in 1843. These children, however, appear to belong to Ellen's sister, Mary, and her husband, Joseph G. Miller. The Abbotts may have fostered them for a period of time, a common practice in those early years of uncertainty.

A mystery surrounds the last son, William Henson Abbott as his name did not appear on the list recorded in Ellen's diary, although he may have been initially named something else, (such as Wilson or Walter). It is clear, however, that he did live to adulthood and was one of the three surviving children named in his father's will in 1875. William attended Victoria College, a Methodist Theological university, originally established as the Upper Canada Academy, in 1856. He became an ordained British Methodist Episcopal minister in 1875.[19] Yet it would appear that William was not immune to the occasional vindictive assault, for records show that in 1879, in response to a wrongful attack upon his character, he withdrew from the ministry after only four years.

The gravestone of Sarah Toyer, wife of Walter Toyer (Ellen's brother), located at the BME Church Cemetery in Buxton, Ontario. Adjacent is the grave marker for Walter, indicating that he was born in Maryland and came to Canada in 1852. He died in 1886.

The Mormon Church of Latter Day Saints records indicate that William and his wife, Louisa James, resided for a time in Atlantic City, New Jersey, although it has not been possible to locate any records of any children or direct descendants. Perhaps he became involved in the African Methodist Episcopal Church while living outside of Canada, since at the time of his father's death in 1875, William was living in Boston, Massachusetts. As one of three heirs, he inherited an equal third of Wilson's estate. City records show that he later returned to Toronto and continued to deal in the real estate market along with his siblings, Anderson and Amelia.

Although the Toyer family appears to have originated in the Caribbean, records suggest that Ellen's immediate family are likely have been slaves in Maryland. Jane, whose freedom was

24

secured by Wilson when she was twenty-one, eventually left the home of her sister and married Adolphus Judah,[20] a successful builder and architect in Toronto. As a staunch Conservative, Adolphus Judah became involved in a number of Black organizations including the British-American Anti-Slavery Society, the Provincial Union Association and the Elgin Association[21] in Buxton. In the 1860s, he served as treasurer and trustee of the Provincial Association for the Education and Elevation of the Colored People in Toronto.[22]

Alberta Judah Price of Chatham in 1991, now deceased.

When I dropped in to visit my cousin Alberta Judah Price, I discovered a tiny and cheerful lady with a smile that spread across her face in sheer delight at the mention of her father, Norman Judah, grandson of Adolphus. She proceeded to fill me in on a very complicated story that involved several marriages, deaths, moves and numerous descendants. Apparently Adolphus and Jane's son, Phillip Judah, lived in Chatham and married Caroline Francis Weaver, the only child of Henry Weaver, the first Black alderman in Chatham, and Rebecca Brown Weaver, owner of a profitable mercantile business in the old Duke Hotel. Apparently "Annie Rebecca" was an enterprising woman and, while her husband ran the store, she cooked meals and rented out the rooms upstairs to other coloured folk. As her great-granddaughter, Alberta told me, "At that time women were not given any consideration when it came to legal investments, but she was able to borrow $300. People said she would never be able to repay the money. But when a coloured travelling band came along and was denied a room in the local hotel, she put them up in her rooms and that's how she repaid her loan!"[23]

When Phillip's wife Caroline died, he married Henrietta Casey, a sister to Mary Ann Casey, Anderson Abbott's wife. Phillip and his second wife lived in Toronto and owned a fruit market, situated at the corner of Queen and Beverley streets. Although they never had any children of their own, they remained highly involved in the life of Phillip and Caroline's son, Norman. That connection would remain strong through the next generation.

Alberta had enjoyed some very special times with her Grandmother Henrietta, and her eyes lit up as she cast back into the past and described her summer holiday in Toronto. "Grandma really fixed me up. If I didn't look right, she'd just die. One day I went up to Toronto to attend a ball and I had a black velvet dress with a little stand-up collar to wear. I weighed only about ninety pounds and looked very small, so she spent all afternoon making a little bustle for me to wear with it."[24]

Gazing into her beaming face, I couldn't help but imagine how much joy and laughter that vigorous bundle of energy would have brought to the sedate lives of her grandparents every summer. Even now in her eighties she exuded an overwhelming sense of warmth and pleasure. By the end of the interview we had become fast friends. It was with great sadness that I received a letter from her niece several months later, informing me of Alberta's death. Although it was but a brief moment in her lifetime, I am ever so grateful for the opportunity to have met Alberta Judah Price—she was a very special person.

CHAPTER 4

EARLY BLACK CHURCHES IN TORONTO

On Sunday, in the church they became deacons, deaconess, the lead tenor or soprano in the choir, or superintendent of the Sunday School...they became somebody, all brothers and sisters, sons and daughters of God.[1]

THE CHURCH WAS TRADITIONALLY one of the oldest, most influential and stable institutions in the lives of the Black community, serving its spiritual needs and acting as a centre for social, recreational and educational activities. For Blacks and whites alike, the church served as a powerful institution that influenced both social and political thought and behaviour. Indeed, one's religious affiliation was recorded on the nominal census data. By 1840, most churches in Toronto boasted a policy of integration as Black and white congregations intermingled freely. However, as the congregations continued to grow, the Black members indicated a preference for a separate form of worship that many of them felt would better suit their more passionate sermons and songs and, subsequently, founded the First Baptist, Colored Wesleyan Methodist and the British Methodist Episcopal churches.[2]

In 1826, a handful of Black fugitives congregated on the shores of the Town of York to pray and thus formed the First Baptist Church congregation. Shortly afterwards, they met in St. George's Masonic Lodge, but by 1834 the congregation had increased to such an extent that they required their own building. Their first property was on Richmond Street and, in 1841, the First Baptist Church was erected at the corner of Queen and Victoria streets.[3]

The African Methodist Episcopal Church (Bethel) arose out of the Anglican denomination but broke its ties to the segregated white congregations of the American south, and was modified and re-established in

The British Methodist Episcopal (BME) Church, located on the west side of Chestnut Street between Armoury and Dundas, as it looked in June 1953. *Toronto Public Library (TRL), J.V. Salmon Collection: S1-960.*

Philadelphia by Richard Allen. In 1816, the church sent missionaries into Upper Canada and enjoyed a good deal of support, particularly after the institution of the Fugitive Slave Laws in 1850 and the consequent massive Black immigration from the United States. In 1854, the Canadian members instituted a Canadian Conference and renamed themselves the British Methodist Episcopal (BME) Church, acknowledging their British benefactors. By separating from the AME Church, they avoided the expectation of having to travel to the United States for annual confer-ences, with the accompanying risks of being taken by slave catchers once they crossed the border.

Ellen and her sisters were founding members of the British Methodist Episcopal Church, originally located on Chestnut Street in Toronto and, in 1840, Ellen became the first president of the women's outreach group known as the Queen Victoria Benevolent Society. It was composed of about forty members who provided care and support for immigrant Black women when they first arrived in Toronto, thus preventing them from becoming a burden to the community. One of their special funds covered funeral expenses of the poor.

Ellen was also active in the Home Mission Society, an international outreach committee of the BME Church that sponsored many mission-aries working in Central America. Their philosophy strongly promoted the concept that education was the best means to achieve social and economic elevation for all Blacks, both at home and around the world. One of the most remarkable and enduring traditions within the Black community was the Canadian Home Circle. This was a large organization, loosely composed of local church families that would meet regularly for an evening of music and entertainment over a light supper, offering a means of partaking in social and spiritual recreation. For the Abbotts and their friends, these pleasant occasions presented opportunities to meet other Black residents, even serving to knit some of the families together in marriage.

In 1828, the Colored Wesleyan Methodist Church[4] evolved out of the Methodist New Connexion, which represented both the True Wesleyans and the Primitive Wesleyans. The Church faced a critical dilemma when Black members of the congregation voiced resentment that their fellow white Wesleyan members continued to maintain an organizational attachment to "slave-holding congregations in the American South."[5] In 1853, some of the Black congregation amalgamated with a white congregation and this group then challenged the remaining Black congregation for entitlement to the church building. Although Wilson does not appear to have been particularly pious, he maintained that the Richmond Street church should be a place of worship specifically for the coloured people of Toronto. When their ownership was threatened by white secessionists, he arose, prepared to fight with both tongue and fist. The supportive coloured members were incensed by the affront and appointed Wilson to attend the church's Quarterly Conference, where he was prepared to present the terms of the trust deed for official inspection. However, when his opponents realized his motives, they took steps to have him barred from the meeting.

In response, Wilson and Reverend Charles Hatfield attempted to take over the building and Wilson engaged in a "disgraceful row," with the church pastor, Reverend Smallwood. As holder of the keys to the church, Reverend Smallwood refused to submit to these demands. Consequently, one Saturday morning Wilson and a colleague, Mr. Jennings, proceeded to remove the locks. When Smallwood arrived, he attempted to prevent the action and immediately a scuffle occurred. "He became so demonstrative that he shoved or pushed both Jennings and Abbott off the platform of the steps, whereupon Jennings threw Smallwood down and took possession of the keys. The doors were opened and the services in the chapel were resumed as usual.[6]

Afterwards there resulted a number of legal actions, including those of trespassing and assault, with Reverend Smallwood continuing "to annoy the congregation, by removing stealthily, at different times, the locks placed on the doors by the Trustees and placarding the same with No Trespassing Notices."[7]

To add fuel to the fire, Wilson was then faced with another crisis. Just as he was about to go to court to face his adversaries, he discovered that the deed for the church property, which he had held in his possession since 1838, was missing! Suspicions ran high, as it was thought that the opposing party had somehow obtained possession of the deed. But after a diligent search, the document, fortunately, was located in Mrs. Abbott's bottom dresser drawer:

After many weeks of hopeless search the valuable document was recovered, just in time to appear in court and secure a verdict, which confirmed the Colored Methodists of Toronto to be in undisputed possession of the property on Richmond Street.[8]

In 1855, the courts finally turned the building over to Reverend Smallwood who was able to reconcile the congregation, and he remained the pastor until his death in 1881. From 1855 to 1875, the chapel continued to serve the coloured community as a public school during the week and place of worship on Sundays. At the close of the American Civil War, the church membership dramatically decreased, as elderly members either passed away or returned to their original homes in the United States. In 1891, the Colored Wesleyan Methodist Church of Canada ceased to exist as a religious body and the Trustees sold the property, distributing the proceeds to the Black community. However long before then, Wilson appears to have given up the struggle and joined his wife at the British Methodist Episcopal Church in Toronto.

During my investigation, it became apparent that the religious affiliation of my Black relatives in both Canada and the United States was a very sensitive subject. The early family members had belonged to traditional Black churches such as the British Methodist Episcopal, Baptist and Colored Wesleyan, but today most of my American cousins are Episcopalian and my Canadian ones are Anglican. Seemingly, the chosen denomination reflects their social class and, when I visited cousins in Detroit, I could not help but notice their distinct pride in their affiliation to a "High" Episcopalian church.

CHAPTER 5

THE ELGIN SETTLEMENT

We came like terrapins—all we had on our backs. We took a house together when we came—the house was bare of furniture; there was nothing in it at all. We had neither money nor food... That is the way the principal part of our people came: poor, and destitute, and ignorant, their minds uncultivated, and so they are not fitted for business.[1]

AS THE RACIAL PRESSURES continued to increase south of the border, fugitive slaves as well as free Blacks streamed through the bottlenecks at both Windsor and Niagara Falls, seeking a haven from racial persecution. The collective effort of both fugitives and abolitionists provided a unique prospect for indigent immigrants who had never lived according to their own volition and had little opportunity to explore other means of sustenance. Consequently a number of Black settlements that epitomized "communal and self-help principles"[2] were established in southwestern Ontario, such as the Dawn Settlement at Dresden, the Refugee Home Society outside of Windsor and the Wilberforce Settlement in Middlesex County near London. In time, each of them faced a variety of internal and external challenges including allegations of financial mismanagement and increasing racial prejudice.

The new Elgin Settlement initiated a different tactic, for it was managed by a group of Black businessmen who formed the Elgin Association, along with a separate group of Elgin residents who, as a committee, ran the Buxton Mission, which concentrated its efforts on the business of religious and academic education. Thus, Wilson Abbott joined forces with other business associates and served as Treasurer for the Elgin Association. While land records do not clearly indicate that Wilson actually purchased any property in Buxton, he most certainly invested both time and money into the project.

Reverend William King (1812–1895) brought his own 14 slaves to the then newly created Elgin Settlement in 1849. There they would be free men and become self-sufficient members of a community. *Courtesy of Bryan Prince, Raleigh Township Centennial Museum.*

William King,[3] credited as the founder of the mission, was the youngest son of a farmer. Born in Ulster, Ireland, in 1812, he was raised as a staunch Roman Catholic, and was fortunate to have the opportunity to study under the classical tutelage of a Roman Catholic headmaster. However, in 1826, he attended a boy's academy near Coleraine, where he was profoundly affected by the Presbyterian headmaster, Reverend Mr. James Bryce. During his second year, King confirmed his new Protestant convictions by converting and joining the Presbyterian church, hoping one day to become a minister himself.

His first experience with the antislavery movement occurred while he was attending the University of Glasgow. It was the vehement protestations of the British common people, who opposed those who financially and politically benefited from trading with the American slaveowners, that eventually led to a series of reforms and finally culminated in the official abolition of slavery within the British Empire in 1834.

Like many of the Irish farmers, the King family faced the inevitable problem of a lack of land to pass on to future generations. Thus, in 1833, when the Kings harvested an excellent crop of potatoes, William was appointed to go to America to search out new opportunities for the family. William proved to have a sound sense of business and had no trouble selling his quantity of potatoes in Philadelphia for a good profit. The rest of the family immediately sold their holdings in Ireland and joined him in New York City, where they would wait for spring to then travel on to Canada where they hoped to establish their new homestead.

But William, impatient to learn what he could about the New World, chose to travel on to Northfield, Ohio, to join a friend who was teaching school. After one year, he moved on, hoping to find a suitable location for his family's farm. Eventually, with the help of his brother John, they chose an area in the Six Mile Woods in Ohio, where markets would be readily accessible via the new railroad lines and canals that extended between Lake Erie and the Mississippi River.

Once again, in 1834, William became a full-time farmer, honing his agricultural and labour skills by clearing land, tilling the soil and erecting a house, finally creating a family homestead. During this period he was exposed to the North American brand of racism for, although Ohio was considered a free state according to the Northwest Ordinance of 1787, its residents proved to be equally divided over the question of racial equality and, by 1804, had passed the first of the Ohio Black Laws. These laws were common throughout many of the southern and northern states and basically required all Blacks to produce legal documentation demonstrating their "free" status, and pay an annual fee of twelve and half cents to the authorities. In 1807, the cost of such bonds went up to $500. To add further insult, Blacks were not allowed to testify against a white person in court, nor could they serve in the militia or attend public schools.

In 1835, William left the family farm and resumed his teaching career in Alabama, with the hope of earning enough money to pay for tuition at Divinity school. No amount of student protesting, abolitionist lectures or scholarly philosophizing could have prepared William for the iniquities of slavery he encountered in the deep South. Fortunately, as William had excellent references and letters of introduction, he was able to secure a teaching position and, in time, build himself a reputation that elicited respect from even the most impertinent sons of passionate slave owners. His school flourished and, in time, he had to call upon his brother James to join him as an assistant.

In 1841, William met and married Mary Mourning Phares, a sister of one of his students and a daughter of one of the most prominent slave owners in the area. As husband to a woman who owned slaves, he would eventually inherit her slaves. He thus found himself in a dreadful dilemma, for he had developed a strong friendship with his students and their families, and yet he also cared deeply for the happiness and welfare of Mary's slaves, who had been with her for many years.

He wanted to set them free. One alternative would have been for him to send them off to Liberia, as others in his position had done. However, he felt this would only be condemning them to an even worse situation, for they were sure to remain what he considered "heathens" forever and would have had no preparation for African life. Furthermore, to simply turn them out in Louisiana, or send them to fend for themselves in a northern state like Ohio that condoned Black Codes, would be extremely cruel. Ultimately, he decided he would have to wait for a sign from God.

However, by 1843, William was disillusioned and disgusted with the prospects of his future. Now, with a wife and a newborn baby boy, Theophilus, he thought only of the bleakness of a life overshadowed by the hell of slavery. Even more distressing was the fact that he himself had succumbed to the need for reliable help and had purchased a trustworthy slave by the name of Talbert, who was subsequently placed in charge of all the domestic duties. This included overseeing the hiring and supervising both the Black and white employees. Despite the relief from domestic worries, William could not overcome the overwhelming guilt he suffered through being an owner of slaves.

Interestingly enough, his brother James had no such problems. He was more than happy working and living alongside slavery, as long as he did not become an owner himself. Eventually he too married a woman who possessed slaves. His solution was to promptly free them and send them to Liberia in Africa. He continued at the Academy, which William had founded, later becoming a mayor of Jackson and then governor of a lunatic asylum.

William was determined to continue his theological studies and made plans to return to Edinburgh, Scotland, but first he had to ensure the welfare and security of his family. Although quite unhappy about the whole business of slavery, he managed to become even more deeply entrenched in the mess, as he again purchased another man, Jacob, to assist Talbert with the labours involved in running the farm while he was away.

After seven years of interruption, he finally resumed his studies and entered the New College of the Free Church of Scotland in Edinburgh. Eventually, he sought to bring his wife and his son and newborn daughter over to join him, but sadly they took sick and died before this could be achieved.

Thus, by 1846, William King was once more alone. Upon the death of his wife and family, he inherited their slaves. This brought his human assets to a total of fourteen. To make matters worse, he found he could not legally set his own slaves free. By then the law required a special act of the Louisiana legislature to release the enslavement of any Negro under the age of thirty years, unless they actually saved the life of their master. In fact, even upon release, any freed slave could not leave the state unless the owner posted a one thousand-dollar bond and, by 1842, no slave could be liberated at all, even upon the request of the master. Thus, William's only recourse appeared to be to take them with him to a free state where he could then issue them manumission papers.

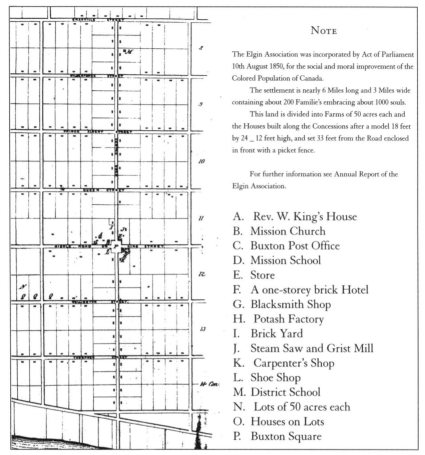

The Elgin Association was incorporated by Act of Parliament 10th August 1850, for the social and moral improvement of the Colored Population of Canada.

The settlement is nearly 6 Miles long and 3 Miles wide containing about 200 Familie's embracing about 1000 souls.

This land is divided into Farms of 50 acres each and the Houses built along the Concessions after a model 18 feet by 24 _ 12 feet high, and set 33 feet from the Road enclosed in front with a picket fence.

For further information see Annual Report of the Elgin Association.

A. Rev. W. King's House
B. Mission Church
C. Buxton Post Office
D. Mission School
E. Store
F. A one-storey brick Hotel
G. Blacksmith Shop
H. Potash Factory
I. Brick Yard
J. Steam Saw and Grist Mill
K. Carpenter's Shop
L. Shoe Shop
M. District School
N. Lots of 50 acres each
O. Houses on Lots
P. Buxton Square

"The Elgin Association was incorporated by Act of Parliament on 10th August, 1850, for the social and moral improvement of the Colored Population of Canada. The settlement is nearly 6 miles long and 3 miles wide, containing about 200 Families embracing 1000 souls." *Courtesy of the Raleigh Centennial Museum.*

One would presume that such hardship and loss would drive a good man against the will of God but, to the contrary, William seemed to see these events as a precursor to the path he was meant to follow. He wrote, "I could now see the dispensation which appeared so dark and mysterious to me at the time I lost my whole family, that it was preparing the way for me to manumit the slaves that were coming to me by inheritance."[4]

In 1846, at the age of 34, William King was appointed to Canada by the Colonial Committee of the Free Church of Scotland, under the direction of the Presbytery of Toronto, and, in 1848, he proposed a plan to the

Presbyterian Synod to establish his slaves and other fugitives on land in Canada. It was recommended that King seek the advice of a committee which included King and six of the other ministers, as well as several elders of the Presbyterian Church of Canada, and a group of prominent members of the clergy community, including Dr. Robert Burns, Moderator of the Presbyterian Assembly, Dr. Michael Willis, Principal of Knox College, and Reverend Alexander Gale of Knox Church. Other members of the committee, drawn from the business and political fields, were John Redpath, a wealthy trade and shipping merchant from Montreal, Judge Skeffington Connor, James Scott Howard, Nathan Gatchell and James Gibb of Quebec City.[5]

William King was definitely well-equipped to seek out appropriate lands and direct the kind of work that needed to be done to prepare the land. He had selected a choice Clergy Reserve Tract of land in the Township of Raleigh, just outside of Chatham in North Buxton, Canada West. It proved to be a propitious location for future businesses and enterprises as it was located near the shores of Lake Erie, directly in line with the expanding railroads and local waterways. The Great Western Railway was just in the throes of construction and there was no shortage of work for the new settlers. It was in this favourable and insulated environment, that King brought his own former fourteen slaves and several other Black fugitives to settle where they could learn to fend for themselves and become regular members of the larger community.

> I told them that in two weeks I was going to leave for Canada and take them with me. The journey was long and I wished them to be ready by that time. They seemed not to understand what was meant by going to Canada. Most of them thought it was some new plantation I had purchased and was going to take them to it."[6]

When he told them that he would give them their freedom and settle them on their own farms where they could learn to support themselves:

> …the good news seemed to have little effect on them. They had come to consider that slavery was their normal condition. They did not know what freedom meant. They thought that to be free was to be like their master, to go idle and have a good time.[7]

Over the next two months stockholders gathered to form the Elgin Association. Reverend King was named the Managing Director with Archibald

McKellar as its chairman. The first challenge to face was the local volatile political and social climate, as the Chatham area was not ready to accept its own Black community despite the relative success of other Black villages like the Dawn Settlement[8] near Dresden, and even larger Black communities in towns like Amherstburg and Windsor. Yet, Canada West was so close to the American border that the anti-Negro attitudes, which had caused riots in most of the Northern cities, crossed the border with every American newspaper and visitor. Violent incidents had occurred as early as 1826, and the social ostracism of the Blacks was as severe in some of the Canadian communities in southwestern Ontario as it was in America. King wrote in 1849, that "…the prejudice which exists against the Coloured Man in the Northern States has followed him even into this free country and operates against his moral improvement."[9] However, Canada did offer certain amenities: it had already passed anti-slavery legislation, it had proven reluctant to return fugitive slaves to the United States and it had developed both in theory and practice a "…color-blind political and legal system,"[10] even if not yet a social one.

During that period, the settlement provided ample security with its collective arrangement and numbers. Its vulnerable residents lived in fear of American "bounty hunters"[11] who often were sneaking over the border, eager to snatch an unsuspecting fugitive to be returned to a slave master in the United States. Under the auspices of the Fugitive Slave Act of 1850, slave owners or agents were legally allowed to seize ex-slaves and return them to their master's bondage. Consequently, all Negroes above and below the border lived with this threatening reality. Many agents were truly no more than bounty hunters, and made little differentiation between freed or escaped victims.

King hoped that the settlers would strengthen their self-sufficiency, without any help from charity or handouts and thus prove themselves to be successful models for future Black fugitives. He set out a number of stipulations: each male resident had to purchase a parcel of land, clear it and erect a house, built to specific standards, which could not be sold to a white person for a minimum of ten years; everyone was to grow their own crops and raise their own livestock to feed and clothe their families. They could pay back their debts by earning income from the sale of their crops or from outside employment, which was readily available for those skilled individuals who had learned such trades as iron working and stone masonry on the plantations. Some brought with them extensive experience from their days of navigating the Ohio and the Mississippi rivers, and were able to pole barges up and down the local Thames River.

Hardwood lumber and potash, used in the production of bricks, proved to be the most profitable resources, and subsequently a sawmill was erected on the settlement, providing even more jobs.

In 1851, the Abbott family was entrenched in the development of the Elgin Settlement. Regrettably, very few anecdotes have been recorded concerning the Abbotts' experiences during these exciting years in Buxton. In his memoirs, Anderson recalled the time he attended the Buxton Mission School. When not immersed in his studie, he was put on duty as the security guard for the general store:

> The Indians visited the settlement every winter on the way to their hunting grounds. They frequently stopped at the store to purchase supplies at which time we had to keep a sharp lookout because the squaws had no scruples about purloining anything that they could conveniently secret about their clothing. They generally carried the articles out and stowed them away under the blankets covering their ponies.[12]

Since Wilson was not a fugitive slave, he did not need to fulfill the same requirements as the other settlers and, instead, his contribution was made in the form of service. He aligned himself with Henry K. Thomas from Buffalo, a freed slave who had moved to Buxton in 1851 to avoid the dangers imposed by the American Fugitive Slave Act. Together the pair solicited funds from other wealthy Blacks in Toronto and Buffalo for the purpose of financing the sawmill. Other businesses also sprouted up and, in 1852, a general store enterprise, known as the Canada and Mercantile Company, with $4,000 in capital, became a reality in Wilson Abbott's capable hands as the Treasurer. Their constitution stated:

> We unite ourselves together in order to establish a sawmill, a grist mill and a good country store, believing that this is the only way for us to become independent and respectable in business transactions.[13]

The association successfully resisted the opposition to the settlement by local white residents. At the time, at least a third of the population of Kent County was Black and racial violence was cited in Chatham as early as 1826, when the white community opposed the integration of Black settlers. Benjamin Drew conducted a study of the experiences of fugitive slaves who had settled in Canada and he noted in one of his interviews the feelings of some of the white inhabitants:

School Section no. 13 Raleigh, North Buxton (1861–1968). This school defied the tradition of separate education and drew both Black and white students from the surrounding area. *Courtesy of Bryan Prince, Raleigh Township Centennial Museum.*

> The truth of the matter seems to be that, as long as the colored people form a very small proportion of the population, and are dependent, they receive protection and favours; but when they increase, and compete with the labouring class for a living, and especially when they begin to aspire to social equalities, they cease to be "interesting Negroes" and become "Niggers."[14]

When the Buxton Mission School was established, Wilson and Ellen Abbott enrolled their children with the expectation that it would offer them a good classical education. Traditionally teachers had been hired solely on the strength of oral examinations that were administered by school trustees, some of whom could barely read and write their own names. The Buxton School hired John Rennie, a divinity student who had graduated from Knox College in Toronto. The school was originally established for the education of the Black children from the settlement, but within a short time it had earned such a superior reputation for its quality of instruction that, despite the segregated policy of the public school in Chatham at the time, white parents eagerly sought a placement for their own children. At this time, it was common for public schools to be segregated, but in 1850 a Separate School Act provided the legal option to integrate schools, thereby eliminating the practice of segregating children based on their race and religion.[15] Within two years Buxton boasted the first racially integrated public school in North America with an enrolment of 250 pupils from across the county. By 1856, the Buxton School was able to turn out seven students qualified for Knox College.

> No where else in Canada, the United States or in England had the anti-slavery societies, the interested churches or the Quakers, established Negro schools to prepare pupils for the standard classical education."[16]

King believed that offering only vocational training to the Negro merely perpetuated the assumption that they would remain forever, "drawers of water" and "hewers of wood." It was the beginning of a difficult struggle, for many Blacks in the United States had been discouraged from seeking higher education that was normally reserved for the white race. Rather, they were encouraged to be content to be excellent labourers. The famous Booker T. Washington (1856–1915), the first Principal of the Tuskegee Institute in Alabama,[17] himself a teacher and former slave from Virginia, disregarded his own higher education when he professed that "there is as much dignity in tilling a field as in writing a poem."[18] Influenced by social and political pressures during the tumultuous period of Reconstruction in the South, Washington promoted the belief that Negro interests could be best served through the acquisition of an industrial education. However, W.E.B. DuBois vociferously opposed this philosophy, with the words, "we shall hardly induce Black men to believe that if their stomachs be full, it matters little about their brains."[19] King applied this latter philosophy in his educative endeavours for the adults in his community and opened a night school "It was interesting to see men and women from twenty-five to thirty years of age and some even older who had never tried to learn before, begin with their ABCs..."[20] The accomplishment did much to cultivate the advancement and intellectual education of the Black community and provided them with a welcome source of self-esteem.

King then joined Dr. Thomas Cross in successfully establishing the first collegiate institute when the Chatham Collegiate Institute opened its original doors in the old military barracks in Tecumseh Park.

In February 1850, a committee of the Elgin Association, composed of Wilson Abbott, Adolphus Judah and David Hollin, appealed to their local MP, Malcolm Cameron, the prevailing leader of the growing anti-Tory Reform Party (Grits). As their association had not been granted incorporated status, the committee submitted the following request:

We the undersigned committee, have been appointed by a number of colored stockholders of the Elgin Association to ask your views on a subject that chiefly concerns our civil rights. Your long residence in the western part of the province, where most of our people are settled, makes you well acquainted with our condition and the many disadvantages under which we labor, in consequence of an unjust prejudice, which deprives our children, in a great measure, of the use of the common schools and excludes us from participating in the rights and privileges guaranteed to us by law. This prejudice has lately assumed a hostile form, in an address published at Chatham in August last, the object of which is to prevent us from settling where we please and if carried into effect, would eventually drive us from the province. As you represent the county where the Elgin Association has purchased land for colored settlers they wish to know if you are in favor of our settling there, or any other place that we may select in the province and if you will aid us in obtaining the rights and privileges we are entitled to by law. An answer at your earliest convenience will oblige the committee.[21]

Cameron welcomed their message and replied that the Reform Party intended to uphold the civil liberties of all Canadian citizens. This was considered a most valuable weapon in the Black settlers' uphill battle towards equal recognition within both the local community and the country as a whole. Prepared to support their request, Cameron responded as follows:

In reply to your letter of this day I beg leave to say that the evil you complain of, relative to your position in common schools, was fully provided for in the new school bill which I had the honor to conduct through Parliament last session and which comes into operation in January next.

I regretted very much the tone and sentiments of the resolution and address to which you allude as having been passed at Chatham in August last and I feel quite sure they are not the sentiments of the great mass of the County of Kent. For my own part I have ever advocated the perfect equality of all mankind and the right to all every civil and religious privilege without regard to creed or color. And under the constitution we now enjoy all men are really 'free and equal' and none can deny to the African anything granted to the Scotchmen and Irishmen or the Saxon; they have the right to purchase where they please and settle in groups or singly as they like; and wherever they

The British Methodist Episcopal Church in Buxton, Ontario, as it looks today.

are, they will find me ready to defend and maintain the principles of civil and religious freedom to all, as the principle I hold most dear to myself and most sacred to my country.[22]

These efforts served to establish a commitment from the Reform Party to any opposition instigated by their Tory foe, Edwin Larwill, when the Elgin Settlement charter came up for legislation.

The Abbott family intermittently lived in Buxton for about three years, during which time it appears that their main purpose was more one of contributing rather than receiving, as Wilson proved himself highly interested in promoting the achievements and abilities of the Black community. Their son Anderson was enrolled in William King's first class, along with six other young "intellectuals," including Jerome Riley and James Rapier. "No single community in either the United States or Canada contributed so much to the emancipated Negroes as the sons and daughters of Buxton."[23]

In 1894, despite growing racial unrest throughout the rest of the province, Dr. Anderson Abbott penned the following memoir describing life in Buxton:

A large number of white settlers now occupy the land, but that makes no difference. The two classes work together on each other's farms, go to the same churches, their children attend the same schools, the teachers are white and colored, and the pupils fraternize without any friction whatever. The teacher of the North Buxton School, Alfred

The grave site of William King located in the Maple Leaf Cemetery
in Chatham, Ontario.

Shadd, is an Afro-Canadian. He holds a second-class certificate from
the normal school, Toronto, and has been a successful teacher for a
number of years. One-third of his pupils are white. There are three
hundred pupils in the schools. The various offices of the municipality,
such as councilors, school trustees, pathmasters, constables and justices
of the peace are fairly distributed among both classes. The colored
farmers who now occupy the land are of the best class. Very few of
them had any means at first; their only resources were their courage
and determination to succeed. When they appear in the Chatham
market side by side with their white neighbors, as vendors, there is
nothing to distinguish but their colour.[24]

When the Abbotts left the Elgin Settlement and returned to Toronto,
their children continued their formal education in integrated schools. A
decade after the settlement had successfully been established, Elgin
residents began to filter into the white population, both as individuals
and in small groups. Although a small, Black community remains in the
village of Buxton to this day, many of the original settlers and supporters
of the settlement have long since drifted away. Over the years, as their
need for refuge gradually dissipated, many of the American fugitives
either returned to their homes in the United States or quietly integrated
into the local population of their Canadian communities.

CHAPTER 6

BACK IN TORONTO

It was the best of times, it was the worst of times, it was the age of wisdom, it was the age of foolishness, it was the epoch of belief, it was the epoch of incredulity, it was the season of Light, it was the season of Darkness, it was the spring of hope, it was the winter of despair, we had everything before us, we were all going direct to Heaven, we were all going direct the other way—in short, the period was so far like the present period.[1]

IN THE MID-1800S, grand visions of freedom and a life without pain and humiliation were often shattered in the struggle for dignity and equality, even in Toronto's rapidly growing Black community. Large Canadian urban centres like Toronto and Hamilton were able to absorb all sorts of new immigrants because of their prosperous economies and the building trades were able to employ many Blacks and Irish semi-skilled labourers. Fugitive slaves were increasingly seeking sanctuary in Canada, coming north via the Underground Railroad, the clandestine means of transportation offering a system of safe houses and secret routes. Although the beginnings of systematic prejudice had begun to smoulder, more immediate crises, like the threat of American invasions, the repercussions of the Fugitive Slave Acts, the impetus of the Irish immigration and the impending American Civil War were of foremost concern to Canadians.

The "Abbott Collection" identifies two separate early initiatives to establish abolitionist groups in Toronto—one in 1833 and the other in 1840. Seven years later, in 1847, Wilson joined forty-five others in relaying their appreciation to the Attorney General of Canada East, the Honourable W. Badgely, for his support of an American abolitionist, Samuel Young:

We the undersigned coloured citizens of Toronto and vicinity, loyal and dutiful subjects of Her Majesty's just and powerful government, take pleasure in availing ourselves of this opportunity to express to you our sincere thanks for the courteous and Christian-like manner in which you have recently received our kind and worthy friend, the Rev. Samuel Young of New York, who is known to have been deeply interested in the protection and welfare of our afflicted brethren in the U.S.A. especially as evinced in the case of the innocent and grossly injured and persecuted man who has lately found his way to this asylum, from the midst of republican despotism and slavery.

Signed

W.R. Abbott & 45 others[2]

In 1840, when the Abbotts resided at the corner of Terauley and Albert streets,[3] Wilson took his causes and ambitious spirit to the municipal podium and won, by a margin of 40 votes, a seat on the Toronto Council as the representative of St. Patrick's Ward.[4] The *Toronto Directory* of 1846-47 indicated that at least 81 coloured men lived in that area, working as labourers, skilled tradesmen, business proprietors and ministers.[5] By 1859, Wilson was serving as a member of the Reform Central Committee, and stood prepared to challenge any issue that struck him as illegal, unjust or tasteless. For example, one of the most aggravating situations for the people of colour in the City of Toronto involved the performances of some American travelling theatrical groups that sometimes

The site of present-day Toronto City Hall once held the homestead of Wilson Abbott and his family.

cast Blacks as buffoons and scapegoats in "nigger minstrel" acts. Usually white performers in "black face" took these roles, but the effect was still exceedingly demeaning. Wilson Abbott submitted a petition with eighty-five signatures to the Toronto City Council in 1840:

> The subscriber of this humble petition represented to his worship, the Mayor and the corporation that they have remarked with sorrow that the American Actors, who have from time to time visited this city, invariably select for performance plays and characters which, by ridicule and holding up to contempt the colored population, cause them much heart-burning and lead occasionally to violence. They therefore respectfully entreat his worship and all those to whom the right pertains, to forbid in future the performance of plays likely to produce a breach of the public peace.[6]

Unfortunately, Council did not have the authority to censor such performances, but it did institute a requirement that the troupes had to procure a license. In 1843, Wilson noted that Kingston, the newly appointed capital city of Canada, had passed a bylaw that banned any racially offensive performances. So, with another petition in his pocket, he appealed to Mayor Henry Sherwood to enact a similar bylaw that would empower Council's "right to licence or refuse requests for the exhibition of shows" and "to make such laws as will tend to the peace, welfare and safety, of the inhabitants of this City."[7] Mayor Sherwood agreed to grant the offending travelling circus a license only "on the condition of their not singing Negro songs—this to save the feelings of the gentlemen of color."[8]

During the 1850s, Black voters began to lend their support to Reform candidates. As the social and political climate shifted, Reform candidates were quick to realize the potential of the Black vote and strove to address their concerns. In 1850, a second Fugitive Slave Law had been passed in the United State, which reiterated and strengthened the original terms, preventing any fugitives from testifying on their own behalf and penalizing any official that did not uphold the law. As a result, Black fugitives began entering Canada at an even faster rate than before. White communities in northern states expressed concern about the increasing Black populations within their midst. It was during this period that the largest wave of Black refugees to date immigrated to Toronto, swelling the Black population to about one thousand.[9]

On February 26, 1851, the Anti-Slavery Society of Canada was established in Toronto. Wilson joined the mayor and his strong ally, George

Brown,[10] to support an effort on the part of other Toronto Blacks to establish an official policy that would provide refuge for these fugitives. Although the organization was mainly composed of white sympathizers, three of the fourteen vice-presidents were Black, including Wilson Abbott and Samuel Ringgold Ward, the well-known African-American anti-slavery activist. Dr. Michael Willis, Principal of Knox College, was nominated as the president. During its first year of existence, members chose to concentrate on relief activities such as raising funds to feed and clothe of indigent Blacks and sponsor motivating public speakers such as Frederick Douglass. Ultimately, the society was seen as merely a local factor and no Canadian political party ever made race a part of its platform.

Urban life was not always blissful and, consequently, Vigilance Committees were formed in cities like Toronto, Chatham, Windsor and London

Samuel Ringgold Ward, originally from Maryland, toured the province giving speeches on anti-slavery. He was one of the first Black students at Knox College. From Samuel Ringgold Ward, *Autobiography of a Fugitive Negro: His Anti-Slavery Labors in the United States, Canada and England* (London, U.K.: John Snow, 1855) Frontispiece. *Toronto Public Library, Special Collections, Genealogy & Maps Centre.*

where there was a perception that "Negro vagabonds" would prey on fugitives for the purpose of financial gain. On August 9, 1854, Wilson joined forces with Thomas F. Cary,[11] and led a group of thirty-five others to create the Provincial Union Association in Toronto,[12] an organization that sought to encourage regular school attendance and discourage any further fragmentation within the Black churches. Its members tried to persuade new Black refugees to disperse throughout the province in order to hasten racial integration, deplete the potential for racial conflict and allay prejudice by decreasing the concentration of Black populations in any one area.

That same year, Wilson chaired a meeting of Toronto Blacks, to address the objectives of the Colonial Church and School Society, an English-based missionary association that wanted to establish an all-Black school in Toronto. The Toronto Black community was against the idea, for it

The original Trinity College was erected in Bellwoods Park on Queen Street West in 1852. New land was purchased after the First World War was over, and today's Trinity College established. The old site was sold and the buildings demolished.

believed that such an institution would only serve to reinforce an image of Blacks as poor, helpless, begging indigents who were dependent on charity. The general consensus of the group was that Toronto schools should not make any distinction based on race and thus segregated schools in Toronto were unnecessary.

Wilson's son, Anderson, later joined Alfred M. Lafferty and Samuel Ringgold Ward, who as an infant had escaped slavery in Maryland with his parents, at the Toronto Academy of Knox College, where they became its first three Black students. Alfred Lafferty, also Toronto-born and a Buxton School graduate, became a teacher in Richmond Hill and then a Headmaster at Guelph High School. From 1875 to 1882, while living in Chatham, he served as the principal of the Wilberforce Educational Institute. Samuel Ringgold Ward became a Presbyterian minister and continued to actively promote self-sufficiency and education among the Black refugees and, in 1853, he founded the highly reputed Black newspaper, the *Provincial Freeman*.[13]

Before the Civil War, the town of Oberlin, Ohio, had served as a main Underground Railroad terminus. In 1856, Anderson Abbott enrolled in the Preparatory Department of Oberlin College. Interestingly, Anderson makes no mention of any concern regarding either the Black Codes or the Fugitive Slave Act. The college reiterated its strong moral philosophy by ardently supporting abolitionist efforts and opened its doors to a modest intake of Black students in 1835. Although Oberlin served as a "conservative oasis" from the world at large for many middle-class students, it held the distinct honour of being the first co-educational college, and consequently its programs provoked a certain degree of scepticism. Students explored philosophies pertaining to Christian Perfectionism, family relationships, the communal sharing of property, the abolition of slavery and even women's rights.[14] Although manual labour was originally an important component of the curriculum, students tended to spend more time philosophizing than labouring in the fields. This aspect of the school's mandate was later modified into a physical education program, which again proved to be one of the first of its kind.

It was in such an innovative and stimulating atmosphere, that Anderson Abbott completed his secondary education. Soaked with a generous share of philosophy, religion, art, music, literature and other intellectual studies, he would continue to pursue these interests throughout the rest of his life. The opportunity to be able to consider possible alternative roles and rights or prospects for children, women and minority races would have exhilarated such a mind. Amidst such political and social activists, he would become adept at strategies that he later used to buffet the most vicious blows from his future adversaries.

In 1857, Abbott enrolled in University College in Toronto to study Chemistry and in the following year entered the King's College Medical School, which was affiliated with the University of Toronto. He was an outstanding and dedicated student and for the next four years, became truly

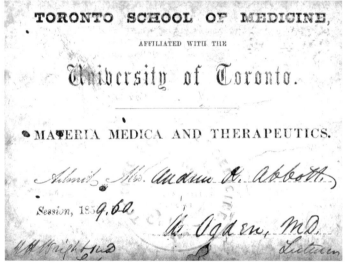

One of Anderson Abbott's "Perpetual Tickets." These were used as admission passes and for attendance to the university lectures. Handwritten on the back and signed by the MD lecturer are the words "very regular attendance certified April 14th 1860." *Abbott Collection, Toronto Pubic Library (TRL): S-90.*

In 2002, Dr. Anderson Ruffin Abbott was recognized as one of the University of Toronto's "Great Minds" honorees. His banner tribute was displayed on the lamppost at the corner of Bloor and St. George streets in Toronto.

entrenched in the mystery and revelation that the study of science could offer. He took courses in the Principles and Practice of Medicine, Materia Medica and Therapeutics, Surgical Anatomy, General and Descriptive Anatomy, Practical Anatomy, Institutes of Medicine and, of course, Obstetrics and Diseases of Women and Children.

His "Perpetual Ticket"[15] for the Toronto General Hospital indicated that he practised in the hospital from October 5, 1858, until April 1, 1861. Many of his handwritten notes, including a number of lectures, have also survived. During his years at medical school, Anderson Abbott was to deepen a friendship with one of the most influential men in his career. Dr. Alexander T. Augusta[16] became his teacher and mentor and led the way to dreams once thought utterly unattainable by a Black man. Dr. Abbott graduated from the Medical College and became the first Black Canadian-born licentiate of the Medical Board of Upper Canada in 1861. He was only twenty-three years old.

CHAPTER 7

OFF TO WAR

*...while all of Canada was struggling toward Confederation, all the
United States were whirling toward disunion.*[1]

IN 1861, THE UNITED States was split between the Union and the
Confederate causes and Canadians were caught in an enormous tide
of fluctuating loyalties. Primarily they were loyal British subjects, but
many still cultivated a strong affection for their birth countries, either
in Europe or the United States, some even lending sympathy to the
Confederate side. Strong familial and economic ties frequently bound
many southern families to the British aristocracy, and even some
Canadian newspapers like the *Toronto Leader* and the *Montreal
Gazette* publicly pronounced their sympathies for the South. By 1862,
the Union blockade of the Southern ports had effectively depleted
the cotton trade, creating extensive unemployment in the textile
industry in England. Although Britain officially remained neutral
throughout the Civil War, she lent her support to the Confederate
states in subversive ways.

> Anglo-Canadian support for the Confederacy developed for a variety
> of reasons including economic ties, disgust for American tariff policies,
> a belief in the inherent right of self-determination, recognition that the
> Union's main purpose in fighting the war was not the abolition of
> slavery and a suspicion that the North might invade Canada once the
> South was defeated.[2]

At any rate, shots were fired and so were the spirits of the people, not
only above and below the Mason Dixon Line, but also above the Canadian-
American border. It was the beginning of a frustrating two years for Dr.

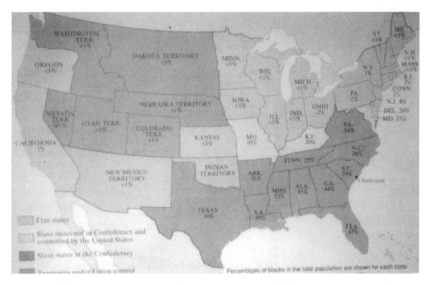

A map of the United States, 1861, showing the Slave and the Free Areas. According to the map, California, Oregon and Kansas were free states, while Kentucky and Montana were slave states, but not aligned with the Confederacy. *Courtesy of Bryan Prince, Raleigh Centennial Museum.*

Augusta and Dr. Abbott. Alexander Thomas Augusta (1825–1890), born a free Black in Norfolk, Virginia, worked as a barber when he lived in Baltimore, Maryland. He developed an interest in medicine and, when the University of Pennsylvania refused him admission based on his race, he sought out some private tutoring from one of the professors. Eventually he enrolled in Trinity Medical College in Toronto and, in 1856, was the first Black graduate in the field of Medicine in Canada. He subsequently established a practice, was appointed in charge of the Toronto City Hospital and set up a pharmacy on Yonge Street in the Central Medical Hall in Toronto.[3]

Augusta, with the assistance of Dr. Abbott, regularly attended the patients sequestered at the poorhouse.[4] Many hospitals for the poor and asylums for the insane were serviced by doctors at no charge, in return for the opportunity to use patients for practice and observation. During this Victorian period, when body modesty was extremely prevalent, it was decidedly difficult for doctors to find patients, particularly women, who would agree to be models for instructional purposes. Many of the recent immigrant Black women accepted free medical attention in return for the use of their cases for medical instructional purposes. Another

> ## CENTRAL MEDICAL HALL
> ## A.T. AUGUSTA
>
> Begs to announce to his friends and the public generally
> that he has opened the store on Yonge St. one door south
> of Elm Street, with a new and choice selection of
> ### DRUGS, MEDICINES,
> Patent Medicines, Perfumery, Dye Stuffs, etc.
> And trusts, by strict attention to his business,
> to merit a share of their patronage.
> Physicians' prescriptions accurately prepared
> Leeches applied
> Cupping, Bleeding and Teeth Extracted
> The proprietor or a competent assistant, always in attendance.[5]

regular problem encountered by doctors-in-training was the shortage of cadavers for use in anatomy and physiology labs. It has been suggested that grave robbers were able to find a ready market for their wares.

It is unclear whether or not Doctors Augusta and Abbott were paid for their charity work in cash, but certainly they would have gained considerable practical experience prior to their work at Freedmen's Hospital during the Civil War. The poorhouses would have provided them with a valuable opportunity to learn about the principles of disease control and hospital sanitation, very useful for their later work during the Civil War in the treatment and prevention of disease.

In those days, while Black students were able to mix freely with white students in the City of Toronto, they usually lacked the necessary finances to further their education. The availability of educational opportunities for Blacks was a real concern to Dr. Augusta and he became involved in the Educational Institute, where he frequently offered Lyceum lectures[6] to the public. As an intellectual, he was very interested in the practice of free expression, especially pertaining to civil rights, and he often delivered lectures on racial issues to the members of the Provincial Association for the Education and Elevation of the Colored People of Canada, a so-called literary society. Naturally he was also an active member of the Anti-Slavery Society.

A.T. Augusta must have possessed a certain degree of boldness, coupled with a good helping of defiance, for upon his graduation from medical school, he applied for the position of Coroner for Kent County. Doubtless,

Dr. A.T. (Alexander Thomas) Augusta was a mentor to Anderson Abbott. Originally from Virginia, he received his medical training in Toronto. A distinguished surgeon, he was the first Black major commissioned in the Union Army.
Courtesy of Bryan Prince, Raleigh Centennial Museum.

he would have been alert to the political and social opposition to Blacks within the Chatham community, but he would also have been aware that such a position could provide a stable and respectable future. Predictably, the community turned down his application; it was clear that they were not yet ready for their first Black Coroner. However, he would live to see the tide change, as his prodigy, Dr. Abbott would one day snare the position and treasure the accomplishment with great pride.

Dr. Augusta, a graduate of the University of Trinity College, Toronto, was the only available man at that time, so his application was sent in for the appointment of Coroner. How was it treated? Why it was thrown in the scrap basket and Dr. Lawlor, an Irishman, received the appointment instead of Dr. Augusta.[7]

In 1847, Dr. Augusta married a woman by the name of Mary, who held the distinction of being the first Black businesswoman in the City of Toronto. She ran a couturier shop on York Street, between Richmond and Adelaide, where she found herself in great demand, offering the latest designs from Paris and London to the ladies of the town. When Mary relocated to Washington with her husband, she was able to maintain her contacts and courted a close friendship with Mrs. Keckley, the lady-in-waiting and dress-designer for Mrs. Lincoln.[8]

Coloured recruits, and even coloured contract surgeons, were not considered potential candidates for service in the companies of the Union Army until 1863, when President Lincoln declared them to be legitimate citizens of the United States of America. At that point, a large number of them flooded across the border to serve in combat regiments from Massachusetts, New York and Michigan. Both Mary Ann Shadd[9] and Martin R. Delany[10] were instrumental in the recruitment of Black Canadians. In fact, Martin Delany and Josiah Henson,[11] of Dresden, proposed a unique solution to President Lincoln's need for troops:

I propose, sir, an army of Blacks, commanded by Black officers. This army will penetrate the heart of the South, with the banner of Emancipation unfurled, proclaiming freedom as they go. By arming the emancipated, taking them as fresh troops, we could soon have an army of 40,000 Blacks in motion. It would be an irresistible force.[12]

Although Anderson Abbott was Canadian-born, he was also keen to participate in the Union effort. But it was a complicated process to legally enlist in a foreign army, since International Law prevented outsiders from joining the forces of another nation. Dr. Augusta, however, was American-born and, except for his "objectionable" race, would have been an acceptable candidate. He was made a Major of Cavalry when he first entered the Union Army and he left as a Brevet Lieutenant Colonel, the highest rank achieved by a coloured, commissioned officer during the Civil War.

Abbott recounted the advent of Dr. Augusta's military service in 1863, where he reflected on the "sanguinity" of the good doctor to assume that the government would consider the commission of a coloured man as a surgeon. But much to everyone's surprise, Augusta was ordered to appear in Washington before the Board of Examiners for Military Surgeons. He was received by Secretary Edwin M. Stanton (1814–1869) and referred to Surgeon General Hammond for examination. Hammond, however, did not make any effort to convene the Examination Board and delayed the process for more than three weeks. Finally, Augusta again applied to Secretary Stanton, who immediately issued a peremptory order for the examination:

Accordingly, he appeared before the Board on the day appointed and was subjected to a rigid examination and recommitted for an Assistant Surgeon. But Secretary Stanton said that if he had been able to pass that Board, he was entitled to the full Surgeoncy and he so appointed him Surgeon of the 7th United States Colored Troops, with the rank of Major of Cavalry. As soon as the Doctor received his commission, he was appointed in charge of Camp Baker [Barker] Hospital in Washington, D.C.[13]

This made Augusta the first Black man to be awarded the rank of Major in the United States Union Army.[14] Dr. Abbott added an amusing story regarding Dr. Augusta's initial recruitment:

Apparently, Dr. Cronyn, who was President of the Examining Board, having occasion to go into Surgeon General Hammond's office a short time after Augusta had passed, was asked by the General, "I say, Cronyn. How did you come to let that nigger pass?" Cronyn replied, "The fact is General, that the nigger knew more than I did and I could not help myself."[15]

As Surgeon-in-chief of Freedmen's Hospital,[16] Augusta was also the first Negro to head any hospital in the United States. In the winter of 1863, he was assigned to Camp Birney, a recruiting station, where new recruits were examined medically. Next, he was assigned to a hospital in Savannah, Georgia, as Surgeon-in-chief, where he remained until the end of the war. Afterwards, he assumed charge of Lincoln's Hospital in Savannah, Georgia, under the auspices of the Freedmen's Bureau, where he promoted the popular policy of self-help, encouraging freedmen to contribute their personal support for the hospital. When he returned to Washington in 1868, he set up a medical practice, specializing in the Diseases of Women and Children, while teaching part-time at Howard University.[17]

It appears Dr. Augusta had more than one run-in with the authorities while stationed in Washington. Rushing to a court martial hearing, to which he had been summoned, he hopped on a streetcar at Pennsylvania Avenue. The conductor immediately expelled him from the interior of the car and the Doctor was consequently late for the hearing. Upon receiving his explanation, the judge ordered Augusta to submit a statement in writing to the Senate. Washington DC was not a state and, thus, was answerable only to Federal governmental jurisdiction. Senator Sumner read the report and the situation was discussed in the Senate. As a result of the incident, separate streetcars were made available for the Blacks but eventually, even this distinction was abandoned, and public transportation was integrated:

> Thus it was through Dr. Augusta, that the colored people of Washington came to ride in the streetcars. Until that time, the only concession that had been made to them in that respect was to allow them to ride on the front platform and it was a common sight to see colored men, women and children riding in front of the car with the driver.[18]

Soon after receiving his commission to Freedmen's Hospital, Dr. Augusta became a celebrity. *The Star*, a Washington newspaper, reported that Dr. Augusta attended an anniversary celebration of the signing of the Act of Emancipation of April 16, 1862, which freed the slaves in the

District of Columbia, at the 15th Presbyterian Church in Washington. The article, entitled "Emancipation in Columbia," described the effect of his presence to the congregation:

> The appearance of a Colored man in the room wearing the gold leaf epaulettes of a Major was the occasion of much applause and congratulation with the assembly. The individual thus distinguished was Dr. A.T. Augusta, who received a surgeon's commission last week from the Secretary of War.[19]

Travel in or out of Washington was very difficult during those times, with the quickest route being via the Baltimore & Ohio line on one of eight passenger trains. Each trip took about an hour and half and cost $1.60. The trip itself could prove to be sometimes even dangerous for travellers. Dr. Abbott recalled an incident when Augusta rather injudiciously wore his uniform when travelling home on the train from Baltimore. While waiting in the car at the Baltimore Depot, he was accosted and forced to defend himself, until a squad of soldiers came to his "rescue." They arrested him for impersonating an officer and he was marched off to the Provost Marshall, all the while followed by a howling mob. When the good doctor was finally able to provide proof of his commission and rank, he was escorted back to the Depot under an even stronger guard of soldiers. Again attacked and knocked down in the ensuing chaos, Augusta managed to slip into a pharmacy and escape via the back door, furtively making his way back to his departure point. Anderson Abbott admonished such disregard for personal safety:

> It was a wonder that he escaped with his life for only a few months [ago] previous Black Massachusetts soldiers were shot down in the streets when going to that City. President Lincoln had been obliged to change his route on his way to Washington for his first inauguration after having received a message that he would be assassinated if he went through Baltimore. It was a foolhardy act and it might have cost the doctor his life. But he had the bulldog tenacity of temperament which cannot be deterred by fear.[20]

Two years later, Dr. Augusta was to experience the profound satisfaction of "riding through the streets of Baltimore in full uniform at the head of 75,000 troops on the occasion of the passage of President Lincoln's remains through the city."[21]

The Freedman's Hospital in Washington eventually became the Howard University Medical School and General Hospital, and Dr. Augusta joined as one of its founding faculty. Incredibly, on January 13, 1870, he discovered that the Medical Society of the District was not prepared to admit any coloured physicians and his application was rejected. The rest of the University faculty responded to the offensive gesture by inviting all of the regular medical practitioners in the District of Columbia to a meeting, where they established the National Medical Society in the District of Columbia. In 1875, they elected the retired Chief of the Freedman's Hospital, Dr. Reyburn, as President and Dr. Alexander Thomas Augusta became one of its first Vice-Presidents. When the school term ended that year, Augusta went on to become a physician at the Smallpox Hospital and Washington Asylum. Dr. Augusta died in 1890, and was buried in Arlington Cemetery.

CHAPTER 8

DR. ABBOTT AND
THE CIVIL WAR

Will the slave fight? If any man asks you, tell him No. But if anyone asks you will the Negro fight, tell him Yes![1]

ON APRIL 16, 1862, slavery was abolished in the District of Columbia and on January 1, 1863, President Lincoln publicly endorsed the Emancipation Act. It was not a popular bill and many of the white citizens of Washington were incensed at the prospect of the inevitable influx of freed Blacks and escaped slaves to the city. Washington, seen as a haven, had attracted many sick, infirm and destitute refugees, creating very serious and disconcerting problems for the authorities. Employment agencies gradually dispersed some of the indigents to other parts of the country, but still many more remained in the hospitals and camps. The City of Washington could not handle the heavy traffic and hordes of refugees surging through the streets, homeless, hungry and susceptible to disease. Public sanitation procedures and facilities were extremely primitive, and temporary camps and hospitals sprouted up everywhere. Ironically, many of the inmates and patients were later moved to the rural setting of Freedman's Village in northern Virginia, across the Potomac River on the Union-controlled estate of Robert E. Lee, the renown leader of the Confederate forces.

In 1861, the problem of so many escaped slaves harboured in the camps around Washington caused the President much embarrassment. Although he did no personally condone returning the fugitives to their bonds, he had committed to upholding the institution of slavery. Yet the army needed labourers and these men were strong, willing and able-bodied. That spring, General Ben Butler, Commander at Fort Monroe, refused to release some runaways to the Confederates, as he realized that they would only be put to use against his forces. Despite the fact that the Fugitive Slave Law remained in effect, Butler was determined to employ these men in support of the Union effort, and the President granted permission for Blacks to be employed as military labourers. Two coloured companies were subsequently raised in Massachusetts, but Lincoln himself demonstrated little confidence in the effort as he feared that their arms would end up in the hands of the secessionists.

Although all fugitive and freed slaves were designated as contraband of war, their prospects and very survival were greatly impeded as the war dragged on. There were so many of them that most had to be released from hospital care under deplorable conditions. They had no homes, no source of income, no food and no means by which to gain employment. Inevitably, they began to congregate along the North/South borders and in the cities, in alarming numbers. Eventually their numbers swelled to ten thousand in Washington and another three thousand in Alexandria, forcing the authorities to establish a new camp at Arlington, called Freedmen's Village, where the "contraband" refugees were organized into teams of blacksmiths, wheelwrights, carpenters, tailors and shoemakers.

Some of the details pertaining to these days are confusing, because the hospital for Blacks operated under a variety of names. Dr. Abbott refers to Camp Barker as Camp Baker, which was later remodelled into the Campbell United States Freedmen's Hospital.[2] In 1865, it was officially proclaimed to be Freedmen's Hospital, when its administration fell under the auspices of the Freedmen's Bureau, along with numerous other hospitals and camps. Some records refer to it as the Abbott Hospital, after Dr. R.O. Abbott,[3] the Medical Director of the War Department.

In 1867, a hospital was rebuilt on the grounds of Howard University and was named Freedmen's Hospital. It later functioned as Howard University Medical School, Pharmaceutical School and General Hospital.[4] Modern medicine was still in its infancy during the Civil War years and those interested in the field were desperate to learn from any available event. Dr. Washington F. Crusor described the school laboratory in his memoirs on October 30, 1899:

> The lectures were given in the front room where dissections were also made, until the fact came to the knowledge of the family below. The subject was then removed to an old building on the same lot, until the family secured more congenial quarters. Dr. Augusta, our Demonstrator of Anatomy, was persistent in trying to overcome all obstacles.

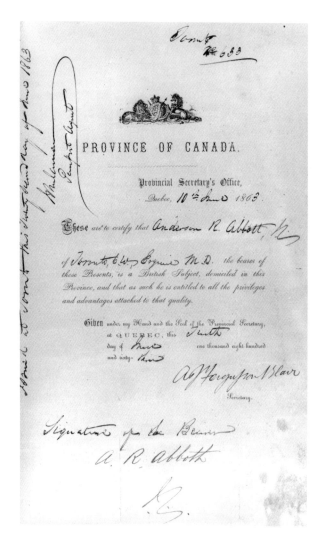

The official document, dated June 10, 1863, stipulating that A.R. Abbott, Esquire, M.D., is a British subject. At the bottom of the paper is the signature of the bearer, A.R. Abbott. *Abbott Collection, Toronto Public Library (TRL): S-90.*

The Professors were gentlemen of ability and several became eminent in their specialties. They were entertaining and pleasing in their method of instruction, courteous and with becoming dignity in their bearing toward the students, whose interest, attention and respect were at once enlisted.... It was the philanthropic spirit that characterized and controlled the Institution in that early period and gave it its great impetus...[5]

As a Canadian, and thus a British subject, Dr. Abbott found himself facing serious obstacles in his quest to join the Union forces. Ultimately, he decided to appeal directly to Mr. Stanton, the Secretary of War:

I learn by our city papers, that it is the intention of the United States government to enlist 150,000 colored troops. Being one of that class of persons, I beg to apply for a commission as Assistant Surgeon. My qualifications are that I am twenty-five years of age and I have been engaged in the surgical medical practice of medicine for five years. I am a licentiate of the College of Physicians and Surgeons Upper Canada—a board of examiners appointed by the Governor General to examine candidates for license to practice. I am also a matriculate of the Toronto University. It is my intention to go up for my degree of Bachelor of Medicine in the spring.[6]

When unsuccessful, he persisted, this time requesting a position as a Medical Cadet on April 30, 1863. In this case, he leaned on the reputation of his former mentor, Dr. A.T. Augusta, who had recently made an appearance at the mustering of the first two companies of contrabands in Washington, "[s]plendid among the shabby field hands...[t]he sight of his uniform stirred the faintest heart to faith in the new destiny of the race, for Dr. Augusta wore the oak leaves of a major on his shoulders."[7]

Dr. Abbott wrote:

I beg most respectfully to apply for a situation as medical cadet in the army. I am a colored man and would desire to be appointed in one of the colored regiments, if you think favorably of my application.

It may be some recommendation to add that I have been a pupil of Dr. A.T. Augusta for several years. He received a commission from you, as you know, recently. He will give you the information you may require concerning my character and attainments.[8]

After several anxious months, Abbott was gratified to be hired as a Contract Surgeon on a salary of $100 a month. He was never commissioned as an officer, but he was awarded the honorary rank of Captain and became one of eight Black doctors in the Union Army and served as the Acting Surgeon-in-Chief at the Freedmen's Hospital for the next two years. Throughout his life Dr. Abbott was acutely dissatisfied with his "unofficial" rank and continued to seek some form of official recognition. He must have been highly vexed, knowing that other Canadians who had not declared themselves as such, had joined and fought with no regard to the international agreement.

Others shared the same frustration and, in January of 1865, Abbott supported an appeal to the President of the United States, requesting recognition. One hundred and eighty-five men put their signatures on the following petition, including those of Senator Charles Sumner, Frederick Douglass, Horace Greeley and Minnesota Governor Stephen Miller:

Anderson Ruffin Abbott, M.D., in Civil War uniform, wearing a green sash to depict the position of medical doctor. *Abbott Collection, Toronto Public Library (TRL): S-90.*

> Sir: In view of the recent Proclamation of the President calling for 300,000 volunteers and appreciating the necessity of an immediate response to this call, we would respectfully petition that permission be given to raise a number of colored regiments to be officered exclusively by colored men.
>
> In regard to the policy of this measure, we would respectfully urge that while many of the noblest of our race have sprung to arms with alacrity in defence of the Government, many others, equally loyal, have hesitated because one of the greatest incentives to enlistment and the greatest stimulus to the strict performance of a soldier's duty—the hope of promotion—has been denied them.
>
> We confidently believe that the removal of this bar to a soldier's ambition would result in an uprising of the colored people, unsurpassed even by the enthusiastic response to the President's first call.
>
> In regard to the capability of colored men to perform the duties of commissioned officers, we would respectfully suggest that there are hundreds of non-commissioned officers in colored regiments who are amply qualified for these positions, both by education and experience and that others of our educated men, anticipating the granting of commissions to colored men by the Government, have applied themselves to the study of military tactics, in order that men properly educated might not be wanting to accept them.
>
> And your petitioners will ever pray, etc.
>
> Lewis H. Douglass, later Sergeant Major 54th Massachusetts Volunteers;

James T. Wormley, Sergeant 5th Massachusetts Cavalry; Benjamin Owsley, Sergeant 27th Colored Troops; Charles R. Douglass, later Sergeant 5th Massachusetts Cavalry Volunteers; John H. Rapier, A.A. Surgeon U.S Army; William R. Ellis, A.A. Surgeon U.S Army; Thomas J. White, David E. Wycoff, later Sergeant 108th New York Volunteers; James R. Martin; A.R. Abbott, A.A. Surgeon U.S Army.[9]

It seems a cruel twist of fate that, in contrast, a white Canadian, Dr. Francis Wafer of Kingston, Ontario, was readily accepted into the 108th New York Corps while he was still a medical student at Queen's University. The American authorities arranged special examinations for him and, upon meeting the minimum requirements, he received a commission as a 2nd Lieutenant and was sent off for duty.[10] It was clear to Dr. Abbott that race very much influenced the granting of commissions to officers.

As Dr. Augusta's replacement at Freedmen's Hospital, Anderson Abbott assumed the role of Chief Executive Officer and Surgeon-in-Chief. He had always been particularly impressed with the flourishing accomplishments of the famous Florence Nightingale, who, with her innovative policies of personal hygiene, hospital sanitation and disease prevention techniques, had recently revolutionized the role of hospitals in the Crimean War. Abbott's memoirs indicate that he excelled in the business administration of the hospital and he took great pride in his ability to achieve similar high levels of efficiency. He had a staff of six surgeons, two clerks, two stewards, two matrons, a large corps of servants and a full staff of nurses. Although the hospital served only the coloured soldiers and refugees or "contraband," as they were called, it was fully equipped with a capacity of two thousand beds.[11] His responsibilities would have included ordering the rations, controlling sanitation procedures, hiring and training the staff, as well as surgery and administering to the patients. In later life he was able to apply these superb skills to his future administrative endeavours, all the while practising and teaching at other hospitals.

During the Civil War, the practice of embalming corpses evolved. Many families sought to have the bodies of their fallen loved ones preserved and returned to their homes, to be buried on the family plot. The procedure of corpse preservation involved injecting chemicals into the vessels and cavities of the corpse. The success of these endeavours and the preservation of the body rested on the efficiency and speed with which the process was completed. Thus, most of the work had to be done out in the field, after the battles had subsided. Soldiers were not required to wear "dog tags," and so often embalmers were responsible for the identification of the corpses.

Detail from a photograph of battlefield remains following one of the Civil War battles. *Courtesy of Bryan Prince, Raleigh Centennial Museum.*

In the case of the coloured soldiers, this practice was probably not as prevalent, for few would have had any family or home left to return the remains of the bodies. Although the majority of Dr. Abbott's Black patients at the Contraband Camp would have been fugitives and refugees, it is highly likely that he would have kept himself abreast of this fascinating subject. Such experiences may well have sparked his future interest in forensics as a prospective coroner.

Following the war, the Freedmen's Bureau took over the administration of fifty-six hospitals, including forty-eight dispensaries, employing one hundred and thirty-eight physicians. Its original purpose was to address the vital needs of the refugees that required assistance in aspects pertaining to money, lands, medical attention, schooling and skilled training. By 1872, most of its duties had been reassigned and the altruistic dreams of its earlier advocates withered away with the passing of the guard, as the phase of Reconstruction commenced.

Although all fugitive and freed slaves were designated as contraband of war, their prospects and very survival was greatly impeded, as the war dragged on. There were so many of them that most had to be released from hospital care under deplorable conditions. They had no homes, no source of income, no food and no means by which to gain employment. Inevitably, they began to congregate along the North/South borders and in the cities, in alarming numbers. Following the war and in response to the crisis, the Freedmen's Bureau took over the administration of fifty-six hospitals, including forty-eight dispensaries, employing one hundred and thirty-eight physicians. Its original purpose was to address the vital needs of the refugees that required assistance in aspects pertaining to money, lands, medical attention, schooling and skilled training. By 1872, most its duties had been reassigned and the altruistic dreams of its earlier advocates withered away with the passing of the guard, as the phase of Reconstruction commenced.

When the war ended, Dr. Abbott was honourably discharged from duty in August of 1865 and, upon his resignation, he received the following commendations:

Washington, May 14, 1866.
War Department, Bureau of Refugees, Freedman and Abandoned Lands
Office of the Chief Medical Officer

I take great pleasure on bearing testimony to the good and faithful service rendered by Assistant Surgeon A.R. Abbott. While Supervisor of Freedman's affairs for the District of Columbia, under the Surgeon General of the United States Army, for a year nearly prior to the organization of the Bureau, my attention was directed to Dr. Abbott, then Executive Officer of the Hospital where his officiary soon gained for him promotion to the position of Surgeon-in-Charge. Since which time he has continued to discharge with credit to himself and the entire satisfaction of his superior officers trustees involving professional and administrative responsibility. His resignation is accepted with regret.

Albert W. Homer, Surgeon U.S Vols., Chief Medical Officer
Headquarters, Arlington, Virginia[12]

January 2nd, 1866
re: A.R. Abbott, Assistant Surgeon of United States Army
Doctor:

I am about to assume duties in another portion of the State and will be relieved from duty here. Before going allow me to return you my thanks for your hearty co-operation in all matters of duty of your profession.

Allow me to say without desiring to flatter that I consider you the most skilful of any surgeon ever in charge of this post (and there have been many). Be assured of my kind regards and wishes for your success.

Very Truly Your Friend,
G.B. Carse, Brevet Major Commanding Post[13]

There is even a record of a letter of commendation from Dr. Reyburn, dated May 12, 1866. On May 15, Dr. R.O. Abbott, Surgeon of the U.S. Army and Medical Director, Department of Washington, also wrote a commendation stating that Dr. Abbott had served well in his department as Acting Assistant Surgeon from June 1863 to August 1865.

After devoting the following year to work with the Freedmen's Bureau, in Washington, DC, Anderson Abbott returned to Toronto in 1866. Deeply sorrowed over the assassination of President Lincoln, he would continue to admire the honourable intentions of his deceased hero and his supreme achievement in securing the Emancipation Proclamation. Although Lincoln had consistently claimed that the preservation of the Union was his first and foremost priority, the abolition of slavery proved to be a fitting end to his term. Several weeks after his return to Canada, Dr. Abbott received a black and white houndstooth shawl[14] from Mrs. Lincoln. It had been worn by the President to cover his knees in the carriage while on his way to his first inauguration. Obviously, Dr. Abbott had made a lasting impression on the First Family:

The remaining weeks that Mrs. Lincoln spent in the White House, after the removal of the President's body to Springfield, Illinois, were spent in disposing of her late husband's personal effects. Several articles that he valued very much and which were much used by him, were given away as mementos to his friends. I received the plaid shawl which Mr. Lincoln was frequently seen wearing of a chilly evening when going to the War Department to consult Mr. Stanton on important state business.... *The New York Weekly News* of October 19, 1867 described the gift as follows:

'The shepherd plaid shawl, which Mr. Lincoln wore during the mild weather and which was rendered somewhat memorable as forming part of his disguise, together with the Scotch cap, worn when he wended his way secretly to the capital to be inaugurated as President, was given to Dr. Abbott of Canada, who had been one of his warmest friends. During the war this gentleman, as a surgeon in the United States Army, was in Washington in charge of a hospital and thus became acquainted with the head of the nation.'

The report that the shawl formed part of disguise is without foundation. At no time during the journey to Washington did the President assume a disguise. He carried the shawl on his arm when entering the carriage, which conveyed him to the railroad depot in Philadelphia. This shawl has been preserved in my family for the past thirty-six

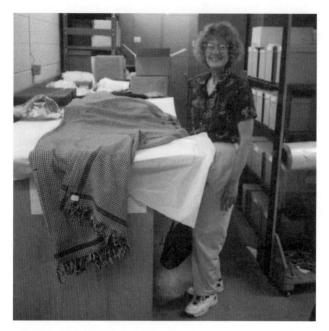

Above: The author's cousin, Bonnie Grosnick of Madison poses with the shawl where it is retained on display at the Wisconsin Historical Society in Madison, Wisconsin.
Below: Enlargement of detail of the pattern of the shawl given by Mary Todd Lincoln to Dr. Abbott following Lincoln's assassination.

years and regarded as a most precious heirloom. During the time Mr. Lincoln was in office he was the recipient of several canes. After his death one was given to the Honorable Charles Sumner, another to the Honorable Frederick Douglass still another to the Rev. H.H. Garnet and I was entrusted to deliver one to the late Rev. Dr. Caldicott of Toronto, Canada."[15]

After Dr. Abbott's death, the shawl was passed on to his descendants. When it came into my mother's hands, she sent it along to her American cousin as a Civil War memento. Of course, at the time, she had no knowledge of the history behind the shawl, nor of how fittingly the black and white threads of its houndstooth weave portrayed the contrasting images

The author's invitation to attend the preview and reception for "Something to Hope For," held on February 7, 2002. This ROM exhibit, organized by the Buxton Historic Site & Museum, highlighted Dr. A.R. Abbott.

of her own family. Today the shawl rests in the capable hands of the State Historical Society of Wisconsin, where it is suitably treasured as a worthy Civil War memorial.

CHAPTER 9

THE GRAND ARMY
OF THE REPUBLIC

It was not a war for conquest or territorial aggrandizement, racial, social or political supremacy. It was not a war for white men or Black men, red men or yellow men. It was a war of humanity. To be sure in the beginning it was a war for the preservation of the Union, but in its ultimate results it transcended all geographical and political lines. It became a conflict between Beautiful Right and Ugly Wrong, between civilization and barbarism, between Freedom and Slavery.[1]

THE GRAND ARMY OF the Republic was a fraternal organization that extended across the United States and even into Canada. Initiated in Decatur, Illinois, by Benjamin F. Stephenson on April 6, 1866, it represented Federal veterans of the armed forces during the Civil War. The uniqueness of the GAR, as it was commonly labelled, lay in the fact that its membership could never grow or change and with each passing year, the roster gradually declined as the list of deceased veterans increased.

In the aftermath of the Civil War, in the early 1870s, the GAR almost disappeared but was revived in 1875 under new leadership. In 1890, when the GAR boasted its largest membership of more than 490,000, it exerted strong leverage on the politics, law and social doctrines of the American way of life. By the late 1890s, the organization mainly served to promote patriotism on Decoration Day,[2] and was usually described in such terms as "...a fraternal lodge, charitable society, special interest lobby, patriotic group, or political club."[3] Each post was developed locally and the members elected their own officers. As Stuart McConnell so aptly wrote:

70

In the Grand Army of the Republic, we see an earlier group of veterans trying to cope with issues that are as relevant now as they were in 1865: the extent of the society's obligation to the poor and injured, the place of war memories in peacetime, the meaning of the "nation" and of the individual's relation to it.[4]

In Washington, DC, on May 23, 1865, some 150,000 uniformed white men marched past President Lincoln in the Grand Review, representing the great force that had miraculously held the Union together and emancipated 4,500,000 slaves. Sadly, the Black troops were not included in the parade that day:

> Neither the Black former slaves nor the free Black soldier was to be the hero of this national pageant; instead, each was relegated a secondary rather uneasy position within it. The exclusion of the Blacks from the celebration was a clear message about the sort of Union the white veterans felt they had preserved.[5]

Many years later, in a Memorial Day address to the GAR, Anderson Abbott overlooked this discrepancy and declared:

> There never was such a gathering of men of all races, kindred and tongues, under our standard, moved by a common impulse to sacrifice their lives for a great principle as in that Civil War.[6]

Nevertheless, McConnell reported that very few Blacks were admitted into the white GAR posts and, where there were large contingents of Black veterans, they maintained their own separate posts. He described the situation, not so much in terms of intentional discrimination, but as a reflection of the ethnic makeup of the nation at the outset of the Civil War.[7] Minority groups like Blacks, women or immigrants were sorely under-represented in the GAR, but so were the wealthy, educated and elite, for they had often made expedient use of their financial or political status to avoid actual recruitment. Most immigration, as we know it today, other than English, Irish, Scottish or German occurred after the Civil War. Thus, the majority of GAR members would have been born and raised in rural parts of the country, having acquired only a modest education.

Dr. Abbott felt very strongly about the preservation of the ideal for which they had fought so hard, even thirty or forty years later. At one of the Annual GAR Encampments, he addressed his fellow veterans:

71

We assemble year by year around the graves of our departed comrades to decorate their graves and thus endeavour to keep alive and cherish their memories. There are few years left to do this. Some have dropped out of the ranks of the Grand Army militant since we last performed this service over the graves of our departed comrades. Others are absent on this occasion by reason of old age and infirmity, but those of us who are left will not fail in discharging this sacred duty from year to year while life and strength last.[8]

One of his deepest concerns was that the post should continue to decorate the graves of the departed comrades, as a gesture of remembrance each May 30, on Decoration Day. He suggested that a special committee administer the necessary funds and delegate the tasks. Other charitable responsibilities of the GAR posts included providing medical services, aiding the destitute and unemployed and providing funeral assistance. Although he does not appear to have actively participated in the organization until the end of the century, it is clear that he was very pleased to be appointed as a member of the Jas. S. Knowlton Post No. 532 in April of 1890. James S. Knowlton possibly saw more active service than any other Canadian until he died from disease while he was with General William Tecumseh Sherman on the famous march to the sea.[9]

James S. Knowlton, Post No. 523, Department of New York, to which I belong is composed of forty-three members, three of whom are Afro-American, A.R. Garrison, Chaplain; Corporal Brown, 7th U.S.C.T. and myself. I do not think that we can complain of discrimination on account of color, seeing that two out of three of us hold important positions. There are now five posts established in Canada: Winnipeg, London, Hamilton, Toronto and Montreal...It is said that there are 150 veterans in Toronto alone. Of course a good many veterans are deterred from joining these posts from the fear that, in some ways, they might compromise their citizenship:[10]

The objects of the Grand Army of the Republic are found to be of a charitable and not a military character...[11]

The post was still active after Anderson's death and, in 1914, had twenty-six remaining members. It closed down in 1949 with only six survivors left. There is no evidence to suggest that he was denied the privilege based on his race, but he did not join the organization until his retirement in

Erected in 1999, this African-American Civil War
Memorial is set in Washington's Shaw District.

Toronto. During this time, he travelled to Buffalo for the annual meetings
and regularly addressed his fellow comrades in commemorative speeches.

On November 21, 1892, Anderson was appointed the Aide-de-Camp,
to the Staff of the Commanding Officers of the Department of New York.
In 1890 and 1891, rulings were established which asserted the rights of
Blacks to join the same encampments as the whites in the South. Upon
his resignation, he was awarded a dress sword and the traditional green,
medical officer's sash and belt by the officers and comrades of the post.
These items have been preserved with pride by my family and will
continue to be passed down to future generations of Abbotts.

The National Park Service has developed a project called the Civil
War Soldier System (CWSS) and has computed information pertaining
to the 5.5 million men who served in the Civil War. The African-
American Civil War Freedom Foundation has documented the names

of those who served in the United States Colored Troops during the Civil War. In 1996, the African American Civil War Memorial Project joined the endeavour to provide a monument that would commemorate the service of 178,000 Blacks in the Civil War. The memorial is a semi-circular, three-foot high, curved stone wall bearing stainless steel plaques engraved with the names of the soldiers and their white officers. It is fittingly located in Washington's historic Shaw District, named for Colonel Robert Gould Shaw, the famous Commander of the 54th Massachusetts Colored Volunteer Infantry. A.R. Abbott's name is not included on the memorial as he was a contract surgeon and not an American citizen.

CHAPTER 10

EARLY MEDICAL PRACTICE IN THE NINETEENTH CENTURY

The paths of pain are thine. Go forth,
With healing and with hope;
The suffering of a sin-sick earth
Shall give thee ample scope.[1]

EARLY MEDICAL PRACTICE AND the criteria for the qualification of practitioners were considerably different than today. The techniques they used were sometimes extremely crude and often questionable. Many settlers, living miles apart and far from towns, had to rely on self-taught, traditional remedies for sickness or injury when competent doctors were out of reach. In some cases, the local doctor turned out to be simply an individual who was bold enough to attempt to alleviate the suffering of his neighbours with the primitive tools and limited knowledge he possessed. In many instances, their expertise could not be surpassed by some of the formally trained doctors.

During the early nineteenth century, most doctors adhered to the belief that disease resulted from the presence of toxic substances in the body and specifically in the blood. The most common method of releasing the "poisonous" blood was to bleed the patient by severing some of the blood vessels or by applying blood-sucking leeches to the skin. Sometimes toxins were "purged" by inducing vomiting, or ingesting laxatives. Surgeries were atrociously gruesome and most patients succumbed to severe infections that inevitably erupted from the unsanitary conditions prevalent both during and after surgery. It was not until the late 1800s that the newly acknowledged "germ theory" prompted practitioners to modify

Top, Anderson Abbott's lecture admission card for "Principles and Practice of Medicine," dated 1858–59; *bottom*, An invitation to a "Conversazione" addressed to Mr. A.R. Abbott, dated January 3, 1862. *Documents courtesy of the Abbott family.*

their approach to the treatment of infection and disease, and the use of modern antiseptics and medicines became more prevalent. Once doctors began to study disease with more insight into the intricacies of human anatomy and physiology, more preventative techniques were established. Vaccinations against the dreaded smallpox became safer and more effective with the use of the newly developed cowpox serum.

Scientific medicine was maturing very slowly. Most patients were extremely unreceptive to the vulgar and debilitating methods condoned by the trained doctors of the time. Electrotherapy necessitated the wearing of electrical garments like corsets and belts and mesmerism involved the manipulation of body fluids using magnets, while hydrotherapy advocated the flushing of the body orifices with water. The study of phrenology, which delved into the physiology and function of the brain, attempted to interpret and qualify behavioural and physical characteristics according to an individual's degree of inherited talents and ability. The science of Eugenics advocated the practice of breeding specific characteristics into future generations of human beings. Such philosophies, however, stimulated curiosity and experimentation and were eagerly received during those years when religious revivalism was rampant, providing stimulating fodder for public debates.

Homeopathic remedies and patent medicines were also very popular, and newspapers jumped at the unlimited possibilities that advertisements for such miraculous cures provided. Although most of the concoctions were relatively tame, containing such ingredients as alcohol and vegetable extracts, some did conceal dangerous toxic substances like mercury, arsenic, lead, and even stimulants like opium and caffeine. A clever doctor often found it to his advantage to gain the confidence of his patients by combining a few of the popular alternatives with some of the old standby remedies.

Medical practice was not a lucrative profession and many doctors supplemented their meagre incomes by operating pharmacies and taking it upon themselves to mix their own patent medicines. Although many practitioners would be considered "quacks" by our standards today, their presence inadvertently served to effectively provoke a necessary reassessment of the status quo of traditional medicine. Some of the newest medical treatments began to promote a sound and sensible approach to the maintenance of good health, based on the practices of good hygiene, well-balanced diets and plenty of fresh air and exercise.

Anderson Ruffin Abbott, M.D., in his academic robes. He graduated from the Toronto School of Medicine in 1861. *Abbott Collection, Toronto Public Library (TRL): S-90.*

The advent of the Crimean War of 1853 to 1856, the Civil War of 1861 to 1865 and the Spanish American War of 1898 all provided a plethora of opportunities for the development of new medical knowledge. Doctors and military commanders readily confirmed the fact that more men were dying from infection, disease and dysentery than from their actual battle wounds. Horrific injuries provided plenty of opportunities for surgeons to hone new techniques and develop better anaesthetics. Since 1846, surgeons had been using sulphuric ether as an anaesthetic, which allowed them to undertake much more complicated and extensive surgeries, while keeping the patient safely unconscious for extended periods of time.

Still, the empirical study of medicine in those days was quite a different prospect than it is today. The practice of medicine was so unregulated in United States during the 1840s that the licensing of physicians was virtually abolished in many states, making it perfectly legal to practise medicine without a license. In an effort to curtail the practice of quackery, the government began to stipulate stringent legal regulations regarding the licensing of doctors. By the 1850s, the Thomsonian Medical Society, an American organization, promoted the science of Botanics or Eclectics[2] and gained so much credence that the legislators granted them licences to practise medicine.

Early in the 1800s, two Canadian doctors, John Rolph and Charles Duncombe both of whom practised medicine in St. Thomas, Upper Canada, developed an academic program of medical studies. Yet, after two years, only one student appears to have completed the series of courses. In 1843, the first official medical school in Toronto opened its doors at King's College and, shortly afterwards, Queen's University established a school in Kingston. At that time the University of Toronto was composed of a conglomeration of separate colleges, each affiliated with a religious denomination: King's College was Anglican, Victoria College was Methodist, Knox College was Presbyterian and St. Michael's College was Catholic. The government did not want to provide financial support to the policies advocated by minority parties, like the Reformers, nor were they interested in supporting colleges affiliated with any of the other churches. It was commonly known that King's College, with it affiliation to the Church of England, received more government funding and preferential treatment under the umbrella of the British crown. But, in 1848, by virtue of the Baldwin Act, King's College was turned into a non-denominational institution known as University College, and was thus granted some public funding. Even still, the High Church Anglican candidates were given admission preference, and the endowment, which

STUDENTS—SESSION 1861-2.

*Abbott, A. R.	Toronto.
*Aiken, E.	Jarvis.
Armstrong, T.	Yorkville.
Baldwin, W. A.	Toronto.
Baxter (M.D), B.	Fort Erie.
Barrett, C.	Toronto.
*Bell, W. H.	Amherstburg.
†*Bolster, J.	Uxbridge.
Braithwaite, F.	Toronto.
Buchanan, C. W.	Toronto.
Burgar, W. E.	Welland.
Burnham, E. La F.	Port Hope.
*Campbell, A. W.	Brooklyn.
*Cassady, J.	Goderich.
Chapman, O. W.	Welland.
Cook, M. W.	Cooksville.
*Covernton, W. H.	Simcoe.
*Craig, T.	Kemptville.
*Dack (B.A.), F. B.	Toronto.
†*DeGrassie, G. P.	Toronto.
*De La Haye, A. J.	Humber.
Dillabough, J.	Easton's Corners.
*Douglass, C.	Streetsville.
*Eby, Aaron	Berlin, C.W.
*Eckardt (M.D.), F. P.	Markham.
Fair, R.	Mariposa.
*Forrest, R. W.	Uxbridge.
Hampton, W. B.	Toronto.
Hardy, R. M.	Uxbridge.
*Harley, J.	Toronto.
*Henry, J.	Sand Hill.

The opening page of the "Annual Announcement" for the Toronto School of Medicine, 1862–63. A.R. Abbott's name heads the alphabetical listing of students for the Session 1861–62. The asterisk beside his name identifies him as "Matriculate in Medicine in the University of Toronto."

had originally been awarded to King's College, was used exclusively for University College and not for any of the other sectarian universities.

Bishop Strachan further appealed to the British government for more funding to establish yet another medical school. He felt that the moral and religious training of King's College medical students was sadly

79

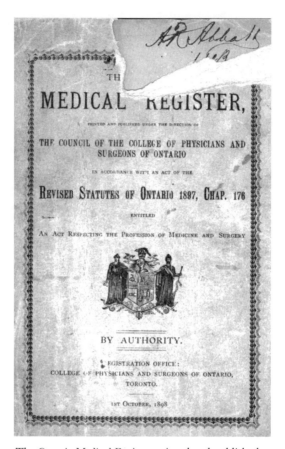

The *Ontario Medical Register*, printed and published
under the direction of the Council of the College of
Physicians and Surgeons of Ontario, published
October 1, 1898, lists Anderson Ruffin Abbott of
Toronto at 245 Ossington Avenue.

neglected in the curriculum and believed that "religion should form the
basis of the whole system of education, being by far the most important
part of knowledge that man could attain, and that neither the advantage
of individuals nor the prosperity of the State could exist unless guided
by religious principles."[3] Strachan's ardent plea was heard and in 1850
he returned to Canada with enough funds to establish the Upper Canada
Medical School, this time under the auspices of the new Trinity College,[4]
which once again represented the Anglican faith. The first Medical School
campus was located at Queen Street and Spadina Avenue in Toronto and
a prestigious faculty was retained to conduct the lectures.

In order to receive the Degree of Medical Doctor, the candidate had to fulfil a number of criteria. They were required to complete a full-time medical program, pass all examinations, be at least twenty-two years of age and earn a degree in the Arts. Each intern was required to work at a recognized hospital for eighteen months and then at an Obstetric Institution for six months. If all went well, they then wrote and defended a thesis approved by the Dean of the college. The Bachelor's Degree (M.B.) in Medicine, involved four years of Professional work and a sound background in Divinity, Classical studies and Mathematics. The only other medical program in existence in Toronto at the time was Dr. Rolph's Toronto School of Medicine and those graduates were granted certification through the University of McGill College in Montreal.

The licensing of physicians presented certain problems.[5] The Upper Canada Medical Board, appointed by the government of Upper Canada, licensed medical graduates from their provincial universities and apparently gave little consideration to graduates from private institutions, like the Toronto Medical School. Finally, in 1869, Parliament appointed the Council of the College of Physicians and Surgeons of Ontario for the purpose of overseeing the licensing process, thus eliminating any favouritism. All applicants were required to attend at least one session of courses in an Ontario medical school and to submit to an oral examination administered by the Council. This was particularly pertinent to physicians who were licensed elsewhere and had immigrated to Canada.

The Upper Canada Medical College continued to endure more organizational changes over the next few decades. Finally, in 1887, Trinity College severed its affiliation with the University of Toronto and applied for its own incorporation, so that it would then be equipped with the power to grant its own degrees in medicine, surgery and midwifery.

When Dr. Abbott left for the Civil War, he had already earned his M.D., but upon his return in 1865, he re-entered Trinity College and, in 1867, graduated with a Bachelor's Degree in Medicine. He became a member of the College of Physicians and Surgeons and the Ontario Dominion Medical Association.

By that time, a number of hospitals were already established in Toronto, namely the Toronto General Hospital, the Toronto Eye Infirmary, the Toronto General Dispensary and Lying-in Hospital, the Provincial Lying-in Hospital and Vaccine Institute, the Maternity Lying-in Hospital and General Dispensary, the House of Industry and the Catholic Orphan Asylum. The original building of the Toronto General Hospital was located on a lot the size of the entire block, bounded by King, Adelaide,

John and Peter streets. A Deed of Sale found in the Abbott Collection indicates that Wilson Abbott had, at one time, owned the property where the original hospital once stood.[6]

Interestingly, there is no evidence to suggest that Dr. Abbott actually set up his own medical practice in Toronto. It would be reasonable to expect that as a "coloured" man, he would have most often attended coloured or Black patients. However, it is well documented that the racial atmosphere in Toronto at that time was unique and people were often judged by their social and financial status rather than simply by the colour of their skin. In 1867, the Toronto General Hospital was closed because of heavy financial losses, but was reopened in 1868 under the direction of a Dr. Hampton. It is known that Dr. Abbott acted as Surgeon-in-Chief of the Toronto General Hospital for about two years, during the temporary absence of Dr. Hampton. In this capacity he was responsible for all of the patients in the hospital. These would have included people of all races, not just Blacks.

Anderson remained critical of the medical institutions and the way they abused the sensibilities of the medical students. The following is a letter that he penned to the Editor of the *Globe:*

Sir,—While the Hospital question is rife, I would call attention to two or three other resources of the institution not mentioned by "Medicus," which, with a little improvement in their management, would render the institution more useful in subserving one of the purposes for which it was intended, namely: a practical school of medicine. We are compelled to attend the practice of the Hospital for at least twelve months. I agree with "Medicus" in saying that it is so much time lost. When the medical officer does attend, he spends a short time admitting the "outdoor" patients and prescribes for them in that off-hand style which evinces little disposition to let us understand the nature of the case or indications for the treatment. Surely a few words explanatory of these is not too much to ask. It would be highly interesting and instructive to the students and they would be enabled to spend their time more profitably while in the Hospital than in reading newspapers, gazing out of the windows, or playing tricks upon one another.

The bedside of the patient affords more facilities for obtaining a practical knowledge of medicine than any other means; therefore, it is very desirable that those examinations should be conducted with care and attention. Unfortunately, as they are conducted at the Toronto General Hospital, we receive little or no instruction from them. The

A view of the original Toronto General Hospital (1856–1913), located on the north side of Gerrard Street East, by eminent photographer William Notman of Montreal, circa 1860s. *Toronto Public Library (TRL): T30148*

students are not allowed to enter the wards unless the medical officer is present; and when he is present, he manages to walk his rounds with amazing rapidity, while the students follow him at a rattling pace, terrifying the poor patients with the noise of their footsteps and the velocity of their motion. When the bedside is reached, a few hasty questions are put to the patients; something is muttered to the clinical clerk, the purport of which is unintelligible to the students; and some orders given to the nurse. At the next bed this formula is repeated.

I do not think the medical officers are to be blamed for these hasty proceedings. Probably they spend as much time as the distance of the Hospital from the city, their private practice and collegiate duties will admit of. But why cannot we have a clinical lecture to the Hospital, whose duty it would be to make himself acquainted with the different cases and give us a course of lectures upon them. I am satisfied the students would be willing to pay a fee that would remunerate him.[7]

Most doctors were not able to generate a regular income from their medical practice and often had to forego payment for their administrations. It was not unusual for doctors to practise law, or to hold political office at the same time. Even the well-known Dr. John Rolph had been educated as a lawyer while still practising medicine and had sat in the Legislature and on various Medical Boards for the universities. Even Dr. Augusta probably earned more income from his pharmacy in Toronto than from his medical practice.

Anderson Abbott was no exception, and it seems he too found himself compelled to find outside sources of income. It would not have been a simple matter to develop a lucrative medical practice with only coloured or Black patients in Toronto at the time, and this may explain some of the reason for his move to Chatham. It was certainly fortunate that he had enough "family money" acquired through his inheritance to sustain himself and his family.

CHAPTER 11

SETTLING DOWN

Oh Mary dear, I come not here
With blandishment to woo thee,
I know the secret of your heart,
I know full well you love me.[1]

AFTER THE CIVIL WAR, as new immigrants continued to pour into
Canada, racial strife began to rise within many Canadian communities.
In his book, *The Blacks in Canada: A History*, Robin Winks notes that
Canadian Black immigrants could not ignore the ever-present reminders
that their "haven" was still considered more a legal one than a social one.[2]
By the time Anderson Abbott returned from the Civil War, he would
have integrated his experiences into the makings of the man who would
eventually make his mark on Canadian history. By now he was more
than ready to assume a leading role in the turbid waters of the growing
civil rights movement of the 1870s. The Reconstruction Period after the
Civil War saw some of the new concepts of the Emancipation Act carried
out, but as the United States reeled from the tremendous human and
economic losses suffered, by both the North and the South, the actual
effectiveness of the new resolutions began to erode. There were so many
changes needed and not enough manpower, authority or expertise to
implement them. As time went on, opposition from the old South
regained momentum and the dreams of true social justice and harmony
flew by the wayside. In a few short years, many of the original intentions
of Reconstruction had been undone or overturned. For the most part,
Blacks in the South remained downtrodden and destitute, with little
opportunity for education, employment or civil liberties for almost another
century. In the North, things seemed somewhat different at first, since
the Abolitionists were fairly abundant, influential and compassionate.

A formal portrait of Anderson Ruffin Abbott in his later years, wearing his academic robes. *Abbott Collection, Toronto Public Library (TRL): S-90.*

However, as immigration from Great Britain and Europe increased, many of the opportunities shifted from the plate of the African descendent to that of the white refugees. Tremendous political agitation and controversy resulted and most Blacks retaliated by thronging together in ghettos, instead of integrating with their fellow citizens.

The place of the African-Canadian was slightly different, as it was not yet solidly established and many of the better-educated and wealthier Blacks actively resisted the forces intended to curb their civil liberties. Dr. Abbott rose to the task. Though often a voice in the background, he wrote voluminous essays and letters questioning, probing and stridently evoking thought and action from his people. He constantly strove for equality and fairness for all races, and his boldness, race pride and even his seeming arrogance were important factors in transmitting his message as he ardently opposed any demand to submit to oppressive measures. He proposed that his people should be valued as human beings, with their contributions to society based on their accomplishments. To this end, he set himself the incredible challenge to represent himself as a living example. No doubt, it was often a thankless task, but he never relented and went to his grave with the same pride and fortitude that had sustained his forebears for decades.

By far, the most challenging of his converts were the coloured people themselves, for frequently he ranted about their unfortunate lack of self-esteem coupled with a reluctance to assume responsibility for their own welfare and future:

We have as yet to learn the full scope and application of the sentiment expressed in the motto, "United we stand, divided we fall." Union and harmony are the moving springs of all great actions, whether they pertain to the moral or physical world. If there is not a harmonious correlation of forces, chaos and confusion result. If we search history we find numerous examples of the demoralizing and disseminating effects of disunion and discord...What we need especially is "coherence," if we ever expect to rise to that level of respect, ability and influence which other classes enjoy...There is no shutting our eyes to the fact, that we labor under the ban of ostracism and we may expect this state of things to continue until we aspire to the wealth and enterprise of those who have them in the most abundance...Numerically speaking we are in a minority in this country and if we become divided in sympathy and interest we render ourselves powerless in the hands of our enemies and incapable of accomplishing anything for the good of ourselves or prosperity. Let us therefore be united in spirit and purpose and as we have been...by a common bond of sympathy. Let that bond still continue to unite us throughout the ever-varying phases of our growth in prosperity.[3]

While in Toronto, Anderson began to court a young woman, Mary Ann Casey, from St. Catharines, Ontario. During his courtship he penned a number of poetic tributes to his sweetheart. One such poem, entitled "The Rover's Bride,"[4] depicts himself as a "young rover," away at war and Mary Ann as his "beloved." In November of 1869, he declared his love and proposed to her in a poem entitled "The Declaration."[5]

Mary Ann's mother, Mary Ann Adams, was white and of Scottish descent. Records located in the St. Catharines library indicate that she was the daughter of Elias Smith Adams, the first mayor of St. Catharines. In 1852, he founded the interracial Refugee Slaves' Friends Society to assist American fugitive slaves. Mary Ann's father, Thomas Powers Casey was described as coloured. There is some indication

Mary Ann Casey, daughter of Mary Ann Adams and Thomas Powers Casey, circa mid-1870s. *Courtesy of the Abbott family.*

87

that Thomas may have worked as a court clerk in Ireland before coming to Canada, but other census documentation suggests he migrated to Canada from the United States. When he settled in St. Catharines, he opened a barbershop and, along with shaving and hairdressing, he advertised other speciality services, such as bleeding and dentistry! The shop was located in the old Welland Hotel in St. Catharines for many years, but when a fire destroyed the building, he moved across the road and expanded his facilities. An excerpt in the Thorold newspaper of April 21, 1882, reported an interesting bit of gossip. "Tice Egerton paid dearly for boisterously embracing Thos. Casey's wife while visiting en route for home, whereupon Casey returned home and a scuffle ensued, involving a neighbour and Tice was almost killed."

St. Catharines was considered one of the major gateways to the "promised land," prior to the Civil War and a haven to where many Underground Railroad conductors furtively guided their charges over the Niagara River into Ontario. Gradually many of the refugees dispersed across the province and settled in other cities or rural communities. The people of the Niagara belt were strongly influenced by the political climate in the northern United States, and Black refugees could not escape the repercussions of the racially discriminating and segregating practices of the Jim Crow[6] phenomena that had spread northward.

Prejudicial behaviours were observed in 1852 when a coloured militia joined a white militia in a parade exercise and the coloured militia suffered taunts and assaults from white spectators. The white fire brigade responded to the alarm with the understanding that the Black militia had instigated the conflict and the resulting riot preceded a brutal attack on the residents of the Black community. In 1854, the *Provincial Freeman* reported that the coloured waiters of the major hotels went on strike to protest on-going acts of discrimination like the "...cruel prejudice which denied colored persons, however respectable, the use of public conveniences to and from the railroad station and steamboat."[7] The threat was taken seriously by the owners of the hotels and, shortly afterwards, they amended their policies. In 1855, the St. Catharines School Board refused to admit coloured children to the white school. But again, after sufficient protest, the decision was reversed and, in 1857, coloured students were finally allowed to attend the upper levels in white schools, as long as they sat in a separate area. Primary schools remained segregated in that city until 1883.

Although well-respected in St. Catharines, the Casey family must have considered the more privileged position they would be able to enjoy by

Left, Mary Ann Adams, mother of Mary Ann Casey, was the daughter of the first mayor of St. Catharines; *right*, Mary Ann's father, Thomas Powers Casey, was owner of a successful barber and hairdressing shop in St. Catharines until he relocated his family to Toronto in 1867. *Photographs courtesy of the Abbott family.*

living in a metropolis like Toronto, which was more racially tolerant. Around 1867, they left their home and moved to Toronto, where Thomas set up shop in the old Queen's Hotel, the present-day Royal York Hotel, located on Front Street.

An interesting story about the Casey girls has been handed down through the family. Apparently Mary Ann and her three sisters, Henrietta, Hannah and Sarah Jane, attended a private school, known as the Bishop's Palace, in the old Grange building situated in Toronto at the corner of present-day University and Wellington streets.[8] If the story is accurate, the girls' inclusion in such an elite group would certainly have reflected the unique attitude prevalent in the city during that period. Or, perhaps it was the result of an early but subtle form of racial passing. Unfortunately, there are no registration records or other evidence to substantiate the story.

On August 9, 1871, Thomas Powers Casey gave away in marriage the hand of his daughter Mary Ann, at the age of fifteen, to Dr. Anderson Ruffin Abbott. They were married at St. George's the Martyr Anglican Church in Toronto. Shortly afterwards, they moved to Chatham and

Mary Ann's sister, Henrietta Casey, who had married Phillip Judah, accompanied them in the new adventure. Her father-in-law, Adolphus, a carpenter and builder by trade, erected a house set side-by-side for each of the families on Park Street. At that time, it was quite common for families, often linked by marriage, to live and operate in close association with one another. Like the Toyer girls before them, the Casey daughters also married into other "old-line" Black families, such as the Watkins, the Lightfoots, the Judahs and the Hubbards. Relocating from place to place together, they were thus able to establish and maintain a strong source of family support.

When Anderson and Mary Ann chose to settle in Chatham, they intended to be long-term residents. Anderson set up his medical practice in the Hunton Block on William Street, but also travelled throughout the countryside making house calls. A newspaper clipping reveals the details:

Dr. A. Abbott
Licenciate of the Medical Board of Upper Canada, 1861;
Primary Bachelor of Medicine, University of Toronto, 1867;
member of the College of Physicians and Surgeons, Ontario;
member of Dominion Medical Association;
exassistant Surgeon U.S. Army; for three years in charge of
Camp Baker Hospital, Washington, DC, and for some
time acting resident physician of Toronto General Hospital;
Coroner for the County of Kent.
OFFICE-King Street, in Hunton's Block.
RESIDENCE-Colborne Street[9]

Other Black physicians practised in Chatham between 1850 and 1870, including Doctors Riley, White, Aray and Martin Delaney. However, when the prospect of becoming Coroner of Kent County arose, it was Dr. Abbott who boldly, and successfully, applied. On March 4, 1874, he received the following letter from the Provincial Secretary's Office in Toronto:

Sir,
    By command of the Lieutenant Governor, I have to inform you that he has been pleased to appoint you an Associate Coroner, in and for the County of Kent.
    Your Commission will be forwarded to the Office of the Clerk of the Peace for the County upon payment to this Department of Thirteen

90

Dollars, the necessary fee thereon. The Clerk of the Peace will also be directed to administer to you the Oath as prescribed by law.[10]

Ultimately, this event made Anderson Abbott, M.D., the first Black man to hold that position, and even quite possibly the first Black Coroner in Canada. Politically speaking, a dream had been fulfilled, for a decade before, Dr. Augusta had been denied the honour because of his race. Although Anderson Abbott never appears to have sought election into political office, this appointment would have carried a significant amount of official prestige, making him a Civil Servant, as well as providing him with a regular income. Even in the 1870s, the Coroner's position would have demanded a certain degree of investigative and analytical work. Dr. Abbott's extensive experience with Civil War deaths would have combined nicely with his deep interest in the interpretation of the law, and would have contributed to the makings of a formidable medical examiner. Unfortunately, most of the early Coroner records have been destroyed by fire, so this portion of his career cannot be traced in more detail.

Death means different things to different people and, in the 1800s, death occurred frequently, as a routine fact of life. Many children died at young ages and the Abbotts lost two of their own while living in Chatham. Several years later Anderson had the bodies of his children exhumed and removed to join their ancestors in the Abbott crypt at the Necropolis Cemetery in Toronto.

Dr. Abbott's adherence to high professional standards gained him a good deal of respect from the community and, when he was elected Chairman of the Kent County Medical Association in 1878, a local paper smugly announced the following:

> At a recent meeting of the Chatham Medical Association our esteemed townsman, Dr. Abbott, presided, having been appointed Chairman by a unanimous vote. This may be a small matter for comment, but it is said, straws show how the wind blows and this little circumstance is another proof that condition, not color, is what operates to the disadvantage of the colored race.[11]

In another article, Abbott was described as one "who has proven himself to be very skilful. Many, we have reason to believe, would have been called to stand in their lot, had they been left to other hands."[12]

It may be that Anderson Abbott chose a career in medicine for some very specific reasons. He was highly motivated and intelligent enough to learn meticulous information, and he was extraordinarily inquisitive and fascinated by the intricacies of all the arts and sciences. As well, such a career would have provided him with a tangible means of helping his people, while at the same time gaining a social status that very few coloured physicians enjoyed at the time. Finally, he would have viewed the profession as a very concrete way of highlighting the limitless possibilities for other members of his race. He may have been perceived as somewhat arrogant and self-involved, but quite probably those were the traits required to confront the obstacles of racial discrimination of the day.

CHAPTER 12

THE COUNTRY LIFE

Those who profess to favour freedom yet deprecate agitation, are men who want crops without plowing up the ground; they want rain without thunder and lightning.... Power concedes nothing without demand.[1]

BY THE 1870S, A NUMBER of Black fugitives had returned to the United States. This exodus depleted the markets and clients for a number of the remaining Black professionals and businesses. Many were consequently forced to move to the cities to seek employment or better business opportunities. The little General Provisions store in Chatham owned by Commission Merchants Weaver, Judah and Boyd proved to be an exceptional enterprise, conducting its business transactions all over the world. By this time, some of the previous racial tension had eased, as the small communities regained their white majority. Dr. Abbott's appointment as Coroner of Kent County indicated that some changes had transpired, on the outside at least.

However, strong discrimination and apprehension continued to prevail beneath the surface, as many whites were supremely concerned with miscegenation. When Thomas Pinkney, a Black Anglican minister, married Elizabeth King, a white teacher in the Negro school, a great outcry ensued as the local whites demanded new legislation to prevent such "...desecration of the white man's lineage, his breed and his distinctive features and characteristics."[2] In 1863, while forty thousand Canadians were fighting for the American Union and freedom of the Black slaves during the Civil War, Canadian government officials could be heard making wide, sweeping discriminatory statements. The Chatham mayor professed that "...only the most abandoned whites married Blacks..." and a white schoolteacher stated that "...when white women married Black men they were disowned by their race."[3]

Alderman Henry Weaver was a respected businessman in the Chatham area in the mid-to latter 1800s. *Courtesy of Gwen Robinson, Heritage Room, WISH Centre, Chatham, Ontario.*

In 1864, S.G. Howe conducted the Freedmen's Inquiry Commission in Canada and reported that during the early years of immigration, Black men often married white women, especially those of Irish descent.[4] A similar instance can be seen in the marriage of Thomas Powers Casey who was of Black/Irish descent and Mary Ann Adams, of Scottish descent. Although many whites could not accept the practice, Bishop Green of the BME Church declared that the Black community had "too much good sense to think a woman is degraded because she marries a Black man. A respectable colored man and a respectable white woman are looked upon as a respectable family...they treat them as if they were both colored"[5]

But still prejudice persisted. Howe reported the opinions voiced by some of the white residents that he interviewed, as follows:

"The feeling against the colored people has been growing ever since I came here and more particularly since your President's Proclamation. They are becoming now so very haughty that they are looking upon themselves as the equals of whites!..."

"I think the prejudice against the colored people is stronger here than in the States..."

"You will find a great many colored people about Chatham—too many ..."

"The colored people generally live apart. There has been, hitherto, a very strong prejudice against them and the result is that they are, generally speaking, confined to a particular locality of the town..."[6]

Perhaps the saddest note was struck by Mr. Sinclair of Chatham, when he declared that, although Canadian law firmly regarded all Canadian citizens as equal, in reality, "...the colored people are considered inferior and must remain so for many years, perhaps forever, because their color distinguishes them."[7]

Top, Henry Weaver's store was located at the intersection of Duke and Park streets. *Bottom*, a view of King Street in Chatham, circa the 1870s. The imposing building in the right foreground, owned by Nathaniel Murray, housed Black businesses. *Photographs courtesy of Gwen Robinson, Heritage Room, WISH Centre, Chatham, Ontario.*

This was the atmosphere that the Abbotts faced, as they settled into the community of Kent County. Such were the times, when many people openly speculated about the physical and mental attributes of the Negro, regardless of the fact that none of it was based on scientific fact. Charges of laziness, dishonesty, lack of physical stamina, infertility and sickliness

95

were freely and irresponsibly flung about at random. Howe's study summarized the situation as follows:

> As long as the colored people form a very small proportion of the population and are dependent, they receive protection and favors; but when they increase and compete with the laboring class for a living and especially when they begin to aspire to social equality, they cease to be "interesting Negroes," and become "niggers."[8]

Before the Civil War, the Canadian economy had prospered and, in 1860, Kent farmers produced an admirable, agricultural output. Black or white, they could be seen profitably selling their wares, side by side at the Chatham market every Saturday morning. Anderson's memoirs record his impression of the dramatic urbanization that unfolded in the County where, not long before, the land had lain a pristine wilderness and "...the axe and the bullet had not yet greeted their ears." As industrial development spread, machinery was used to cultivate the land and farmers were able to increase their produce without the need for costly manpower. Farms became more prosperous and the future seemed to hold unlimited possibilities. The Black pioneers had come a long way since the early arduous days. Abbott observed that the elegantly furnished houses were built with good taste and surrounded by extensive and ornamental gardens:

> No more apparitions of physical distress, or brawny sunburnt arms, toilfully swinging the flaming scythe...The muddy wagon tracks, rendered almost impassable by obtruding roads and stumps had given place to dry and level roads. New, well-cultivated farms stretched far away on every side...Thrift and enterprise were apparent everywhere.[9]

In another article Anderson reported that many of the coloured people owned some of the finest homes in the area and their barns were large and spacious, being well-stocked with herds of sheep, cattle and swine. Most families owned several horses along with a selection of threshing, mowing and reaping machines. None of them owned less than fifty acres of land and some as much as three hundred acres:

> A gentleman counted, in my presence, 3,300 acres owned by coloured men and all within a circuit of four miles.[10]

Dr. Abbott was very much interested in the day-to-day events that affected the townsfolk. An interesting letter to the Editor of the *Chatham Planet* makes a practical commentary on a recent bylaw, restricting the running at large of cows in the township. Here he uses his medical expertise to fairly weigh the need for public health and contentment of the community:

Sir:—The By-law passed by the Council respecting the running at large of cows and which comes into force on the 1st prox., has had the effect of stirring up the indigestion of a large number of our citizens. It would be a strange thing if someone did not protest against a measure so harsh and arbitrary. It is repressive in its character and evinces an utter disregard of the interests, comfort and convenience of a large number of our citizens, because the condition and circumstances calling for such a By-law do not obtain in this community. The idea of applying the municipal regulations of such a place as Toronto, with its thickly populated districts, to the wide-spread area over which our population is scattered, is simply preposterous; and such legislation by our town fathers is both ill-advised and meddlesome. If they would concentrate the mental focus of their assembled wisdom upon some method of exterminating the rats, mice and cockroaches, one might at least give them credit for good intentions. But to drive from our midst those animals which administer to our comfort and necessities, evinces a disposition to follow in the footsteps of those who, being clothed with a little brief authority, are very apt to overstep the bounds of prudence and sound judgement. This I am sure the Council does not wish to do. But the effect of the By-law will be to give that coloring to their actions. It will deprive many poor families of their principal means of subsistence. It will compel those in better circumstances and to whom a supply of pure healthy milk is a necessity to resort to the heterogeneous mixture peddled around the streets, the use of which, during the hot months causes many cases of diarrhoea, dysentery and typhoid fever...It will raise the price of milk, with the inconvenience and uncertainty of dealing with a few vendors. It will render the cost of keeping a cow so expensive as to place it beyond the means of all but a very few and thereby create a milk monopoly. It will deprive many families of a plentiful supply of one of the most nutritious and essentially necessary articles for dietetic and culinary purposes. It will necessitate, in many cases, the hiring of a boy to drive the cow to and from the pasture with the cost in addition of $1.50 per month for very poor pasturage. If the animal be housed and fed it will not only increase materially the cost of keeping but it will impair its health and render the milk impure. It will force the sale at a great sacrifice at this time of many valuable animals and in many other ways I could mention, it will do a positive injustice to a great many in an endeavour to prevent a possible injury to a few...I hope, sire, that steps will be taken at once to quash this By-law as being arbitrary, selfish and repressive in its character and as calculated to do more harm than good.[11]

Three churches received strong support from the townspeople, the Presbyterian, the British Methodist Episcopal and the Union. Reverend King's Presbyterian Church was still going strong. When Anderson visited Buxton he would sometimes attend the services. He described one such visit:

As I sat there and thought of faces once familiar and voices mute too soon, all my affections seemed to gather round the old kirk and I loved it with a sort of personal love. Sunday I heard a very instructive sermon from the Rev. Mr. King and my impression is that, as the old gentleman grows weaker physically, he grows stronger intellectually and spiritually. He is still as zealous in his self-sacrificing labours as he was on the first day I first saw him.[12]

The brick British Methodist Episcopal Church in Chatham was constructed on the same property as the original frame structure, known as the BME Victoria Chapel. The first church remains today as a Mason's lodge. *Courtesy of Gwen Robinson, Heritage Room, WISH Centre, Chatham, Ontario.*

This young women's group, known as the Buds of Promise, learned how to conduct themselves like ladies under the tutelage of Helena Lynn, a music teacher at the Woodstock Institute, a school in Chatham. A non-denominational group, they met at the BME Church. *Courtesy of Gwen Robinson, Heritage Room, WISH Centre, Chatham, Ontario.*

On another occasion he attended a service led by Reverend Jon Riley, formerly a protege of Reverend King's who later settled in Leavenworth, Kentucky:

> I had heard much of this gentleman's abilities as a speaker while he was attending Knox College in Toronto and therefore had some curiosity to hear him.... Mr. Riley possesses a good countenance, a sympathetic eye, a clear, musical voice, a distinct enunciation, a good command of language and is happy in the expression of those higher emotions of the heart inspired by deep religious fervor. I am much mistaken if his eloquence be not felt beyond the limits of his own denomination.[13]

Although Anderson and Mary Ann had been married in the Anglican Church, in accordance with Mary Ann's denomination, they became

One of the last congregational conferences held in the BME Church before it became the Community Church for a period of time in the 1930s. By 1950, it had reverted back to being a BME Church once more, but was demolished in 1989.[14] *Courtesy of Gwen Robinson, Heritage Room, WISH Centre, Chatham, Ontario.*

steadfast supporters of the BME Church while they lived in Chatham. The building was eventually destroyed by a fire and the congregation had to pool their resources to replace it with a fine brick edifice, 80 by 60 feet and able to seat 1,200 people. Reverend S.C. Gossely publicly acknowledged, with admiration, the Black craftsmen who had built the new church. Each Sunday hundreds of worshippers would attend the Morning Service and another three or four hundred would arrive for the Evening Service. Abbott took the work of the Church very seriously, believing that it offered a fine foundation for racial uplift:

> The church has a great work to perform in the cause of education. There cannot be any antagonism between these two humanizing and evangelizing agencies. They must work together for the up-building of our race. Life is a reality, something to be made practically useful, not only to ourselves, but to those around us. It is the duty of the Church

to teach people how to live, as well as how to die. She should be the focus, from which should spring all those moral, social and intellectual influences, which make men wiser and better. She should foster and encourage all those innocent social enjoyments which young people delight to participate in.... Therefore there can be no antagonism between religion and education. They are two of the most powerful agencies at work in the up-building of our race.[15]

The Sabbath School served as an important aspect of the community's religious life and contributed greatly to the advancement of their education. A full program of religious education included enthusiastic sessions of scripture readings and hymn singing, which were held every Sunday afternoon, for more than two hundred students. In an anniversary address to the Sabbath School, in 1874, Anderson Abbott proposed that the lessons should be made as palatable as possible, by de-emphasizing "the mere enunciation of religious principles and theological dogmas."[16]

While living in Chatham, Dr. Abbott became a prolific writer and found the perfect venue for delivering his messages, when he became Associate Editor, along with Reverend R.R. Disney, of the *Missionary Messenger*, the bi-monthly newspaper of the BME Church. He was proud enough to compare the quality, usefulness, endurance and longevity of the paper in comparison to other Negro publications like the popular *Voice of the Fugitive* and the *Provincial Freeman*.[17] Abbott believed that the *Messenger* stood ready "...like a battle-scarred veteran, with powers unimpaired to battle for the cause of religion, education, morality and temperance."[18] Although he saw the paper as a reflection of the "... indomitable zeal and enlightened sentiment for the ministry,"[19] he also recognized its usefulness as a vehicle for extending his own views on many local social, political and cultural subjects:

To this end the clergymen of the B.M.E. Church have established and sustained with commendable success, that creditable little sheet the Missionary Messenger, which, for over nine years, through heat and cold, prosperity and adversity, success and discouragement, has not failed to visit your firesides, to instruct and amuse you. While other enterprises of this kind have broken upon the intellectual atmosphere, like a comet for a time; this little sheet has been growing stronger and stronger in intellectual vigour and can tack, now, its victorious standard to the mast and boast that it has never once been obliged to strike its colors.[20]

The Charity Block, located at King and Adelaide streets, was
a well-known business centre. James Charity sold shoes on
the upper floor, while the *Provincial Freeman* was published
on the lower level. *Courtesy of Gwen Robinson, Heritage
Room, WISH Centre, Chatham, Ontario.*

The practice of "begging," on behalf of the "poor, unfortunate Negroes"
was common among some Black communities and created a great deal
of embarrassment for many others. In Amherstburg the True Band
Society formed to combat such activities and became so popular in Canada
West that it increased its numbers to 600 members within 14 Bands spread
across the land. Likewise, Anderson was very concerned that this practice
reflected poorly on his people and he publicly denounced the participants
as swindlers:

> They generally pose as preachers or agents and represent themselves
> as authorized to collect funds for some alleged church or society among
> the colored people. It is needless to say that the funds never reach the
> objects for which they were donated. These men are impostors of the
> rankest type. They associate themselves with some religious or philan-
> thropic institution in order that they may more easily swindle the public
> … The colored people as a class are not known as beggars. This reputa-
> tion they would like to maintain. But it is difficult to circumvent the
> surreptitious methods of these impostors who possess neither honesty
> nor self-respect.[21]

His own public image was also a serious consideration and in one instance,
while living in the United States, in his reading of an Indianapolis journal,

he learned of an imposter who engaged in "begging" and in so doing had taken advantage of a friend. Abbott quickly moved to counter any association with the individual. "While we can appreciate the good, but misdirected effort to assist a fellow creature, at the same time we cannot but express our regret that so many of our friends have been victimized on our account."[22]

When Booker T. Washington agreed to visit Toronto and address the Black community, Anderson sprang into action. He saw the event as an opportunity to clarify the situation of the Canadian Negro and to publicly dispel some of the falsehoods berating the Black race. Furthermore, he was concerned that Washington admire the progress of the Toronto Blacks and not harbour an image of them as poor, helpless and indigent, for all who attended were intelligent, well-dressed and obviously able to readily pay the admission fee:

> It is hoped that the attendance of a large number of intelligent, well-dressed colored people at the lecture has disabused Mr. Washington's mind of the impression that there is any considerable number of his race in this city who were too poor to pay the price of admission.
>
> It is for this reason and others that I could mention that I consider Dr. Washington's visit timely and profitable. It is seldom that the citizens of Toronto have the opportunity of hearing colored men of talent and oratorical ability.[23]

Dr. Abbott's keen interest in all manner of social welfare issues led him to eagerly embrace any opportunity to learn from experience and he would often travel to the United States to observe how things were done there. Assimilating new ideas, he would then return to Canada to share and apply his new knowledge to parallel situations at home. In 1878, he participated in a tour of the prison facilities in Detroit and brought back many ideas regarding the philosophy and practice of incarceration. "We were very much pleased with what we saw in the little time that we had at our disposal and feel much obligation to the gentlemanly official who conducted us through the buildings."[24]

It would appear that Anderson Abbott enjoyed a rather different life than his father before him. He was born into a favoured class and received a classical academic education to become a medical doctor, whereas his father had to raise himself up from illiteracy, through the ranks of apprenticeship and labourer to become an astute businessman. Nevertheless, Anderson, like his father, did like to challenge the status quo and constantly devoted himself to acts of resistance to the social forces that persistently oppressed marginalized people. Although he was cognizant of his own social privilege and class, he did not turn his back on those of lesser means. Rather, he endeavoured to use his good fortune to further the interests of others through the promotion of education, Christian principles and civic responsibility.

CHAPTER 13

EDUCATION–SEPARATE
BUT EQUAL?

*Of all the manifestations of Negrophobia the attempt to deny Negroes
the equal use of public schools was the most successful. In communities
where problems of land sales, voting rights, or jury service never arose,
a large number of white inhabitants agreed with efforts to keep Negro
children from the schools.*[1]

VERY LITTLE IS KNOWN about the personal side of the Abbott family
life while they lived in Chatham, raising their five surviving children: three
daughters, Helene, Ida and Grace; and two sons, Wilson and Gordon, all
of whom were born in Chatham except Gordon, who was the youngest.
It is interesting to note that while Anderson's parents, Wilson and Ellen,
and indeed Mary Ann's parents, Thomas and Mary Ann, took great pains
to educate their children in private schools, Anderson and Mary Ann did
not. They chose to fight for the right to send their children to public schools,
despite the threat of racial discrimination and segregation.

The public school system presented an excellent backdrop for Dr.
Abbott's activities, and he leapt into yet another worthwhile project when
he was elected as a trustee to the school board. By the time he had returned
to the Chatham area with his own children in the 1870s, the social scene
had changed dramatically since his boyhood days at Reverend King's
Mission School. The Buxton schools, which had previously admitted
children of all colours, had become mere shadows of their former selves
as their population diminished. The question of segregation had never
been truly swept aside and, once the quality of the white schools was
restored, school children were again segregated in the town of Chatham.

In 1850, the Ontario Common Schools Act was passed, to allow any
racial or religious minorities to establish separate schools for their children,

105

A sketch of the "Old King Street School." The building
was located on Princess Street in Chatham, Canada
West. In 1858, the American abolitionist John Brown
and his supporters held a meeting here to seek support
for the proposed liberation of slaves and the establishment of a free society. *Courtesy of Gwen Robinson,
Heritage Room, WISH Centre, Chatham, Ontario.*

an act that pleased both Protestants and Catholics. Protestants could
continue to proselytize to their heart's content and, with the help of
teachers and lay ministers, ultimately "rule the conscience, regulate the
pulsations of the heart and restrain the passions."[2] Catholics, likewise,
were free to continue to regulate their religious instruction through the
clergy. However, some school boards took advantage of the Act to ensure
that Black children remained segregated, based on the wishes of the
majority of the local inhabitants.

The coloured people were acutely aware that their children were not
receiving an education equal to that of the white children, despite the
fact that they contributed a full sixth of the total taxes for this lack of
privilege. Back in 1824, the Princess Street Public School in Chatham
was specifically opened to coloured students, after the children of Israel
Williams, a Chatham butcher, were refused admission to Central Public
School in town. By 1858, the Princess School building had fallen into
disrepair but was eventually renovated. However, in 1861, the Chatham
school board established boundaries for separate schools that were
completely unreasonable, and it appeared obvious that the purpose was
to exclude Black children from the white school district. Such action was
declared illegal and, in 1864:

> ...Chief Justice William Henry Draper ruled that if a separate school
> had been established for Negroes and then allowed to fall into disuse,
> Negroes must be admitted to the still-functioning common school.[3]

The Black residents persisted in their demand for integration. They wanted to enrol their children in the best school, regardless of the "…unlawful, unjust and unreasonable proscription."[4] In the heat of the ensuing outcry, the Board of Trustees hastily called a meeting and unanimously passed the following resolution:

> That the inspector of the Public Schools be and is hereby instructed to notify the Head Teacher of each Public School in this town, that no child of school age, whether white or colored, is to be excluded from any of the Public Schools in this town, provided the average attendance of any such school, as shown by the Registry Book, will, according to law, warrant their admission.[5]

Dr. Alfred Shadd was the last teacher to serve at the "Old King School" just before Chatham's schools became integrated. *Courtesy of Gwen Robinson, Heritage Room, WISH Centre, Chatham, Ontario.*

In Anderson's words: "Thus you see by a determined and united effort on the part of our people this vexed question has been settled now and forever."[6] And he did his part to maintain the status quo. In 1875, the local paper recorded the results of his first attempt to become a school board trustee. The sentiments of the coloured community are clearly biased in his favour:

> In Eberts Ward, the candidates were—Dr. A.R. Abbott (colored) and Mr. John A. Hoon (white). The latter was elected by a majority of ONLY ONE VOTE. Considering that Dr. Abbott was unavoidably absent from town on the day of polling and that he is a colored man and a comparative stranger in Chatham, he may well feel proud over the result of the contest. Had Dr. Abbot been present at the poll and had not his opponent VOTED FOR HIMSELF, he (the Doctor) would have beaten the other candidate all hollow.
>
> We are informed that steps are being taken to protest the election, as it is alleged the poll was closed SEVEN MINUTES before time, thus preventing four persons from recording their votes in favor of Dr. Abbott.

In 1873, the Wilberforce Educational Institute came into being in Chatham as a result of the merging of the Nazrey Institute and the British American Institute in the Dawn Settlement. Originally on Wellington Street, the school was relocated to this site on King Street. Another school known as the Woodstock Institute also offered a range of courses during this period. When the original Woodstock Institute was torn down in the 1980s, money was raised and property acquired, and the WISH (Woodstock Institute Sertoma Help) Centre came into being. The centre continues to teach skills to community residents. Gwen Robinson was instrumental in establishing the WISH Centre. *Courtesy of Gwen Robinson, Heritage Room, WISH Centre, Chatham, Ontario.*

It is also said that two minors were allowed to vote. There is no doubt but that another poll will be obtained and Dr. Abbott's friends—both white and colored—say he SHALL BE ELECTED, providing he is present on the day of "combat." It is very necessary that he be present and we sincerely hope that he may, in order that the colored citizens of Chatham, conjointly with the unprejudiced whites, may be able to establish a precedent in the municipal history of this ancient borough.[7]

Abbott studied the American education system extensively as a means of gathering data on Civil Rights that could be applied in Canadian schools. Perhaps his keen interest in this area sparked the attention of his daughter, Helene, who later became one of the first Black kindergarten teachers for Black children in the United States. In the following excerpt, Anderson cites the attention awarded to the education of kindergarten students in the integrated Detroit schools:

> In an interesting account of a visit to the Detroit Schools, published in the *Canadian Monthly*, J.M. Buchan, M.A., Inspector of High Schools for this Province, gives some facts which show that the principle of Civil Rights is fairly carried out by the Detroit Board of Education. He says: "Not only are colored children to be seen in all the schools, but at least one colored teacher is employed by the Board. On my visit to the kindergarten, which occupies a room in the Everett school, I was astonished to find that its conductor was a colored woman. She proved to be a remarkably intelligent and able person and a lady in the best sense of the word. She was in charge of about thirty-five children of all colors and I was informed and can readily believe, that she is very popular with the white parents. The exhibition of the kindergarten method, which she was so good as to make for my benefit, was exceedingly interesting. No one, after seeing it, could doubt that the system is beneficial to both the minds and bodies of the children.
>
> The peculiarity of the Kindergarten system is that it develops the whole nature of the child by natural methods. While learning their alphabet and beginning to read, the children become acquainted with various kinds of lines, the names of Pythagorean solids and of various natural and artificial objects; they play games, sing, act and applaud, in concert; they draw on their slates, prick figures in paper and perform many other exercises.[8]

One person who made a serious commitment to the betterment of the education for Black students was Bishop Nazrey of the BME Church. He established the Nazrey Institute College as a boarding school on his own farm just outside Chatham. Adhering to the philosophy of the church, it offered a stimulating atmosphere in a country setting where God, life and nature could be studied and appreciated to their fullest. Trade and skilled craftsmanship night courses were available. Later it amalgamated with the British American Institute in Dresden, to become the Wilberforce Educational Institute, which strove to prepare Black high school students for university. It was a non-denominational school and, in 1873, was incorporated by an act of Parliament so that it could qualify for public funding. Quite naturally Dr. Abbott became involved in this a worthwhile venture and served as President from 1873 to 1880.

Henrietta Virginia Dolly
Scott taught music at the
Wilberforce School. *Courtesy
of Gwen Robinson, Heritage
Room, WISH Centre,
Chatham, Ontario.*

All his life, Dr. Abbott was to fight for desegregation in the schools, as he could never accept the "separate but equal" concept. Yet, until 1891, such was the law in Chatham, when the last separate Negro school finally closed. In 1951, a Royal Commission on Education in Ontario repealed the offending clauses of the Common School Act. Even then, several Kent County delegations expressed the opinion that Black children were receiving a better education in the segregated system. Incredibly, it was not until 1964, when Leonard A. Braithwaite, the first Black man elected to the Ontario Provincial Legislature, demanded that all references to Black separate schools in the Common School Act be removed.

Although vestiges of inequality continue to plague our schools and educational institutions today, it has not gone unnoticed and perhaps this consciousness will eventually become a strong enough force to impel our society to balance the scales in a productive and innovative manner. Until that time comes, we must press on, prodding and provoking, antagonizing and challenging, just as Dr. Abbott did over a century ago.

CHAPTER 14

THE POLITICAL ARENA

Ald. Hubbard: "Well, when two of us come together with our skates on, somebody's got to be underneath."
Chairman Lamb: "Alas, that somebody is me, I've got the Hubbard squash."[1]

EMANCIPATION DAY WAS, AND still is, celebrated on the first of August, commemorating the day, in 1834 when the British government granted liberty to all the slaves within its domain, including its colonies of Canada and the West Indies. The Black citizens of Chatham usually looked forward to the festivities and would flock to the picnic grounds early in the morning to meet the delegates. This particularly prominent occasion was not only a chance to express their appreciation to the British Crown, but more importantly, it was an opportunity to celebrate their own achievements and the unique role they had played in the making of Canadian history. In just a few short decades, they had shed their shackles of bondage and overcome great obstacles of ignorance, oppression and prejudice. They had worked hard to become enlightened and educated and had earned the right to vote on important issues pertaining to their civil rights, liberties and freedom. Although the negative implications of British colonization had to be acknowledged, many people felt some degree of gratitude that at least they were relatively free from the threat of American slavery. Although clearly sexist and a product of his time, Abbott did not hesitate to acclaim the attributes of his fellow "colored" citizens:

Tell me not, that the colored men are an undesirable class of emigrants. They have given irrefutable evidence that they are capable of attaining to all that pertains to moral, intellectual and industrial progress. Any man with instincts above the level of a brute would see in this, evidence of providence and industry. And as for their loyalty, they are far more loyal than a great many in this country, who left the land that gave them birth and cursed it because it could not, or would not give them a living. Within less than half a decade we have seen men of our race step from the condition of serfs, to take a position in the highest executive chamber of the neighbouring Republic and if our progress in future shall be in a corresponding ration as in the past, there is no telling to what possibilities we may attain. The time has gone by when one race was regarded as the sole possessor of intellect and genius. It has been shown that the same qualities may lie beneath a Black skin and under favorable conditions will break forth like a sunburst upon our senses and radiate with its effulgence, the whole intellectual atmosphere.[2]

Abbott was quick to remind his people that they had earned the right to be acknowledged as loyal, steadfast citizens, offering up their very lives for their country, whenever the need arose. They should not have to apologize for expecting to be treated as equal and deserving citizens:

Our fathers sealed our heritage with their life's blood and we do not intend that either a vitiated public sentiment or the numerical force of European emigration shall drive us out of the country, or dampen the ardour of our patriotism. Here we intend to remain and fight out the battle of equal and exact justice to all men, no matter what may be the ado against us.[3]

His greatest challenge was to create awareness among the Black communities. He repeatedly impressed upon them the need to acknowledge their own achievements by making them known, for even back in the 1870s, Abbott was well aware that African Canadians were already being ignored in the Canadian history books. With a trace of bitterness he wrote:

I do not mention these facts for the purpose of calling attention to my personal history, for they are the history of hundreds of colored men in this country. To be sure you will not find the part they took in the rebellion recorded in the history of our country. The literature of the 19th century with all its intellectual developments has not yet reached the dignity of doing justice to the heroic deeds of the colored man. Who has heard of that gallant band of colored men who seized that schooner or American gunboat in the Detroit River and brought her safely to the Canadian shore—a valuable prize to the British Government. You will look in vain for a record of it. The eye of the historian

112

of today is too jaundiced by prejudice to notice such things. How many of us can declare that we were taught this history even in our modern schools with their enlightened curriculum? How many of our own children have heard of these events?[4]

Like his father before him, Anderson came to believe that the Conservative Party had begun to neglect the needs of the Black voters and that governmental policy needed to be reformed:

> The Conservative party represented the established English oligarchy in Canada. Until the mid-nineteenth century, Conservatives dominated the political and economic life of the country through the appointed executive and legislative councils.[5]

Despite his profound loyalty to the Crown and Queen Victoria,[6] Abbott found himself pitted against the Tories. He publicly charged that some renegade Tory representatives were deliberately working against the interests of the Black people and regarded them as a "...nondescript class, enjoying a nominal citizenship and living here by a sort of sufferance until such time as Providence may see fit to remove them."[7]

When Reverend King first organized the Elgin Association back in 1849, a subcommittee was appointed to ensure the civil rights of the settlers. Adolphus Judah, J.G. Joseph, Wilson R. Abbott and David Hollin, as members of the committee, became locked in battle with Edwin Larwill, a tinsmith and real estate broker, who vehemently contended that Raleigh township did not want a Black settlement intruding on their soil. Larwill had encouraged the Raleigh Town Council to adopt an Anti-Negro petition and then had surreptitiously amended the document to include extra clauses, like the implementation of a poll tax against any American-born Negroes, thereby denying them the right to vote, attend public schools or serve on juries. But Governor General Elgin did not yield to the ploy and the Elgin Settlement went forward.[8]

Dr. Abbott reminded his people:

> You know the class of men who held indignation meetings to protest against your settling in this part of the country, who sent Col. Prince and Larwill to Parliament to offer that infamous resolution in the House to levy a tax of one dollar on the head of every colored man coming into this country. You know that you have received anonymous letters to intimidate you and prevent you from settling in certain communities.

You know you have been discriminated against in places of public entertainment and have been refused the privilege of riding in public conveyances. You know how you have been systematically robbed in your business transactions. Men have come to you with specious professions of sympathy when in straightened circumstances and offered to lend you money at exorbitant rates of interest in order to encumber your property and encompass your ruin.

You know how your houses have been surrounded by an infuriated mob and how you have been subjected to personal violence. You know how your mothers, sisters, daughters have been insulted on the streets and how every means that a diabolical ingenuity could devise has been brought to bear in order to drive you out of the country, or to render your stay here as disagreeable as possible...[9]

King did encourage his settlers to use their votes to block adversaries like Edwin Larwill, who eventually was replaced in 1856 by the formidable George Brown.[10] Although Larwill rallied the following year, he was overthrown on the strength of the Black voters led by Archibald McKellar, a Chatham lawyer and a Clear Grit (Liberal).

A man of firm convictions, Anderson detested the apathy of some of his people and the neutrality of others:

There never was a more insidiously dangerous idea advanced by an intelligent man. Stand aloof from both parties, they say. Neither one is disposed to do you justice...for when you throw away your franchise you are prepared to sink into barbarism; throw away your ballot and you throw away the only weapon that civil government has given the governed for the protection and maintenance of their rights...I earnestly hope to see the day when all divisions and dissension, national, civil or religious shall have ceased, as we, as one people, shall have

William Peyton Hubbard in the backyard of his home on Broadview Avenue in 1908. Born in Toronto in 1842, Hubbard began his career as a baker, then opened a livery business with his brother. An astute business man, he entered municipal politics, serving as Acting Mayor periodically from 1897 to 1904. *Courtesy of the Abbott family.*

William P. Hubbard and his wife, Julia (Luckett) lived at 662 Broadview Avenue (the home to the right). Following the death of Anderson Abbott, Mary Ann lived with them. Next door, 660 Broadview Avenue, was the home of Phillip Norman Judah and his wife Henrietta (Casey), sister of Mary Ann. *Courtesy of the Abbott family.*

> united in the promotion of one object—the glory and prosperity of our common country.[11]

Politics, on any level, had always piqued Dr. Abbott's instincts and he cultivated a keen interest in municipal affairs while living in Toronto. He was a hearty supporter and close friend (and father-in-law) of William Peyton Hubbard, who probably best exemplified the essence of Abbott's teachings. As a child, Hubbard had had to contend with poverty and social disadvantages, but he rose to become the "Cicero of Council," in Toronto politics. He was elected Alderman for five terms and served as Deputy Mayor of the City of Toronto from 1904 to 1907. He was instrumental in securing the institution of the Toronto Hydro-Electric System and later, Ontario Hydro. Today, his portrait graces the halls of the Toronto boardroom of Ontario Hydro.

Although always a staunch Conservative, Hubbard set aside partisanship and often took the side of the "little man," advocating their interests in municipal affairs. He concentrated on such tasks as public control of the city's water supply, improved fire regulations, public support for the city's destitute and homeless and the direct election of the city council controllers. One of the highlights of his career was to ascertain public

115

William P. Hubbard has been honoured with a building
bearing his name, the Hubbard Park Apartment, situated on
Hubbard Avenue in the area of Toronto known as The Beach.

control of the city's hydro-electric power company. At the time, private
businessmen were vying for control of the new innovative and controversial hydro-electric power industry, but Hubbard supported one-time
Mayor of London and later chairman of the Hydro Commission, Adam
Beck,[12] in the belief that control was best left in the hands of the people.
On May 2, 1911, the Toronto Power Company flooded the city of Toronto
with electricity.[13] Many of the later Hubbard and Abbott descendants
remained closely connected to the company and were later employed by
Toronto Hydro and then Ontario Hydro.

The following essay was published in the *New York Age*[14] on January
27th, 1898. It is written out of immense pride, deep friendship for W.P.
Hubbard and displays a certain optimism in the tides of change, which
he felt were largely due to people like this "grand old man" of Toronto.

A Canadian Councilman Alderman W.P. Hubbard
Re-elected for the Fifth Time
Toronto, January 11th, 1898

An Afro-Briton has forced his way to the front of this community in such
a rapid manner that he is likely to make history before his career is ended.
A community whose institutions are founded upon a monarchical system
and whose sentiments are moulded, to some extent, by the mildew relics

The gravestone marking the Hubbard Plot in Toronto's Necropolis Cemetery sits not far from the Abbott family burial site.

of an obsolete feudal system involving considerations of caste and accidents of birth, would in the reasonableness of things, be least expected to raise a colored man from the humble walks of life and place him in one of the highest positions of trust and responsibility in its civic affairs.

This distinguished honor has been conferred upon Alderman W.P. Hubbard, who has been re-elected for the fifth time as a representative from the fourth ward of the Toronto City Council. This ward is one of the largest and most populous and contains the residences of the wealthiest and most influential citizens such as Sir Oliver Mowat, Sir William P. Howland, Mr. Goldwin Smith and many professional and businessmen. Last year Mr. Hubbard was returned at the head of the polls. This year notwithstanding there were eleven candidates in the field, he came within sixty votes of the same result. Among the successful aldermanic candidates for re-election he stands in the first rank and the confidence and enthusiasm manifested by his supporters at his first election have in no way abated. Such a marked recognition of his ability is very gratifying to his friends and must be regarded by him as an unqualified expression of the esteem and regard in which he is held by his fellow citizens of all classes.... [15]

The Hubbard/Abbott friendship was augmented by the fact that Anderson's daughter, Grace, married William's son, Fred Hubbard, also a prestigious Black citizen of Toronto in his own right, who served as a Commissioner of the Toronto Transit Commission. Fred and Grace's son, Frederick, served with distinction with the Tuskegee Black Flyers[16] as a Warrant Officer during World War II. The documentary, *The Tuskegee Airmen*,[17] provides an excellent accounting of the situation for Black airmen in the United States at that time. Frederick was also an accomplished musician, who could play several instruments, but he is particularly remembered for his piano and violin solos given in both public and church concerts.

In their twilight years, after returning to Toronto from Chicago, Anderson and Mary Ann resided at 662 Broadview Avenue, along with their daughter Grace and her husband. Right next door, at 660 Broadview, lived their nephew, Phillip Norman Judah and his second wife Henrietta, sister to Mary Ann—as always, a very close family indeed!

CHAPTER 15

THE DUNDAS YEARS

When all is done, say not my day is o'er,
And that thr' the night I seek a dimmer shore;
Say rather that my morn has just begun—
I greet the dawn and not a setting sun.[1]

IN 1881, AT THE age of 44, Dr. Abbott retired from his coroner's position in Chatham and established a medical practice in the town of Dundas, where the family remained for the next nine years. Historical records suggest that racial prejudice had continued to rise and had become a chronic hazard for Black families in Kent County. Surely such attitudes would have worn down the most resilient contender, and even Dr. Abbott must have realized what kind of prospects his children would have to face if they remained in such an environment. Perhaps the Abbotts had begun to feel the limitations of the parochial effects of the town of Chatham, and hence sought to widen the cultural and social horizons of their adolescent children.

Dundas was located closer to the cosmopolitan centres of Toronto and Hamilton, both well-known for their more liberal and tolerant racial climates. It was in this neighbourhood that coloured families hoped to be able to integrate with the white folk. The Abbotts probably assumed that their sincere sense of civic duty might pave the way for them in this new community as they settled into their new home. Again the familiar Home Circle[2] became an important part of their lives, as the following notice indicates:

Dundas Home Circle—Emminently Successful—
The first reunion of the Dundas Home Circle was a remarkably pleasant affair and gave satisfaction to every one who attended. Dr. Abbott did himself and the Lodge credit as chairman. The speeches

119

from Rev. Mr. McKay and Dr. Laing were excellent indeed and much enjoyed by the audience. The musical and literary programme was exceptionally good. The supper prepared by the lady friends of the Circle was quite a seasonable feast. In fact the evening passed so delightfully that it was 11:30 before the affair concluded.[3]

Anderson continued to hone his writing skills and became Assistant Editor of the local newspaper, the *Dundas Banner*. Not one to pass up an opportunity to spread his views, Dr. Abbott set a rapid pace and wrote and spoke to his heart's delight. Many of his papers reflect the type of topics commonly debated among the townsfolk. He assumed several *nom de plumes* when writing about issues concerning the welfare and civil rights of the coloured people. Three of his favourite aliases were "Uno," "Ethiope," obviously referring to himself as an African Canadian, and "Plutarch," from the name of an ancient Greek philosopher. Under these pseudonyms, Anderson attacked any unfair and misleading published and oratorical views that depicted his race as inadequate, dishonest, unworthy, or objectionable in any way. He made every effort to expound on the achievements of his race and their ability to succeed under fair and just conditions.

As Anderson turned his attention to new dimensions of civic life, he quickly realized that he was still going to encounter "breakers ahead." Once again, he proved himself a venerable contributor as he shouldered administrative responsibilities for the The Dundas Mechanics Institute,[4] the Internal Management Committee, St. James Anglican Church and the Dundas High School Board of Trustees. However, this time he was met with a very different reception than he had received in Chatham, for his ideas regarding politics, education and scholastic standards were often vehemently opposed and he was frequently challenged on the grounds of favouritism, ignorance, justice and local politics. Yet he persisted in engaging in these activities for the entire time that the family resided in the town. It is difficult to determine whether or not the resistance he faced was due to issues of race, personality conflicts, generation gaps or power struggles. In any case, his medical practice thrived and his oldest children completed their high school education in this community. In 1885, Anderson and Mary Ann's last child, Gordon Anderson, my grandfather, was born.

In 1889, the Abbotts lived briefly in Oakville, where a small, but active, Black community was solidly established, but I suspect the family encountered a strong level of racial prejudice and therefore elected to return to

The Abbott home in the Parkdale district of Toronto, acquired in 1890, as it looked in the early nineteenth century. The house still stands today on the corner of King and Dowling but the upper floor is gone and apartment buildings tower over the once elegant house. *Courtesy of the Abbott family.*

Toronto a year later. They retired to a large home at the corner of Dowling Avenue and King Street, in the Parkdale district. Although Abbott still owned several houses and properties, his main residence in Toronto thereafter remained at Dowling. The Abbotts would later move to Chicago for a period of around ten years, where the family enjoyed the lifestyle of elite African Americans. However, in the early 1900s, Anderson, Mary Ann, their daughter Grace and their son Gordon all returned to Toronto.

CHAPTER 16

THE CHICAGO YEARS

White congregations and individuals seemed to have been active in rendering financial assistance, in giving moral support, and in encouraging Negroes to develop a secular leadership of businessmen in addition to clergy, There was much emphasis on the middle-class virtues of thrift, sobriety and decorum.[1]

IN 1891 THE ABBOTTS immigrated to the bugeoning metropolis of Chicago which, at the time, was the second-largest city in America.[2] During the 1890s, Chicago was the host to a budding, Black community, and most of its residents were relieved to encounter a rather peaceful racial atmosphere. After the Civil War, the people of Chicago developed a uniquely positive relationship between the races, and thus created a city which would have provided a prime location for large groups of Blacks to come together and create a variety of organizations.

However in the early 1900s, this racial climate began to change, as the population continued to swell in response to the influx of thousands of Blacks from the southern states seeking employment in the industrialized cities. It would appear that, once again, a small handful of Blacks could be readily assimilated into the urban society, but as the Black population expanded to over 30,000, racial tolerance began to wane. In 1940, St. Clair Drake's report suggested that only "sympathetic whites" sought to support the welfare of the Blacks in Chicago, during the impetus of the immigration.[3]

It is not clear why the Abbott family left their Canadian roots at such a late stage of life and decided to live in a foreign country, particularly since neither Mary Ann nor Anderson had ever been American citizens. However, it had been a regular practice of several of the family members to regularly traverse the border and work in both Canada and the United

Mary Ann Abbott and Anderson Abbott in their later years. *Courtesy of the Abbott family.*

States at various times over the years. Perhaps, during this period of time, they were able to enjoy a certain sense of community in Chicago that was not readily available to them in Canada. Dalyce Newby suggests that they may have been drawn by the "substantial Afro-American community, especially one in which there was a stratified social system."[4]

As usual, the entire family continued to indulge in musical interludes and Anderson achieved a reputation as a violinist, music instructor, conductor and on occasion, a tenor vocalist. "Conductor Anderson R. Abbott is well-known in this city, having resided here for many years during which he has been giving music instruction prinicipally on the violin."[5]

Anderson continued to project his thought through the local newspapers and at public speaking events. He was appointed as Treasurer and Secretary when he joined the elite Sumner Club,[6] an African-American men's club composed of professional businessmen, doctors, dentists and clergymen. The purpose of the club was to promote professional networking, socializing and the discussion of intellectual and literary topics of interest over a pleasant dinner meeting. Although the membership was limited to forty, any "genial" man could be admitted to the club on the approval of the Executive Committee.

In 1891, Provident Hospital opened its doors to the Black community of South Side Chicago, in response to a desperate need for more medical services as well as to the requirement for a venue for Black doctors to practice.[7] As the first private, non-profit hospital, Provident also was one

Provident Hospital as it looks today, the third structure to be built bearing the same name. The first Provident, built at the corner of 29th and Dearborn in Chicago, was a much more modest three-storey narrow rectangular building.

of the first teaching institutions for Black nurses in the United States, with both Black and white medical staff and indeed "…it became a symbol of the Negro professional man's advancement."[8] The hospital was much needed:

…young black women who wanted to become nurses could not gain admission to a nursing school in Chicago…more young doctors were graduating each year from medical schools, none could practice in the all-white hospitals…no hospital was open to Dr. Williams' patients who needed the services that only such a facility could provide….[9]

Dr. Daniel Hale Williams, a prominent African-American physician was instrumental in founding Provident Hospital and operated it as a holistic facility that offered public health services, training programs for nurses and doctors and, of course, surgery to people of any colour. He was probably best known for performing the first open-heart surgery in 1893 at Provident Hospital.[10] Subsequently, he was invited to assume the position of cheif surgeon at Freedmen's Hospital in Washington, DC, thereby leaving a vacancy that was hard to fill. Thus, in 1894, at 57 years of age, Dr. Abbott stepped out of retirement to replace Dr. Williams, to become the Medical Superintendent of the newly established Provident Hospital and Training School for Nurses, located at the corner of Dearborn and Thirty-sixth Streets. With 85 beds, it was a busy place at this time, admitting more than 2,000 patients and servicing 9,000 emergency patients annually. Dr. Abbott excelled in his administrative duties, not only within the hospital and training school, but overseeing the daily operation of the pathological lab, physiotherapy department, social services and the pharmacy.[11]

Unfortunately, very little was recorded about Dr. Abbott's work at Provident, beyond a few articles. The following notice appeared in the *Conservatore Chicago* in December 1898, welcoming Dr. Anderson Abbott to his new position:

Change At Provident
Dr. A.R. Abbott The New Manager of the Hospital, His Splendid
Ability and Experience in Similar Work, Brilliant War Service
as a Surgeon

Provident Hospital has a new Superintendent in the person of Dr. A.R. Abbott, well-known and universally recognized as one of the ablest colored surgeons in this country. He has been a resident of Chicago only three years, but has already identified himself with the people by his earnest promotion of all movements designed to help his race. He retired from active practice after a third of a century of close application to his profession and the attainment of honors and income equalled by no other colored physician and surgeon in this country. Since then Dr. Abbott has applied his time to literary work, devoting most of his time to the study and consideration of questions that affect the race.

The great need of work at the Provident Hospital appealed to him for it was a service that everybody conceded that he was eminently fitted to perform. It was only a question with him as a sacrifice of his well-earned life of retirement and ease and a re-entry into the busy responsible line of work which duty lay at his door. Friends of the institution appealed earnestly to him to lend his invaluable aid and their arguments finally prevailed. He accepted election as Medical Superintendent of the Hospital and entered at once upon his duties as general director of this great work.

The appointment of Dr. Abbott to the position of superintendent will mark an onward step in the history of Provident Hospital. Hitherto the Hospital has not had the direct and constant supervision of a medical superintendent but that duty has been exercised by the superintendent of the training school. It has needed the firm hand of a man able to act as instructor in training, director in all lines of hospital work and a fully equipped manager of the entire institution.

In Dr. Abbott, Provident Hospital has a man who can fill all these requirements to the letter. He is a physician of thirty-five years experience having graduated in 1861 from one of the finest colleges on this continent, the University of Toronto. He is a man of scholarly attainments ranking high among the scholars of his race.

A surgeon with such a splendid record will be a valuable assistance to the work of Provident Hospital. In him the public will have the most perfect confidence for he has proven himself worthy and capable in the highest degree. The public will find every feature of hospital work carefully promoted by him and his staff.[12]

Despite the profuse publicity surrounding this institution, recorded history of Dr. Abbott's work at Provident is amazingly scant. Possibly this was simply an uneventful period of its history or maybe he was considered a foreigner and therefore not of interest to the American public. His resignation, for business reasons, was accepted by the Board of Trustees with regret on June 10th, 1897. We have no indication what those business reasons were, but the family continued to live in Chicago for several more years. During this period, Dr. Abbott obtained a license to practise medicine in the state of Michigan. Within a few years, the Abbotts would decide to return to Toronto, this time permanently.

CHAPTER 17

DR. ABBOTT'S PHILOSOPHY: AN AFRICAN-CANADIAN PERSPECTIVE

*The problem of the twentieth century is the problem of the color line—
the relation of the darker to the lighter races of men in Asia and Africa,
in America and the islands of the sea.*[1]

ANDERSON ABBOTT EVENTUALLY RETURNED to Toronto in the early 1900s and spent his last decade once again as a Canadian. In the end, it appears that Anderson did not depend on his medical career for a living. Instead, he used his pen to create a resource of articles and commentaries that were widely published in both Canadian and American newspapers. Judging from the volumes in my possession, such an active career provided a steady if modest income and his professional title and his education would have served as important accreditation for his opinions.

Always eager to learn something new and exchange ideas, Anderson continued to be active in a variety of community organizations. Much of his time was spent compiling notes and gathering statistics from all over the world. Although formally retired, he made a concerted effort to gather information and statistics about the history of slavery, as well as about the more recent accomplishments of African Canadians. The following ad appeared in a Toronto newspaper:

I am interested in a work, in course of preparation, on Afro-Canadians. Information is so solicited from those who are holding or have held civil, military, professional, educational, commercial, fraternal, or industrial positions in the United States or elsewhere. If not regarded too

Dr. Anderson R. Abbott posing proudly with his three
daughters. *Left to right*: Ida, Grace (who would later marry
Frederick Hubbard, the son of W.P. Hubbard) and Helene.
Courtesy of the Abbott Family.

inquisitorial, facts concerning family history, business, resources, assets,
married or single, where born or place of residence in Canada, educational or other qualifications; description of workmanship, mechanical,
artistic, invention, agricultural and mechanical data especially desired.[2]

While living in Toronto, Dr. Abbott continued to pursue courses at the
University of Toronto[3] and often presented papers to the Canadian Institute, an organization that sponsored lectures on the latest intellectual
scientific and philosophical concepts of the day. The program for the 53rd
session indicates that he spoke on "Pathogenic Bacteria."[4] His likeness
has also been spotted in a photograph of the Natural History Society in
1909.[5]

Dr. Abbott recorded his thoughts in great detail in his journals and a
few of the following excerpts may suffice to briefly present his philosophy on the implications of slavery and the amalgamation of the races.

...Standing between the two races, the amalgamated man is not so
heartily liked by either. Free from prejudice himself, he is the victim
of the prejudices of the pure bloods of both races from which he is
derived...Many persons who are quite dark are of mixed-blood, while

128

their appearance would lead the casual observer to think them pure-blooded Blacks. Then many colored persons are so fair that they are counted among whites by the census takers, who have no reason to suspect them of being colored. I know that also most all white men pride themselves on their ability to 'know a nigger at sight' but I can produce scores in Cincinnati who could not be picked from a mixed company and classified as colored...thousands of them turn white every decade.

...The law, which governs the evolution of races, teaches us that where two races of different degrees of civilization occupy the same soil the weaker becomes subject to the stronger and more progressive race. Under such conditions peace and civil order can be maintained only when the relation of master and servants mutually acquiesce in, or the dominant race is so entrenched in power as to render resistance on the part of the servile race futile. This was the relation that existed between the white and black races in the South during slavery. When it was disturbed by the emancipation of the slaves it resulted in direful consequences to both races, the effects of which are still manifested in violence and bloodshed.

...The Negro having survived all efforts to reduce him again to a condition of vassalage and all schemes to get rid of him by legislation, emigration and repatriation having failed, there are but two alternatives left; the races must either be exterminated or become absorbed. The former alternative is not within the bounds of possibility, therefore, the absorption into a composite race is, in my opinion the manifest destiny of the Southern Negro. It is just as natural for two races, equally conditioned and living together on the same soil to blend as it is for the waters of two river tributaries to mingle with each other.

...The process of absorption of the Negro race has been going on despite hostile public sentiment, for more than two centuries until now there are 3 million mulattos, quadroons and octoroons in the Untied States, exclusive of an indefinite number that are difficult to classify as mulatto, many of who pass for white and thus escape the scrutiny of the census taker.

...History records many instances of the fusion of races under similar conditions. It is reasonable to suppose, therefore, that as the Negro approaches nearer the stand of the white man in education, culture and refinement, objections to intermarriages will disappear and fusion of the two races will go more rapidly until both races will become blended into a composite race...

Several generations will pass from the stage of action before this change is realized to any appreciable degree. In the meantime the white people of the South will realize the necessity of treating the Negro more fairly than they do now both in the matter of wages and protection of person and property. And the Negro on his part will rise to a more intelligent appreciation of his duties and responsibility as the laboring class upon which the South must depend for its progress and prosperity.

...The Negroes will remain for many generations the industrial element upon which the South must depend for its progress and prosperity. Therefore all schemes looking to their wholesale deportation from the South I regard as chimerical and will as theretofore, come to nought.

...As the Afro-Canadian race expands in intelligence and numbers it will become more identified with the business interests of the country and more intimately incorporated as an important and indispensable factor in the social commercial and political life of the nation.[6]

Thus, Anderson believed that an eventual amalgamation or blending of the races would take place and provide a solution to the racial conflict of his people. Perhaps he might have been right, except that he did not foresee "the importation of a more race-conscious West Indian group and the inauguration of a new...[Black] railroad community" that eventually led to a new wave of racial intolerance in Canada.

Dr. Daniel Hill noted that, in 1905, "Dr. Abbott predicted that assimilation and migration to the United States would cause the gradual disappearance of Negroes from Canada."[7] However, an essential base of Black families remained that tended to restrict their marriages to their own social and racial group. Most of them had integrated into the mainstream institutions and social life of Toronto and had become prominent property owners. In the midst of growing racial tensions in the 20th century, the descendants of these "old-line" families assumed a middle-class standing within the white community, where they shared a common membership in various organizations and participated equally in social life. Abbott remained firm in his convictions:

...The Canadian people, quick to fan the kindling flow of enthusiasm in our youth for higher education, encourage in every possible way the feeblest effort in that direction .... The flower of our youth are leaving us yearly, yet we do not factor in the uplifting of the Afro-American on this continent of supplementing those moral, intellectual and industrial forces which are slowly but surely elevating him to a higher civilization.

...Afro-Americans have shared with others in the rapid growth in value of real estate. I have no means of judging the amount of property they possess; half a million is an underestimate of the value of property owned by them. The constant drain to which our population has been subjected since the close of the Civil War precludes the possibility of any very great increase in wealth or numbers. Our youth evince a strong disposition to cross the borderline as soon as they acquire sufficient knowledge and experience to make a living. In this way we are impoverished and you are correspondingly benefited. By the process of absorption and expatriation the color line will eventually fade out in Canada.[8]

It would seem that Anderson accurately read the writing on the wall, for although he acknowledged that Canada offered an appealing alternative to racial oppression that many African Americans experienced in the United States at the time, he recognized that Canada was not home to most of the former fugitives. Their roots, just as Abbott's did, lay in the United States, despite all of its proscription and injustice. Dr. Abbott must have had a sense of the brewing storm clouds about to descent upon his people and ultimately his own family. Like many African Canadians, he would continue to fight for equality for all Blacks in educational, social and political institutions and to uphold their precious achievements that would in time become valuable weapons in the war against racial oppression.

In the fall of 1913, Anderson developed a case of appendicitis and six weeks after surgery, on December 29, he succumbed to complications. Right up to the end, he was still resolutely engrossed in the throes of the social and political issues of his era.

Anderson Abbott had lived a life as a protagonist. He challenged all Black Canadians to prove themselves equal to white Canadians. He used the tools of culture, through music and literary appreciation, fine manners, good taste and gentility to prove his point. He impelled his people to seek a good education, no matter how demanding their daily menial tasks, for only through a better education did he believe they could ever hope to gain the respect and acknowledgement they sought as equals. Thus, he may have offered a form of advice, prescribing the means and ways to a better way of life for his people. But as the years passed he began to foresee what he thought was inevitable and he believed that peace would eventually come in the form of racial amalgamation. He must have prayed that some day Black and white would mix and his family would truly embody a single race. Only time would tell how his children would cope with such issues. In his wake he left a "Coloured" wife, five "Coloured" children and dozens of "Black" and "white" descendants.

When that day dawns which shall find me dead
And all these dreams within me risen higher,
These be the words you place above my head:
Here lies a bit of dust that once was fire![9]

CHAPTER 18

THE SEPARATION BEGINS

When you're black and white, negotiating racial identity is like going through a revolving door.[1]

IN RESTROSPECT IT SEEMS quite possible that the move to Chicago may simply have facilitated a means of keeping the family together. It was during these years that Wilson Ruffin, the eldest Abbott son, was admitted to Medical School in Illinois and eventually graduated to become a prominent lung specialist. He married three times, always to white women. Gordon, born in 1885, grew up in the Black communities of Dundas, Chicago, Toronto and Buffalo. He later settled down in Toronto and married a white woman and raised a "white" family. Grace married a Black businessman, Frederick Hubbard of the prestigious Hubbard clan, and they also remained in Toronto, but raised a Black family. Both Ida and Helene married Black Americans and remained in the United States, both raising Black families.

Prior to her marriage, Helene spent ten years in St. Louis working as a Kindergarten teacher. Helene's daughter Eleanore explained, "Well, Mama went to St. Louis because Grandpa Abbott was a School Trustee and he often visited the schools in the cities in the United States. They were familiar with the system and, of course, they knew she would not be able to find the same kind of work in Canada." Helene was motivated to enter the teaching profession after a friend, Molly Lambert, introduced her to other professional young ladies who were either teachers or secretaries:

She was always ambitious and eventually entered the Kindergarten Program at the University of Toronto. When she graduated she looked around for a job in the United States and she and Grandpa settled on the city of St. Louis. At the time there was a rule that you couldn't

133

teach if you were married. That was true everywhere even in Toronto. You would have been taking a job from somebody else. Well, she went to St. Louis and she taught there for about ten years before she got married after a very long engagement.[2]

At that time, although educational opportunities were available in Canada, employment was not. In the article entitled "The Colored Woman of Today," Fanny Barrier Williams makes a number of interesting observations:

A little over a century ago colored women had no social status and indeed only thirty years ago the term "womanhood" was not large enough in this Christian republic to include any woman of African descent. No one knew her, no one was interested in her. Her birthright was supposed to be all the social evils that had been the dismal heritage of her race for two centuries. This is still the popular verdict to an outstanding degree in all parts of our country. A national habit is not easily cured and the habit of the American people, who indiscriminately place all colored women on the lowest social levels in this country, has tended to obscure from view and popular favor some of the most interesting women in the land.

But in spite of these prejudicial hindrances and a lack of confidence, the young colored women of this generation are emerging from obscurity in many interesting ways that will happily surprise those who have never known them by their womanly qualities and graceful accomplishments. Such women seem to have no relationship to the slavery conditions of the yesterday of history. In a surprisingly brief period of time they have been completely lifted out of the past by the Americanism that transforms and moulds into higher forms all who come under the spell of American free institutions.

That they appreciate the value of the culture and intelligence is shown in the ever-increasing number of young women who are graduates of those universities and professional institutions whose doors are open wide enough to include all women, regardless of color....

...In nothing is the color-line so relentlessly drawn as it is against the employment of accomplished young colored women in the higher grades of occupations ... School teaching has afforded the best field for young colored women. That profession has laid requisition upon the very best women of the race and they in return have elevated the profession by a great variety of accomplishments. It is easy to find these

Helene Abbott with her teaching colleagues. She is seated in the middle row, fourth from the left. *Courtesy of the Abbott family.*

young women capable of teaching everything that comes within the curriculum of the best American institutions. Miss Helene Abbott, of the St. Louis schools, is an interesting type of the young women who bring to the colored schools of the country everything that is best in modern pedagogy....[3]

Between the years 1892 and 1902, Helene was influential in the intro- duction of early childhood education for the Black children of working mothers in St. Louis and Chicago. A lovely tribute to Helene by the Principal of the Dumas and Simmons School was kept by her daughter Lydia. The following quotes include some of the highlights:

Rules largely through love and gets them to love her...has excellent control of her children. She seems to draw out the best in them by the efforts she exerts on behalf of their development.... Has been so well instructed herself that she makes it an important point to see that her children are active, thoughtful and wide awake. She is well-informed and thoroughly interested in the work...and secures commendable

Helene Abbott would marry Benjamin Sayre of Philadelphia. Following his military service in the Spanish American War, he became a dentist. *Abbott Collection, Toronto Public Library (TRL): S-90.*

results from her pupils...quite a student—fond of study and devotes much time to reading the best literature extant.... Attendant of lectures and teachers' meetings.... Agreeable in manners and quite sociable...a most valuable acquisition to the corps. By her deportment exercises an influence for good among parents and children. Quite co-operative in spirit and willing to do anything to further the best interests of the school.

Helene Abbott, fondly known as Miss Helene resigned from teaching in the St. Louis Public Schools leaving an excellent record of 10 years of dedicated service to the boys and girls who came under her care both at Dumas School and Simmons School (1892–1902) Thank God for teachers like Miss Helene Abbott.[4]

Eleanore went on to explain how music played an important part in the adolescent lives of the Abbott children. "Grandpa, way back then, used to have these music students come over for a musicale night and one of these young men got a yen for Mama, but he never got invited back."[5] Helene's husband, Benjamin Sayre, was a relatively young man from Philadelphia when he joined the 23rd Infantry as part of a Black Battalion during the Spanish American War of 1898. He was invited to the Abbott's for dinner one night, before leaving for boot camp in Wyoming. Since the lovely Helene always managed to catch the attention of the male guests, she had agreed, this time, to remain in her room until dinner was served, thus allowing her sisters a chance to attend the officer. However, it was all over for them when she entered the room. She won his heart at the dinner table and that was the beginning of a lifetime romance.

Benjamin was sent on to Cuba as a Lieutenant. It was the practice, during battle for someone else to pick up the flag if the flag-bearer fell and, in one instance, it became Benjamin's duty to do so, whereupon he was later recognized for his bravery. He remained in Cuba for over six months, living in abysmal wartime circumstances.

They lived in tents, just rows and rows of them and the orderlies would go up and down with buckets of quinine water and dippers. In order to prove yourself well enough to be shipped home, you had to be able to walk down this hill and cross a log over a stream and then get down to the beach to get on the sick boat. He failed once but the next time his buddies got down in the creek, on either side of the log. They kept holding him up, so that he could get across. That was the only way he got home to the States. But he was in the hospital for a long time and had a lengthy convalescence at home.[6]

Ida was Anderson and Mary Ann's youngest daughter. She was quite a character and Eleanore remembered her well:

My Aunt Ida had all the curls. She used to buy these separate curls and put them up in her hair. Oh, I loved her! She lived in Grand Rapids, Michigan, and then eventually she moved to Chicago. Her husband, Charles Stevenson, was a mail carrier. After their marriage they went to Biloxi, Mississippi, because it was a new little town and he was going to be in charge of the post office. But it turned out to be some sort of place on stilts and Aunt Ida only stood one winter there. She had three children, including twins by this time, and she couldn't take another winter, so she returned to Chicago and her husband eventually followed. He couldn't take it either."[7]

Ida Abbott, described as the most outgoing of the three girls, married while in Chicago. She remained living in the United States with her husband, Charles Stevenson. *Courtesy of the Abbott family.*

Wilson, Anderson's oldest son was born in Chatham and raised there, and later in Dundas. He followed in his father's footsteps and acquired an impressive education, attending the University of Toronto, Cornell University and then the Medical College at the University of Illinois where he received degrees in Pharmacy and Medicine. He then became a professor of biology and chemistry at the latter institution and

Wilson Ruffin Abbott II, Anderson's eldest son, standing on the dock of the Nightingale summer home on Lake Geneva, Wisconsin. A doctor like his father, he became a highly qualified heart and lung specialist in Chicago. *Courtesy of the Abbott family.*

published a number of medical papers. Later he worked as Clinical Director of the Chicago Tuberculosis Institute until he was appointed Chief of Staff at Henrotin Hospital, Chicago, and Chairman of the Medical Executive Committee of the Hospital. During the war he served as a Major and Chief of Staff at Fort Bayard, New Mexico, at the United States Veterans Service.[8] As a highly qualified heart and lung specialist in Chicago, he became renown for his innovative treatment of tuberculosis, an approach which involved the collapsing of the lung.

Wilson turned out to be a rather debonair sort of fellow. In Chicago he became acquainted with the Nightingales, a well-established white family stemming from the Mayflower Quakers. A daughter, Florence Nightingale (not the famous nurse) was one of nine children. Her grandfather had been a railroad doctor, stationed in Iowa, and had accumulated enough money to retire in comfort, even purchasing a lovely summer cottage at Lake Geneva in Wisconsin. Eleanore recounts, "They were real gents and the ladies wore French dresses. They left Chicago and moved up to a suburb and they had this lovely home on the river with a wharf."[9] Florence's father, Augustus Nightingale, began his career as a teacher and served in a variety of high positions, as President of the Board of Trustees of the University of Illinois, as Principal of Lake View High School in Chicago and as Superintendent of Cook County Illinois Schools. Apparently he was instrumental in establishing the secondary schools in Chicago. He was very much involved in the politics of the day and acquainted with such men as Theodore Roosevelt and Woodrow Wilson. An affiliation to such a family would have blended well with the interests and concerns of the Abbotts.

It would appear that the Nightingales were undaunted by Wilson's race, but as the couple resided in the northerly white part of Chicago, they obviously assumed a white identity, despite Wilson's familial ties to the southerly Black section of town. However, they all handled the situation with discretion. His niece told me that, as a loyal brother, he visited his sister Ida, faithfully each week, but would never allow his family to accompany him. During his boyhood, Wilson's son, Augustus born in 1906, was strongly discouraged from inquiring about his father's profession or family. "What limited knowledge I have came from other relatives."[10] He remembers asking if he could accompany his father to work on the occasional weekend, but soon learned that this would be inappropriate. Apparently Wilson would volunteer his services to the Black community on a regular basis, without the knowledge of his white family or community.

When Eleanore was asked if his patients were Black, she answered:

"No, his practice was among whites mainly. But he took care of me one time when I had pleural pneumonia. I was engaged to a fellow whose family lived in Wyoming and he was studying medicine in Minneapolis, ...and he was graduating that year in June and I called to tell him that this had come on me. In those days they didn't have antibiotics, so my father had a little room built off the porch and I had to lie there with a sandbag on my chest for months and months. I'd look out the kitchen window and they would pass food to me through a little window. Anyway this fellow's family heard about this and said I could come to Wyoming to stay. Uncle Wilson said I had to live in this kind of climate if I was ever to get better and that if I had T.B. I would have to stay in Wyoming and not come back, but I was only on the verge of it because I had the fluid."[11]

Florence Nightingale, wife of Wilson, with their son Gus (Augustus) aged 8 months. *Courtesy of the Abbott family.*

Poor Eleanore, as a young lady of twenty-one she was relegated to the "Wild West" for four years where she gradually recovered from a severe case of pleurisy.

139

When Florence died, her parents (Augustus and Fannie Nightingale) took over the upbringing of young Gus, shown here at about age ten, seated between his maternal grandparents. *Courtesy of the Abbott family.*

Florence Nightingale's mother, Fannie Chase Nightingale, was both a teacher and a proficient artist and pianist. Her daughter, Florence was one of the five surviving children: Florence, Pearl, Jessie, Winifred and Harry, who later became a professor at the University of Illinois. Florence died when Augustus was only six and her parents took over his upbringing, while his father Wilson continued to pursue his medical career. Hence, Gus grew up with his cousins who were like brothers and sisters to him, and so it was that he was raised in a "white" family, as the "white" son of a prominent doctor.

When Wilson married a second time, to his wife's cousin, Ruth, Gus finally got his very own brother, but sadly this young lad drowned in an accident at Lake Geneva, Wisconsin, at the age of three. Cousin Eleanore recounts:

Uncle Wilson married Ruth who was Aunt Florence's cousin and she had Billy and they had him well taken care of. She had some business in a bank one day and she left the nanny and Billie across the street in a store. While she was gone, the child ran down the hill and onto the

140

wharf. He couldn't have been more than two or three and he ended up in the water. The nanny ran out into the water after him, but was terribly bogged down with all her skirts and petticoats. They managed to get her out, but it was some time before the found the body of the child. That was such a tragedy.[12]

After the death of Billy, Wilson and Ruth divorced and eventually Wilson married a third time, while working in the Public Health department at Fort Bayard as a tuberculosis specialist. His new wife [Lee] was a Major on the base and predictably she was also white. Eleanore reported:

Mother and Aunt Ida and Aunt Grace were very upset about this because she was a Southerner who hated all coloreds. We were all different colors then, some good gold, some good other. …[when] he came back with her photograph to Chicago and announced the marriage, Grandma [Mary Ann] came around to see the picture. Mama and Aunt Ida had a look over. None of them were taken with her. We really never got to know her. When they returned to Chicago she joined the Women's Club. Mother and everyone were not very happy about the marriage because of the woman's attitude. Uncle Wilson called his mother and said, 'Well I guess you won't get to know my wife.' They weren't married that long before he died.[13]

In 1892, Anderson Abbott wrote about the Manasseh Society of Chicago, a group made up of interracially married men and women. Their intentions were somewhat ideological, but they were well-accepted by the local Black community and, in fact, served to lend moral support to the mixed couples involved. Wilson and his last wife were active members of this fraternal organization. "This club had a dual significance, however, for on one hand, the Chicago society was not so rigid that intermarriages were taboo, yet, on the other hand, such couples were sufficiently alien to both the Negro and white communities as to make it desirable to organize among themselves for mutual aid and recreation."[14]

Gordon, born in Dundas, Ontario, in 1885, the youngest son of Dr. Anderson Ruffin Abbott and Mary Ann Casey Abbott, was still a child when the family moved to Chicago. As his older brother and sisters wielded their way between racial barriers, Gordon was benevolently protected and indulged, especially by his eldest sister Helene or Nell, as he called her. As an adolescent, Gordon had his own agenda in mind, quite unlike his siblings, all of whom had attended university and settled into dignified lifestyles,

Ann Leworthy, the author's grandmother, was the daughter of English-born market gardeners. She became the wife of Gordon, Anderson's youngest son. The Leworthys had a market garden farm in the Don Valley, not far below the Necropolis Cemetery and lived on Charles Street. *Courtesy of the Abbott family.*

although later, he was to deeply regret foregoing the opportunity for higher education. Gordon impulsively chose to follow the lure of car racing, which had become so popular during his youth. At the time, automobiles were very new and exciting and, around 1910 to 1912, they beckoned him to Buffalo where he joined the famous Thomas Flyer Company. On weekends, he teamed up with a driver, serving as a racing car mechanic. One day he even drove the Thomas Flyer entry in the important cross-country race, from New York to Buffalo.

Perhaps Gordon had his fill of noble and ardent gestures on the part of the Black race, like his father, but as my Uncle Bob put it, "Frankly, I think he was a bit of a rebel. It was as if everyone else was seeking to be part of the 'upper' class and that just wasn't his thing."[15] However this period of Gordon's life is also a bit of a mystery. Not very much is known about his time in Buffalo. My Uncle Bob believes that he lived as Black until he returned to Canada and only began to pass as white after he met and married my grandmother:

I never asked about it because I knew I was not supposed to ask.... In later years I have always been sorry that I had not made a point of sitting down and talking to my dad about it. At the time there seemed to be a veil and one knew that the questions would not be appreciated, although Dad was certainly not the type that would have ever turned you off. It was just a sense that I had...I guess my biggest regret is that I never took the opportunity to share more time with him and learn from him—just to get to know him a little better.[16]

After finishing high school in Toronto, Gordon, with his love of cars, moved to Buffalo, and was employed by the New York Railway Signal Company. There his job consisted of installing and monitoring railway signals on the New York Central Line that ran from Buffalo to New York City. There, he lived with a Black family. In 1915, he decided to return to Toronto where he eventually married my grandmother Ann Leworthy, a white woman. We have a wonderful collection of love letters that they exchanged, sometimes several times a day, so I suspect it was a very romantic courtship. My mother has attempted to interpret the situation that Gordon and Ann must have faced in their racially mixed marriage:

> I realize now that this was quite a daring move. Although my mother's family must have harboured serious objections to the interracial marriage, they openly and warmly accepted him into their family. Still it was probably very difficult for the Leworthys to see their daughter beginning life with someone who was different, no matter how nice he was, knowing that the couple was sure to encounter extra hurdles in the future. Marriage is enough of a challenge without the problems that would invariably crop up due to racial discrimination.[17]

She told me that one night she was in the kitchen finishing up the dishes with her Aunt Winnie (Leworthy) when Winnie commented on how good her own family had been to accept Gordon. My mother's astonishment to such a statement must have given poor Aunt Winnie heart failure, as she realized her *faux pas*, having almost let the secret out of the bag. Her flustered response was simply that he was so dark. Even then, incredible as it seems to us now, my mother did not clue in and just dismissed the comment with indignation. However, it obviously stuck in her memory, for as I persistently prodded through the cobwebs of the past these kinds of little clues repeatedly surfaced.

In any case, the marriage proved to be based on deep, mutual devotion and I suppose they made the decision together to deal with racism in a practical manner. Ann had been a typing and shorthand teacher at the Wells Business School before they were married. Some of their letters mention a Mrs. Wells and we have considered the possibility that she may have had something to do with their meeting. As Gordon was already in his thirties by the time they married, they wasted no time in starting a family and within a few years had two sons, Don (Gordon Junior) and Bob. Ten years down the road my mother Marion was born.

By 1930, Gordon was employed by the privately-owned Toronto Power Company, which generated power from a plant just above Niagara Falls, transmitting it through to Toronto. He worked as a stationary engineer at a steam plant on Terauley Street (Bay Street), between Queen and

Gordon Abbott, the author's grandfather, became a valued employee of
Ontario Hydro and was a leader with the field of employee relations.
Courtesy of the Abbott family.

Dundas streets. It was not long before Ontario Hydro, or then the Ontario
Electric Power Commission, monopolized the industry across Ontario.
Gordon moved on to work as an electrical sub-foreman for Hydro at the
Davenport station.

The Hydro managers were impressed by his eloquence and the warm
rapport he was able to establish with everyone he met. They invited him to
develop a Hydro Employee Association, which later became the forerunner
of CUPE and then the Power Workers Union of Ontario. Gordon Abbott
was its first President. Later his son Bob followed in his father's footsteps
and became Manager of Labour Relations for Ontario Hydro:

> Well, to tell you the truth, Hydro itself came to the conclusion that the unions
> were coming and they decided that they should jump the gun and help form

an organization that they could work with—sort of a protective measure. There was no question that Hydro was concerned about the strength and power of the big international unions and the inroads that they were making and the effect on the public utility, should they become unionized.[18]

My mother, Marion added:

Dad recognized that there needed to be some sort of arbitration system between the company and the employees of Ontario Hydro. This was quite a departure from the norm in society at the time and I'm sure that, although it took several years for their legitimacy to be recognized, when it finally was, it was mainly due to the respect that Dad and his reasonable, but knowledgeable manner commanded. Many years later I remember Dad was quite disturbed when CUPE came along with its closed shop and aggressive manner. I think he too realized that since Hydro had become so big the time had come when the problems of the employees could no longer be resolved by a small, intimate bargaining unit. Anyway, he really paved the way for the recognition of employee rights within a crown corporation.[19]

Hydro continued to appreciate Gordon's abilities and later asked him to leave the union and join the management team. Initially he began as a training officer, working at Royal York and Queensway, where he developed and taught courses on Electricity and General Administration, for what was later to become the Lineman Training School. Shortly after that, he was promoted to the position of Grievance Officer and hence forth, handled all the grievances for management for the entire commission, right up until his death. As a Hydro employee, Bob heard a lot about his Dad:

I know of no one who could command more respect from the employees than my dad. When I joined Ontario Hydro after the war in 1945, it was absolutely amazing how universally his name was known, from one end of the province to another. I never once heard a bad word said about him. He was a quiet man and a kind man and he had an abundance of common sense. He had a tremendous ability for the use of extemporaneous words and he was a prodigious writer. I remember being so in awe of my dad, in that he could speak and write like that. In 1950, after his death, I met many people who would go out of their way to come up and indicate to me the great respect they had for Gordon Abbott. It was years before I felt like an individual.

For a long time I really felt that I was just someone with the name of Abbott, who was following the only Abbott that was worth knowing. I had to go another ten years before there was enough turn over in the staff that his name was not always associated with mine.[20]

Thus we see an interesting phenomenon occurring as the Abbott children began to forge their new careers and start families of their own. When Anderson and Mary Ann lived in Chicago their daughters would have been in their twenties, and likely looking for prospective husbands. We note that two of them did marry American Blacks, Helene a dentist, and Ida a postman. Wilson, the eldest son, followed in his father's footsteps, pursuing a medical career and eventually married into the white race. Gordon and Grace returned to Toronto with their parents. Grace resumed her romance with her father's best friend's son, Fred Hubbard, and eventually they married and lived as Black. Conversely, after Gordon finished his secondary education, he went off on his own adventure to live in Buffalo in a Black community. When he returned to Toronto, he disengaged from that community, married a white woman, and essentially assumed a white identity. It is important to note that during this period, between 1911 and 1921, the Toronto Negro population had increased from 468 to 1,236, due to Black immigration from the United States and the West Indies. For the most part, the "old-line" Blacks engaged in white-collar jobs in such as the post office, civil service, small business and even Ontario Hydro, like the Abbotts, and they did not associate with the "downtown Negro." Consequently, the "old-liners" were regarded with scorn by the professionally trained, business-oriented West Indians "who asserted that the East Enders were not "race people" and did nothing to advance the cause of Toronto Negroes."[21]

Therefore, contrary to what Anderson Abbott predicted, the races did not amalgamate but rather differentiated on the basis of skin colour and dominant culture. It may have been very difficult for Gordon to presume to be Black when he had relatively fair skin and straight hair and did not live or work within the Black community. Definitely it would have taken an enormous effort to maintain a Black identity in the midst of the West Indian community and so it is that I am gradually beginning to understand how he may have slipped into the mode of least resistance.

CHAPTER 19

FADE TO BLACK

If you see a tall fellow ahead of a crowd,
A leader of men, marching fearless and proud,
And you know of a tale whose mere telling aloud
Would cause his proud head to in anguish be bowed,
It's a pretty good plan
to forget it![1]

WHEN I FIRST BEGAN to delve into my family history, I could not have anticipated meeting a whole new side of the family never previously known to me. I had no idea that they would be "Black," since I of course was obviously "white." However as I began to correspond with my newly discovered American cousins, increasing evidence suggested that I was going to be in for a few surprises. When they mailed me their family photographs, I was intrigued to observe great variations in their appearances and that indeed some of the cousins were very "black," some rather "dark," and others quite "fair." However, what really amazed me was that their skin colour did not necessarily reflect their choice of racial identity. In one case, I received a photo from a "Black" cousin who so strongly resembled my "white" uncle they could pass as brothers. Each considered himself a fair representative of their chosen race, although I suspect I have now provided them both with some "food" for thought! But really, this race business seemed to me to be not so much a matter of actual colour, but rather one of racial identity and cultural representation. My "Black" cousin, Abbott Sayre, wrote:

Although for the past few decades I've cast my identity with the Afro-American community, there was an ambivalence I had during my young adulthood. My birth certificate identifies my parents as black.

147

The Sayre cousins, from left to right: Jerome David, Abbott
Pannell, Abbott Paul, Iris Marie and Derek Joseph Sayre,
August 1992.

My physical appearance is otherwise. I now realize my ties to family
would not allow me to break away to a totally white identity. Addition-
ally, I could not live comfortably trying to keep one foot in a white camp
and another in a black camp. Events of the sixties, Martin Luther King
and the civil rights movement actually made it more exciting to be black
than white. The choice becomes more difficult for my children. Their
mother is white, so they do feel they have a foot in both camps. Now
in their late twenties, they are going through a search for identity. Unfortunately our society has not progressed beyond that mind-set where
one does not have to choose a racial identity. Having antecedents such
as Wilson Ruffin, Anderson Ruffin and Helene Abbott along with other
illustrious personage to find pride in could make their choice easier.[2]

Some of the Black cousins with fair complexions, especially the Americans, appear to have experienced otherwise. Cousin Bonnie Grosnick,
granddaughter of Helene Abbott Sayre, explained:

Americans tend very much to classify people by race. I think this
probably goes back to the first segregation laws. Not that it was absent
before, but people were then forcefully separated by their physical
appearance. The Black's facilities, from schools to washrooms, were
always inferior to the white's, during segregation, which perpetuated

the notion that they were an inferior race. I find most people today judge others on the basis of individual merit, rather than on the basis of race but when it comes to marriage, a lot of that objectivity flies out the window.[3]

However, perceptions do vary, for Cousin Lisa, while travelling across the United States with her musical band, has found that "...prejudice is alive and well in parts of the south and you do not openly admit to being part Black."[4]

When I visited the Ontario communities of Chatham and North Buxton, I was startled to find a very different racial atmosphere than the one that I had experienced in Toronto. It seemed to me that the Blacks whom I met there were deeply sensitized to racial differences, and yet they too readily overlooked the similarity of their skin colours. To me, many of them looked to be very fair-skinned and at first I was tempted to presume that they were white, but I was quickly enlightened! They assured me that they were indeed Black! Such an attitude surprised me, for at the time I felt it to be so "un-Canadian," or should I say so "American." Later, as my research evolved, I was to discover that this community had suffered a long history of racial conflict. Even today, those who left the community for the big city told me that they would sometimes return to find that the experience had somehow transformed them into "outsiders" with respect to those remaining in the locality.

Thus, I was faced with the inevitable question. If life could be so difficult as Black and one could pass as white, then why not do so? Moreover,

Cousin Bonnie Grosnick, who lives in Wisconsin with her husband, Jim, and Kathleen Curry, who lives in Texas with her husband, Marlo, and their three children, at an Abbott family reunion in 1994.

if one looked white, would it not prove awkward to claim a Black identity? Perhaps the purpose of identifying oneself with a particular race had more to do with the colour of one's state of mind rather than one's colour of skin. Did identifying as Black then automatically imply that one could not identify as white? As one white cousin asked, "When one is of mixed race, where does passing end and identity as white begin? Is it simply based on how you look?"[5]

Another cousin, Kathleen Curry, a beautiful Black woman with a light complexion, curly hair and delicate facial features, mentioned that she always wondered why she was so fair when her brothers were so dark. She described a long-standing desire to justify her right to belong within her own Black family, despite being proud of her African-American heritage. It would seem that armed with new awareness of her family history, she was able to reconcile her appearance with her multiracial heritage.[6]

For the most part, all the responses to my enquiries were positive, inquisitive and friendly. The exception came from my mother's one remaining first cousin, who had initially declined to participate in the venture. "I trust you will realize the attitude on the subject is much different in the United States than it is in Canada...revealing the story will be tragic for my daughter and her four children."[7]

It was a difficult situation, for on the one hand I respected his feelings, but his children were now middle-aged and I believed had a right to know. However, time has a way of healing old wounds and eventually he acquiesced and told his children. Although they were keenly chagrined to think they had been kept ignorant all these years, they grasped their new identity with zeal and enthusiastically sought further information:

> This new knowledge has definitely changed my feelings of identity. I really don't know how to explain it other than to say I never really thought I fit. I was kind of a round peg trying to fit into a square hole. I have always felt there was something missing. I know this sounds strange, as it must seem hard to imagine how one can miss something they never knew they had. I feel that with each new family contact I make, or each letter I receive from relatives, regardless of their racial identity I am a more complete person.[8]

Early in my quest, I came upon Meredith Lewis, another Black cousin. As a professional broadcaster and journalist, he was delighted that someone was finally tackling the project. While discussing some of our common relatives, Meredith divulged another genealogical discovery

Cousin Meredith Lewis, grandson of Helene Abbott Sayre, now deceased, with his family. *Back row, left to right:* Meredith, his wife Darlene (King), and her sister, Cheryl King; *front row*, daughters Malika and Kali. The photograph was taken on the occasion of their visit to the author's home in October 1991.

about his own father. Shortly before he died, Meredith came upon his birth certificate and discovered that his father's last name was actually Wilder and not Lewis. It seems that Meredith's grandmother had been so embittered over her divorce that she had simply assigned her maiden name to her son, Meredith's father. Just how important this historical episode was became evident later, when Meredith and his family travelled to Richmond, Virginia, to attend the Wilder family reunion. On the grounds of the governor's mansion, he met his cousin, Governor Lawrence Douglas Wilder of Virginia. Meredith described the governor's bearing,

151

diction and mannerisms as being very reminiscent of his own father and he described the experience to be like that of a homecoming—truly remarkable.

Shortly after we exchanged a few letters, Meredith arranged to travel to Toronto with his family for the Thanksgiving weekend. This would prove to be our first "in person" contact with them. As the appointed evening approached, the entire family gathered to await their imminent arrival. We had no photos to refer to and so we did not know what to expect. Would they be fair, dark or Black? Sure enough, when the doorbell sounded we eagerly opened the door to reveal some very Black faces. Later we had quite a chuckle about it, as Meredith divulged that they too, had wondered what we would look like and sure enough, as the door swung open, their eyes had settled upon some very white faces.

Although I had found our visit extraordinary, I had not been plagued by any prior anxiety about being accepted by them. I was therefore very touched when he expressed such heart-felt relief and appreciation. "I don't know what I anticipated, but your warm, thoughtful reception for us was much more than I expected. Everyone among your family and relatives made us feel right at home and part of the family and I cannot thank you enough."[9] Since my family considered the reunion a great mutual pleasure, we were quite surprised. I can only speculate about what other types of reception they might have anticipated, for they had made me feel as if we were, in fact, the lucky ones.

I consider my short acquaintance with Meredith to be very special, for he was such an inspiration to me as we embarked together in spirit on a search for our common history. I could tell that "family" meant a lot to Meredith and he was always eager to reach out to support any family endeavour. Seeking out further relatives just seemed to be the next natural step for him, as he very much wanted to see us all reunited. We were able to meet several times and I will never forget how excited he was about the idea of a family reunion. Big plans were in the works, when he suddenly died of an aneurysm, on December 26 in 1993.

Although I had not known Meredith for very long, I felt deeply honoured when his family called and invited me to deliver the Eulogy at his funeral. It proved to be quite an experience for me, as it meant that I had to announce and acknowledge our relationship to strangers who were not aware of the family history. As I stood alone at the podium with nervous anticipation and faced a sea of multi-hued faces, I believed I could sense his presence beside me and then I knew that I could get through the moment. Several days after I returned home from the funeral, I received a subscription to the *Smithsonian Black History* magazine. It was Meredith's Christmas gift to me. That was my moment for tears.

> When all is done, and my last word is said.
> And ye who love me murmur, "He is dead."
> Let no one weep, for fear that I should know.
> And sorrow, too, that ye should sorrow so.
>
> When all is done, say not my day is o'er,
> And that thr' the night I seek a dimmer shore;
> Say rather that my morn has just begun,—
> I greet the dawn and not a setting sun.[10]

CHAPTER 20

CROSSING THE
COLOUR LINE

*The irony of the logic of identity is that by seeking to reduce the differently
similar to the same, it turns the merely different into the absolutely other.*[1]

THE QUESTION OF COLOUR seems to have been pervasive
throughout many generations in my family. My mother does not
remember ever hearing the issue of race discussed among her family
members, but now she realizes that this was how she was shielded from
such knowledge. Of course, in exasperated fun we have since badgered
her many times, "Mom, how could you not have noticed?" However, she
always shrugged it off with statements such as, "They all looked perfectly
normal to me," or "My skin was the same colour as theirs," or "Most of
them were old with white hair," or "No one ever mentioned it!" She does
recall her mother's ever-constant reminder during the summer months,
"Marion, get out of the sun. You're going to be black!" Of course, at the
time she assumed that her mother was referring to her dark suntan and
that she should take care of her complexion. Little did she know!

On one occasion, she recalls a Hubbard cousin coming to Toronto for
a visit with her family. It was then that my mother first noticed that they
looked different, for her cousin's husband and their children were
obviously very dark and had black, curly hair. But, incredible as it may
seem to us now, nothing was ever openly mentioned about their race.
When another "white" cousin voiced a similar observation, he was
shushed with a simple explanation. "They went out in the sun a lot!"

In 1991, my mother and I travelled to Detroit to interview a newly-
discovered first cousin of my mother, Eleanore Osborne, daughter of
Helene Abbott Sayre, and her husband Ralph. We arrived a little ahead
of schedule and drove through a very quiet downtown area, considering

154

the fact that it was the Saturday afternoon of a long weekend. We knew that crime and racial strife had taken a huge toll on the City of Detroit over recent years, but this was a ghost town! We spotted only an occasional person, even in the centre core of the city, walking along our route or waiting at a bus stop. As we wove through the streets in the late spring afternoon, we entered a prosperous-looking but older neighbourhood adorned with wide, spacious boulevards, neatly edged with gnarled, ancient trees spreading benevolently over the ancient lawns and crackled sidewalks. Finally, we pulled up in front of an old, attractive, red brick house, its porch ensconced in the bountiful arms of a magnificent magnolia bush.

Rather hesitant about our prospective encounter, we nervously disembarked, leaving our bags in the trunk of the car, thinking we could always excuse ourselves and escape to a hotel if things became too awkward. We mounted the front steps and rang the doorbell. A smallish, sprightly woman, darkly "tanned," with snow-white hair and a ring of sporadically placed, silver pin curlers fringing the nape of her neck, opened the door and eagerly grasped my mother's hand.

She exclaimed that we had caught her a bit early, but to surely come in and make ourselves at home. Still tentatively perched on the doorstep, my mother began to explain who she was, since naturally Eleanore would not remember her from their last meeting when Mom was only a young child. But she was abruptly cut short, when Eleanore exclaimed that, she certainly did!

"Remember you!" she said in a strong, rather stern voice. Looking my mother directly in the eye, she said, "The last time I saw you, we were all gathered together in your grandmother's house on Broadview Avenue in Toronto. You came up to me and asked me straight out, 'Do you mind being so dark?' I answered, 'Well, I've been this dark for such a long time, so I don't think I mind.' I asked my husband, Ralph, 'Do you mind me being so dark, Ralph?' And Ralph had chuckled and answered, 'Noooo…I don't think so.' But as I turned back to you, you blurted out in my

Marion Abbott as a young girl.
Courtesy of the Abbott family.

155

face, 'WELL, I HATE IT!!' Your mother was so embarrassed, she jumped up and exclaimed to your father, 'Gordon, I think it's time to go!'" Summing up, Eleanore stated with finality, "So, I certainly remember you!"

By this time, my poor mother had turned several shades of red herself and was delicately choking out some kind of a belated apology. She still does not remember the details of the incident but she has a vague recollection of having said something indelicate and thinking, "Uh oh! What did I say? Why are we suddenly going home?" as she was hustled out of the house. Today, my mother believes that she was simply referring to the nuisance of staying out of the sun and certainly did not understand the racial implications of the situation. Nothing further was ever mentioned to her about the incident.

However, in her defence, the old family pictures of our antecedents that remain in our photo albums do depict seemingly fair-skinned people, especially those that were elderly. I am not sure if that is just the result of faded photographs or that their skin actually faded as they got older, but I do know that even I am not nearly as dark now as I was when I was a child. As one Black cousin put it, "As I grow older, I get lighter and my blood leaves me." Although some of the older relatives had curly hair, many of them did not, nor were their features particularly prominent. Everyone in the family looked similar and it would be easy to understand why a child would not raise the question of race.

When my mother and I crossed the Canadian-American border, we also unknowingly crossed the colour line as well. It was a very peculiar feeling to enter a stranger's house as white and then find oneself considered to be part of a Black family. But I must admit, once past the door there was no going back and we immediately became engulfed in a whole new world, where we were made to feel as if we fit right in—kind of an Alice in Wonderland feeling!

From the moment we stepped through that doorway we began one of the most unique experiences of our lives as we engaged in many happy hours, swapping stories, asking questions and just collecting the missing links of the family saga. Eleanore had worked as a social worker and then a teacher in the Chicago public school system for many years and, typical of the Abbott women, she had devoted a great deal of her time to PTA boards, charity organizations and community services. Over the years she had more or less kept track of everyone and, even at the age of 90 while still recovering from a heart attack, she was as energetic and as sharp as ever. It was all we could do to prevent her from traipsing up and down two flights of stairs to dig out some family relic when a story would trigger the remembrance of a long-forgotten treasure or photograph.

Her husband, Ralph, a retired lawyer and Acting Consul to Haiti was also one of a kind. When he excused himself in the middle of the afternoon and stepped out with a young legal cohort, we were quite impressed! Ralph was the son of a white, Jewish father from Liverpool, England, and a Black mother. Later during our visit, he told us a little more about himself and his childhood while growing up in Detroit:

Eleanore Sayre and Ralph Osborne on their wedding day in 1936. Eleanore was the third daughter of Helene (Abbott) Sayre. She passed away in 1993. *Courtesy of the Abbott family.*

When I was going to high school and playing basketball I wasn't really very dark. I never felt inferior or anything like that. But you can see, in this picture, the coach has placed me on the end of the row of players and I was too ignorant to know why. In my first year at Maine State, I was one of the best players. But I couldn't understand why the coach always played this other guy that had played 13th on my team at Eastern High, instead of me. One day, our Alumni rep came down to visit and noticed that I was not playing on the first line. He went to see the coach and then all of a sudden I found myself out on the court!

Another time I hurt my knee in a game and had to go on crutches. The captain of our team said to me, "Well, why don't you go see our doctor?" I said, "I didn't know we had a doctor!" He went in to talk to the coach and when he came out he said, "I just handed in my suit. If I were you, I'd hand yours in too!" Do you know that coach called my office seven times when he was retiring to make sure that I would be coming to his retirement party? Of course I wasn't going.[2]

We continued to chat for several hours and later another cousin, Margaret Hubbard, joined us. She turned out to be the one with the "dark" husband

Karen Osborne Rucker, daughter of
Eleanore and Ralph Osborne.
Courtesy of the Osborne family.

and children that my mother had noticed as a child. Already suffering from diabetes and the beginnings of Alzheimer's disease, she had driven herself over, despite the fact that Eleanore and Ralph were convinced she would get lost and would never make it to their house. She was an absolute delight, very smartly dressed and well-groomed, and she still appeared to be extremely dignified and capable. She was thrilled to meet us and happily gave us some of her own viewpoints pertaining to old family matters. She had been raised in Toronto and had graduated from the University of Toronto as a dietician, but she went to the United States to complete her internship. Several years later, her daughter divulged to me that she could not do her internship in Toronto because of her race! Even in the forties, none of the Toronto hospitals would have her—they would educate her but not hire her. So much for "Toronto the Good."

Eleanore and Ralph's daughter, Karen arrived a little later and then things really started to rollick. As if we had not been thoroughly awestruck with her parent's hospitality, we fell in love with Karen. She was graced with her parents' good humour and her boisterous spirit carried us through a hilariously pleasant evening of old stories, reminiscences, tales of gossip and even a few serious moments.

Later that evening, completely exhausted and exhilarated, my mother and I tucked ourselves into bed. Totally overwhelmed with our reception, we began to giggle under the covers like two schoolgirls as we reviewed the events of the previous hours in gasps of wonder. Clearly, we had sensed no barriers between us and our cousins, for we had immediately felt that special connection that some families just naturally enjoy.

The next morning was Sunday and we had planned to join Eleanore and Ralph at St. Matthew's and St. Joseph's Episcopal Church. We were a little surprised that no one bothered to worry about breakfast before we headed out, but then since Eleanore never seemed to eat anything anyway, we just assumed that she must have forgotten. After some time, Ralph managed to manoeuvre a gargantuan vehicle out of a pocket-sized garage at the back of the property, and drove it around the block to pick us up at the front of the house. Slipping into the back seat, we were totally unprepared for the cruise across town to the church. As we barrelled down the centre turning lane of a main street, Mom and I both glanced at each other and silently wondered if perhaps it might be time for Ralph to give up his license! However, fortunately there was little traffic and no one else seemed to notice anything unusual. Amazingly we arrived at the church in one piece and proceeded to enter the sanctuary.

As we seated ourselves in a pew, it soon became obvious that this was going to be a High Episcopalian service, complete with incense and bells. Just across from us, a group of street people waited restlessly. As the service began, I gazed around the church and was surprised to notice a statue of a Black St. Matthew! Overall, the elaborate service was quite fascinating, but during the long Latin mantras, I recalled a story Karen had told us the night before. She had been describing the difference in skin shades between herself and her adopted brother and sister, who were quite a bit lighter. She admitted that occasionally her lighter-skinned siblings could be rather insensitive on occasions when they told her, "You walk behind us, so no one will think we're Black." One day, as she was attending church with them, she trailed through the vestibule door and the minister bent down and said to her in a kind voice, "I'm sorry, child, but you must have the

A family reunion in Detroit. *Left to right*: Marion (Abbott) Young, Eleanore (Sayre) Osborne, Ralph Osborne, Catherine (Young) Slaney.

wrong church. You want the Baptist one across the street." In these instances, one can begin to appreciate the relationship between skin-colour, social class and even the choice of religion in the case of my family. However, the impact of this realization did not hit me until a little later that morning.

The Abbotts had become very staunch Anglicans or Episcopalians over the last century, although they had once been devout British Methodist Episcopalians. It would appear that one's particular religious affiliation in the Black community, especially in the American Black community, is extremely significant for a number of reasons. Traditionally, most Blacks tended to be Protestant as were most of the Abbotts. The Canadian ones were usually Anglican, while the American ones tended to adhere to the very similar Episcopalian denomination, with High Church being more desirable than the Low Church. It would seem that such an affiliation denoted a certain social class and perhaps a shade of skin colour. It became clear to me that our ancestors had considered their denomination very carefully as they negotiated their rise in social status.

After the church service, we trooped down to the basement where a chorus of delectable odours greeted our entrance. Eleanore and Ralph took us around the room, introducing us as their Canadian cousins. We eventually sat down to a delicious breakfast of grits, eggs, bacon, sausage, home fries, rolls and juices and freshly brewed coffee. Here, I discovered was the reason for the street people's attendance at the service, as they continued to receive their blessings, this time in culinary form. As we devoured our meal we conversed with just about everyone in the congregation and yet we were still oblivious to our situation. Gradually it began to dawn on us that not only were we in the midst of an all-Black congregation, but we were a part of it! As I chatted with one of the members, he began to explain how difficult it had been for him when he was in the armed forces. He told me that while he was stationed in Georgia, he had not dared to go off the base after dark. Well, of course, I was at a loss as to understand what he meant, until I began to realize that, despite his fair skin, his hair was just a little bit frizzy. I was totally amazed, for I could not fathom how or why anyone would have even thought that he was Black. Yet, here he was, decades later, recounting the experience in all its dreadful truth.[3] As we continued our conversations with other members of the congregation, I began to realize that not only were many of these fair-skinned people Black, but that they appeared to accept us as one of them. Maybe I was mistaken, but it certainly felt as if we were Black for the moment. This was definitely an experience of a lifetime, and we will be forever grateful for the opportunity. What an illumination!

160

St. George's Anglican Church in Toronto where Anderson
Ruffin Abbott and Mary Ann Casey were married in
August 1871. *Toronto Public Library (TRL): T10720.*

A year later Eleanore passed away, and I was fortunate enough to be
able to travel down to the funeral with my cousin Lorraine Hubbard and
her mother. It was a sad occasion, but at the same time it was very important to me to pay my respects, for I might never have found the endurance
or courage to continue with this project without her nudging. As keeper
of the family memoirs, Eleanore had passed on the torch. I was deeply
honoured to accept it.

CHAPTER 21

THE PASSING YEARS

...if you are too unlike us, you are inferior, and if you are too like us, you are a ridiculous mimic.[1]

So what really happened to make this family become two separate entities? One all-knowing, the other oblivious to their counterpart! It probably does not take a lot of historical investigation to realize that times had been changing and life could be difficult whether one was white or Black. But the decision appears to have rested in the hands of the parents who wanted what was best for their children, who wanted to wipe away any of the ugliness of racial discrimination, and perhaps to also make life just a little bit easier for themselves. Certainly one's precious children would have provided the final impetus for such a move, for why should the family have to suffer any consequent indignation? Thus one can see how easy it would have been to simply "whitewash" the family history, still noting all the accomplishments and great deeds of the predecessors, but deleting any mention of colour, race, and most emphatically, Black cousins.

But was it really that easy? It would seem that a tremendous amount of carefully staged deceit and co-ordinated effort by the entire clan was invested in creating a believable genealogy. The strategy appears to have allowed those who could "pass" to do so and those who could not or would not were to remain out of sight—forever—for the sake of the others. Throughout my research, I encountered many new cousins and was invariably surprised to perceive no signs of bitterness, jealousy or cynicism. Whenever we met, everyone was simply delighted to become re-acquainted. It was almost as though they had just been politely waiting off stage until we, the white ones, were ready to rejoin the family. When I think of it now, I realize that my small branch of the family was the "exception," for the others all knew what was really going on.

Left, Gordon Anderson Abbott as a young child; *right*, Gordon Abbott in his senior years. *Photographs courtesy of the Abbott family.*

So maybe a closer look at the practice of passing in the early part of the 20th century is in order at this point. Wilson and Gordon, Anderson's two sons, apparently felt the most need, out of all the family members, to do this. In this case, it does not appear to have been a particularly Canadian or American phenomenon, as Gordon lived in Canada and Wilson lived in the United States. Furthermore, class did not appear to be a factor as the profession of the two men did not make a difference—Gordon was a mechanic and Wilson was a doctor. However, the aspect of gender does tend to muddy the waters in this case, when one realizes that only the boys married white and then actively "passed," while all the girls married "back" into the Black race. Perhaps it was just coincidence, but it would appear that for a number of possible reasons, the girls either could not, or would not, cross the colour line, while the boys, after the death of their father, passed readily into the white race. Of course, one must realize that women did not have the social mobility that they have today. As my aunt suggested, they had to wait to be asked. The men on the other hand, as my aunt put it, enjoyed the option of seeking out the lady of their choice and making an irresistible proposal.

However, Judy Scales-Trent notes that "the white community did withdraw privileges from the light-skinned Black community in the mid-nineteenth century, and consequently the light-skinned group started to seek out alliances with darker Blacks."[2]

It is understandable that the boys felt more at ease with passing as they had married into the white race, and reportedly maintained very close relationships with their in-laws. My Uncle Bob suggested that the family deliberately strove to gradually "bleach out" the colour, in order to increase the social and economic advantages for the sake of future descendants. Nevertheless, despite the apparent rejection of their racial identity, the family remained close and visited regularly. My uncle recalls the weekly dinner at his grandmother's house:

> My family usually went to my grandmother's place for dinner every Sunday, at 662 Broadview. We would worry if the Essex would get us there! The house was turned into a duplex in Grandma's day and she lived with Aunt Grace and Uncle Fred [Hubbard]. That was where we visited Uncle Wilson and occasionally we saw Aunt Nell [Helene]. Sometimes she stayed with us, but she never brought her children.[3]

A postcard celebrating the 75th anniversary of this all-Black resort located on the shores of Lake Idlewild, Michigan. When Mary Ann Abbott purchased a lakeside home nearby in 1929, the Abbott family would holiday there every August. *Courtesy of the Abbott family.*

In 1929, Anderson's widow, Mary Ann bought a lakeside home in the town of Baldwin, Michigan, on the shores of Lake Idlewild. Every August all of the Abbotts would congregate for a family vacation. To this day, the property remains in the hands of my Great-aunt Ida's family. Wonderful tales of summer adventures, romances and family events must surely abound among those spirits of long ago.

Idlewild,[4] founded in 1912, had been one of the few places where professional upper- and middle-class Blacks could vacation in those days of segregation, meeting and socializing with other Blacks. Situated close to Chicago, it was a prime location for jazz nightclubs, where famous musicians like Duke Ellington, Louis

The Abbott daughters in their later years (from left to right): Grace Hubbard, Helene Sayre and Ida Stevenson. *Courtesy of the Abbott family.*

Armstrong and Count Basie would be invited to perform in the various dance halls and resorts, where doors were never marked "colored entrance" or "whites only" in those Jim Crow days.

It's funny how different things seem when we think about them many years after the fact, but when I asked my uncle about his summer visits to the lake, he said, "I never realized at the time of course, but the whole community was Black!" Eleanore related a noteworthy incident concerning her cousins, Bob and his brother Don, during one summer holiday, when they encountered other Black children who clearly made no distinction between skin tones:

> The boys had gone down to the wharf and came running back crying that some kids had made fun of them, calling them "niggers." Aunt Ann (their white mother), was quite taken aback and asked Aunt Ida and my mother, Helene, what she should do. They replied, "That's your problem!" and they up and left her to come up with an explanation that obviously never did clarify the situation, for the boys remained ignorant of the fact that they or anyone else in the family were Black![5]

Robert Anderson Abbott (1920–1998)
as he appeared in the late 1930s.
Courtesy of the Abbott family.

Uncle Bob remembered other trips to Idlewild:

I can still see the cottage in my mind. It was like a great family get-together, with my parents, Aunt Nell, Aunt Grace and Aunt Ida. We would stay overnight in Detroit with friends and then drive up to the little town of Baldwin. A little causeway connected the mainland to an island with a wonderful dance hall. They had lots of big bands booked in there and I remember even Della Reese sang there once. One time I remember watching a coloured man at a fair, sitting up in a booth behind some glass and we threw baseballs at him, real baseballs! If you hit him, you won a prize.[6]

Uncle Bob had a hard time coming to terms with his Black heritage in later life. He found it difficult to put aside his early perceptions of the "family secret," and he could not reconcile himself to the possibility of disclosure. Hence he chose to perpetuate the silence that encircled the family business:

It seemed as if there was an unwritten law and the family remained united in its endeavour. Although some of the Americans went back into the Black race, the ones in Canada that had managed to gain a white status were careful to keep it. All of the predecessors knew about the family's ancestors but the next generation was not allowed to get to know the Black descendants.

Of course I knew that Aunt Nell and Aunt Ida must have had a family over there. But, in my day that was a long way away and not until later, did I realize that a decision must have been made that there should be no visits. When we were young, we were often taken along to visit the American side of the family. As we got older, only my younger sister was taken along. I guess they thought that she wouldn't notice, but we boys were left behind when we got older.[7]

When Fred Hubbard died in Toronto, Gus, who had been raised as white, became more closely involved with his Uncle Gordon's family. As both Gordon and Wilson had deliberately passed as white, their sons did not encounter any difficulty relating to each other and had always kept in touch. Bob explained how his Uncle Wilson handled the situation:

> Uncle Wilson had a much more difficult time keeping the families separate. Gus didn't even know that his father had a Black medical practice, or that he volunteered his medical services in the Black section of the city on the weekends. He was never allowed to go along and the odd time he offered to drive his father to work, he was turned down.[8]

Gus' daughter Bonnie told me:

> I know my father didn't want his children relegated to the back of the bus. He thought our lives would be easier if we lived them as white people. I don't know about Canada, but during my lifetime I have seen ...the integration of schools, the elimination of separate facilities for Black and white and the elimination of the 'one drop rule' where you were considered 'Black' if you had more than one drop of Black blood. In the not too distant past, one state still considered you Black if you were 1/32nd Black.[9]

As I delved further into this phenomenon, I discovered to my amazement that, in 1930, thirty-one states considered interracial marriages to be illegal and that it was not until 1967 that the United States Supreme Court actually banned such laws across the nation!

Cousin Eleanore described how they handled Wilson's funeral:

> Well, when Gus' father, Wilson Abbott passed away, Mama and Aunt Grace went with Grandma to the Funeral Home before the service. The funeral was scheduled for 4 o'clock and they went a couple of hours early and signed the register, leaving behind a flower arrangement with a card that said, "From all of us..." When Gus saw their names on the guest register he realized there was something amiss. Before this, everyone had thought, 'Why bother telling him? If anything had shown up in the child...but it didn't. After he was married and moved to Wisconsin he still always wondered about it. Eventually he wrote a letter to the Hubbards in Toronto and Gus was subsequently invited for a visit, where the entire story was finally disclosed.[10]

Gus (Augustus) Abbott and his family circa 1950. *From left to right*: Gus, Bonnie (now Grosnick), Wynn, Wilson and his wife Adele. *Courtesy of the Abbott family.*

In actual fact, it would appear that Gus had been told about his Black heritage by a maternal aunt after his father's death, but no details had been provided. He was always aware of his Canadian cousins, but his father never let him know that he had aunts living in Chicago. However, Gus was quite disturbed by the news and even offered to give his wife, Adele, a divorce if she wanted one!

The families were always careful to make it clear to their children that they were from good stock, cultured and well-respected. My mother and Aunt reminisced:

Mom: I remember my mother often saying as I grew up that Dad came from a very good family. I guess she thought that someone might find out about the Black ancestors and tell me differently.
Aunt: Actually your mother talked it up more than your father—not the Black part—but the "First Family of Virginia" part—they always used to talk about that.
Mom: I guess that's if I ever found out, I wouldn't be ashamed.
Aunt: You hardly ever saw a Black person. You never questioned it. It was like having an alcoholic in the family—you just never asked. It wasn't talked about—that's just the way it was.[11]

My mother does recall an indignant family discussion at the dinner table, when the renown, Black opera singer, Marion Anderson, came to Toronto to perform and was banned from the very conservative Granite Club. In those days, some of the Abbott cousins, like Clarence and Nellie Lightfoot opened their doors to visiting Blacks and put them up for the night when the major hotels and restaurants refused them service.

When the soldiers returned from World War I to a depressed economy, jobs were very hard to find. The Canadian-born Black veterans who had been permitted to enlist could not simply pick up where they left off. The subtle and not-so-subtle forms of discrimination restricted even the well-educated.

Two of my uncles served honourably in the Canadian Armed Forces during World War II, but of course they had been accepted as white recruits. In some instances, self-declared Blacks were only allowed into labour or construction battalions during the First World War. But during World War II a group of Blacks successfully discouraged racial discrimination in the recruitment of labour forces. When my Uncle Bob asked his father, Gordon why he never joined the Armed Forces during World War I, he would always answer, "Oh, well, I had a bad thumb!" Now we wonder if, in fact, there were other reasons stemming from his race, for he had just returned from living in Buffalo as a Black man. Certainly, then, he would have been a natural candidate for the Black Construction Battalion![12]

Surely then, a strong case could be made for the practice of passing as white. Marriage, employment and acceptance into the armed forces were only a few of the obstacles that would need to be negotiated along the way. Many of the Abbotts had entrenched themselves in the hallowed ranks of the Ontario Hydro company. This was, in all likelihood, because of the close friendship between William Peyton Hubbard and Adam Beck. When Beck, as chairman, hired a

Clarence Lightfoot (son of Hannah Casey and Levi Lightfoot) was in the medical corps during World War I as he was not allowed into the fighting battalions because of his race. *Courtesy of the Abbott family.*

169

Socializing with the Black writer Langston Hughes at the Home
Service Association on Bathurst Street in Toronto circa 1940s.
From left to right: Clarence Lightfoot, Langston Hughes, Mrs.
Magse and Clotiloe Ferguson. *Courtesy of the Abbott family.*

Negro as a clerk in London at the Ontario Hydro-Electric Power Commission, North Hamilton's Member of Parliament publicly voiced his
objections. Thus, it would be understandable that when Gordon worked
at Hydro, he would either not be inclined to broadcast his Black ancestry
or perhaps he simply chose to sidestep any potential challenges. After all,
why risk losing a good job over a bygone family issue?

Gordon Abbott died in 1950, just a few months after my mother and
father were married. He never did tell her about her illustrious ancestors. Perhaps he never planned to, but we would like to think that as the
racial tension eased within the prosperous climate of the times, he might
have relented. However, he died so suddenly that no one really had a
chance to think about the future and how the family secret would ever
be resurrected or even resolved. Now in her 70s, my mother attempts to
adjust her racial identity.

I always believed I was a WASP—white, upper middle-class, Anglo-
Saxon—as was my family, or so I thought. I didn't know there was a
Black component until I was 45 years old. In school, I never knew I
was part Black and so as a child, as an adolescent and as an adult, I
was treated the same as everyone else I knew and I felt I fit in well
with my peer group. But I never sought out any special peer group

based on race. My experiences or lack thereof were partly due to where I lived. I knew very few people of different colour or nationality and spent next to no time thinking about it as I was growing up. I was raised to believe all people were basically the same—they just come in different shades.[13]

It is likely that both her parents assumed an illusive role in not teaching her to acknowledge racial difference within her own family. Although she recalls some lively discussions about racial injustices while growing up in Toronto, they did not equate the stories with themselves:

Today I feel like a WASP even though I now know I'm not completely. My parents obviously knew our mixed racial identity and, in order to make my life easier, chose not to tell me. They died when I was still a young woman, but I'd like to think they would eventually have felt confident enough in my strength of character and that of my husband's and also of the ability of my personal friends and community to accept the truth and tell me.

I think strangers see me as white. I feel as if my Black cousins in the States see as one of them—Black, for the most part, although I still don't know them very well. I've changed in my own mind a little, but I don't really think about my race much. If my daughter didn't bring it up so often I probably wouldn't think much about it at all. It's really no more of a factor in my daily life than it ever was— except as an interesting fact. I always believed Blacks were equal, just a different colour, so this revelation hasn't really changed my opinion of myself. However, I must admit that I do tend to take notice of them more than when I was young and uninformed.[14]

My mother does express regret that she did not have an opportunity to talk to her parents about this. She wishes that they had been more open and that she could have reassured them that she did not mind. It was unfortunate that her parents died by the time she was 24 years old, in the early 1950s. She now says she is gradually recognizing her own colour-blindness, as she becomes more aware of the "other" within herself. She believes that she was "blind to colour" because it simply did not matter to her.

In the case of her cousin Gus, she is glad that he was able to live long enough to accede to the revelation and talk to his children about it before he passed on, allowing them to consequently reconcile many identity conflicts that had plagued them as they were growing up. They all now revel in the knowledge of their Black ancestry and take great pains to reeducate themselves and increase their racial awareness.

My Uncle Bob, on the other hand described a number of painful experiences during his childhood despite being extremely popular and talented in high school. He felt a deep sense of rejection when the parents of his wife objected to their marriage based on race. My aunt's parents, the Seons, were from Barbados and identified themselves as white West Indians; her father was white and her mother, including her entire family, passed as white. The Abbotts and Caseys had befriended the Seons when they first emigrated from Barbados and thus the families were aware of each other for many years prior to the romance. When the prospect of marriage and the possibility of Black children became a reality, her father, normally a very gentle and loving man, refused to condone the union, and her parents did not attend the wedding. Gordon stood in to give away the bride. My uncle was devastated, but my aunt says that although she was extremely sad about the circumstances, she accepted his effort to redirect what he believed to be a poor decision. When she returned from her honeymoon, he picked up his relationship as if nothing had happened and became one of the most doting grandfathers one could ever imagine. For my uncle, the fear that this could happen once again to his own children seems to have locked him into a mindset that remained until just before his death. My mother muses:

> I don't know how my elder brother Don felt about the issue at all, but my other brother, Bob, was very upset about it becoming public knowledge and had a hard time accepting the fact that everyone knew. This was true even though his own children didn't seem bothered by the fact when they inadvertently saw a television documentary about their great-grandfather. I don't think, in fact, that my brother ever let many of his friends ever find out.[15]

Although Bob eventually accepted the fact that his father was Black, he never felt comfortable with others knowing about it and always worried about public exposure and consequent humiliation. Before his death, he made a tape for me, describing his feelings, his regrets and his deep love for his father. It would appear that the loving deeds of his parents elicited mixed blessings, for they left him with much to resolve in later life. My mother said:

172

My parents obviously didn't have a problem personally with the difference although they did make every effort to "pass" as white. I don't agree with their decision, yet I understand how difficult it must have been for them in those days. My mother must have been quite brave, although I think her family was very understanding.[16]

She remembers how deeply in love her parents were. However, she rationalizes that social pressures must have influenced their decision to pass, not only for their children's sake, but also for themselves and the sake of her mother's family. Perhaps the emotional upheaval of my uncle's marriage contributed to the perpetuation of the myth.

Today, my mother's present lifestyle emanates from within a white, rural community. She does not encounter many racial or even multicultural situations. Most of her friends are around her age and have migrated from the city to the country to enjoy their retirement years. Their lives involve hobby farming, horses, tennis, informal social gatherings and croquet matches:

My white community assumes that I am the same as they are even though some of them know of my Black heritage. I expect it is because I look much the same as they do. I feel sometimes now when I tell people that I'm part Black that either they don't believe me or they

Marion (Abbott) Young with her husband Howard relaxing at their Muskoka cottage.

173

don't care. Many of my friends think it's very interesting though, just as I do. Sometimes I think they don't quite know how to react when I tell them, especially if I do so after some joke or comment has been made about race.[17]

She does not find her racial mixture a problem in her everyday life. It does not really matter to her what others think of it, as she herself does not claim her identity through race. On occasion she will refer to her racial background in a joke, just to make a point and raise a bit of public awareness:

> I think diversity is good if we can all learn to accept it, but with the understanding that, though different, we are all equal. So in some ways the answer might be to all become melded and the same. I doubt we will ever do that though. I think sometimes being a little different is an advantage because it gives you the opportunity to be more objective about people and judge them all by the same standards despite their differences. I guess racial identity is more important to those people who have been more affected by being different in both good and bad ways. I feel good about my own racial identity, but it's easy for me because it didn't really change anything in my day-to-day life— it just made my ancestors more interesting. I still feel white or whatever I am. Since I found out, nothing has really changed for me. Even though it doesn't affect me, I do identify with being Black to some extent now when I didn't before because I didn't have any reason to before.[18]

Anderson Ruffin Abbott, even in his day, must have been keenly aware of the "passing" process, although it may have taken on a rather different connotation. On several occasions he noted that their numbers were dwindling and that eventually he could foresee an overall assimilation of the Black population into the mainstream. By the time of his death in 1913, no more than a few hundred Blacks still resided in Toronto. How could he have predicted that the immigration of thousands of West Indians and Africans would some day inflate their social profile?

During those years it could not have been easy to find a place in Canadian society, no matter what the shade of one's skin. The tolerant racial climate that Anderson had experienced in Toronto had receded and racial oppression became much more open and prevalent in both urban and rural communities. The pressure to simply slip into the mainstream must have been tantalizingly strong, despite the presence of those who felt that the Black community should foster a positive Black identity. To many "old-line" Blacks, it was a question of equality, not difference that held their concern and passing may have simply become just another reality.

As Anderson Abbot predicted:

> ...The social proscription which meets the colored man everywhere in this country has suggested to many the expedient, of removing from the homes of their youth, to remote parts of the country and there resolutely entering white society, [thus] losing their identity as colored persons.[19]

As many became more involved in the civil rights movement of the 1950s and '60s, anti-discrimination laws were instituted. In 1960, the Canadian federal government passed a Bill of Rights that opposed any form of discrimination based race, religion or sex. In 1962, Ontario established a Human Rights Commission headed by Dr. Daniel Hill, Ontario's first Black Ombudsman, in an effort to promote equal opportunity under the law.

CHAPTER 22

LOCATING MYSELF ON THE COLOUR LINE

Helped are those who are enemies of their own racism: they shall live in harmony with the citizens of this world, and not with those of the world of their ancestors, which has passed away, and which they shall never see again.[1]

WHILE GROWING UP I never thought to question my ancestry and therefore accepted the fact that, although I had a dark complexion, I belonged in the white, mainstream community. My impression in the 1950s and '60s was that one had to be one or the other. Not much acknowledgement was given to multiracial status unless one was openly and equally biracial, that is half Black and half white. However, I never even considered the possibility at that time with respect to my family. Despite my complexion, I do not personally recall experiencing any instances of racial discrimination, while I was growing up in Toronto, or even when I lived in Halifax, home to a large Black population.

That is not to say that such racial discrimination did not exist in these places, but simply that I did not encounter it. Of course, I have always assumed myself to be "white," and perhaps it is that personal sense of self-identity that holds the key. Even though, on numerous occasions, people would comment on my dark skin, I would always respond with the answer my mother was given, before me, to such inquisitiveness, "Oh, that's because I have a Spanish Great-grandmother!" Inevitably they would respond with some positive cooing and positive affirmation. Today I wonder how they would have responded if I had said I had a Black Great-grandmother. It probably wouldn't have taken me long to keep my explanations to myself, for I expect the reaction from many people might have been less than positive. In that case, I must

Left, Catherine Louise Young, great-great-granddaughter of
Wilson Ruffin Abbott (1801–1876) and great-granddaughter of Dr.
Anderson Ruffin Abbott, at age 2; *right,* Cathy Young and her
friend Pam Murphy on the first day of school. *Photographs courtesy
of the Abbott family.*

consider how differently I and my mother might have constructed our
racial identity over all these years!

During my childhood I recall only one playmate who was ethnically
different and as a result, cruelly teased. I still feel uncomfortable with these
memories, because I remember thinking that I knew it was wrong to be
mean to her, but I did nothing to stop it. I did not discuss it with my
parents at the time, for I felt guilty about it and could not comprehend
my feelings. Now upon reflection I realize that I had few tools with which
to work, for I had never been exposed to racism before and for all practical
purposes, I had not been taught about it. I was not exposed to a multicultural curriculum of any kind in school or even in the community. Yet
that experience remained with me and contributed to my appreciation of
discrimination, making me much more aware of the lessons to be taught
to my own children at early ages, as they encounter various acts of racism
in their daily lives. This is very different than when I was young, for as a
family, we did not discuss race very much at all. It just never came up and
it did not seem to be a factor in our lives at that time.

My children, four of whom are adopted, are basically white. One
daughter is Métis, yet they all consider themselves to be culturally "white"
as they have been assimilated into the dominant culture that they were
exposed to during their upbringing. When we became aware of our Black
ancestry, my biological son was about five years old. I can remember the

177

The Young sisters in 1998. *From left to right,* Cathy Slaney, Christine Genovese and Laura Young.

day when the little towhead returned from his Kindergarten class to report that he had announced to the class that he was Black. It was several years before he began to realize that he needed to modify this definition in order to be taken seriously. However, today he is still very proud of all aspects of his heritage and has managed to incorporate it into his own special identity. He does not feel any compunction to explain or justify his image. But he grew up differently than I did. We talked about racial and cultural differences throughout his childhood, we encouraged him to make friends with people of all ages, abilities and ethnicities, he dated lots of girls of different cultures and races and, in my opinion, he sought out "different" people because he considered them to be interesting and friendly. As a mother I am naturally proud of his open-mindedness, tolerance and sense of social justice.

My sister, Christine has also made a conscious effort to embrace all of the cultures within her family and to pass on an appreciation of them to her children. She is well-informed about her Black heritage and encourages her children to make use of the information and share it with their friends. She too learned about our Black ancestry as an adult, but aside from curiosity, has not appeared to be particularly affected by the revelation. Her children think of this ancestry as a novelty, but with their blonde hair and blue/green eyes, do not particularly identify as Black. However, they are alert to their heritage and do not hesitate to mention it if asked about it. I was present, one day when my sister asked her children about their racial/cultural identity and we both registered astonishment when the children all claimed a definite Italian identity since their blond, blue-eyed father is part Italian and part

178

The children of Christine (Young) and Blaine Genovese circa 1993.
From left to right: Meagan, Jacklyn and Mathew.

English. I suppose we were surprised simply because none of them had ever mentioned it before. It was even more remarkable when her husband entered the room and looked at my sister and me in disbelief when asked about his ethnic identity, as if to say, "Well of course I am Italian! What else could I possibly be, with a name like Genovese?"

A few years ago, I attended a writers' workshop intended for women of colour. I had decided that the best way to learn about being Black was to go to the source. When I got there, the facilitator discreetly took me aside and informed me that this workshop was only for Black women, to which I cringed inwardly and replied, "I know." The woman then apologized profusely and made some polite comment about light-skinned Blacks today. Since there was no turning back at this point, I carried on. After all I was there to learn something new.

It turned out to be one more of many enlightening and humbling experiences. In this situation, I was not accepted as Black, nor was I particularly welcome. I did not fit in and could not readily identify with their Black experience from a cultural perspective. I suppose my genetic blood-lines were just too watered down to validate my entry into this exclusive club. Although some of them were very gracious, there was no mistaking the resistance on the part of several group members, for I had invaded their special space in my endeavour to explore the question of race. But, although I was an outsider and did not relish the position, I believe that it was vital to my learning process and I stuck it out.

At this point, one may ask why it mattered so much to them or to me. I do not have any ready answers. It is not a simple question, although it would be easy to contend that we are all members of the human race and colour should not matter. Well, that may be so, but colour indeed matters to many people and therefore whether one likes it or not, the phenomenon rudely intrudes on our rather self-righteous sensibilities that are so deeply offended by situations of inequity, injustice and intolerance.

In 1999 I returned to school to complete my Master of Education degree at Brock University. My initial intention was simply to learn more about the process of education. But as I began to meld my own family experience into new ways of thinking, I was struck by the similarity to the experiences of other families of mixed race and culture. Dabbling in the philosophies of identity formation, I began to consider the experiences of other family predecessors. I conducted a study of multiracial/cultural identities in children and interviewed a variety of mothers whose families had contended with similar issues of racial and cultural identity. It proved to be a fascinating study and re-awakened my personal interest in the realm of mixed race.

The study, "Exploring Multiracial/Cultural Identities through Mothers' Voices,"[2] revealed that the mothers who raised their children in the 1950s and 1960s reported that they had not addressed racial identity issues with their children while they were growing up. The findings of the study related directly to my own extended family. For example, these women, like my own mother, now realize that some of their children may have consequently struggled with their own multiracial/cultural identities. This finding does not necessarily imply that the mothers were responsible, nor did they particularly indicate that they felt responsible, for this phenomenon. Rather, they believed that their approach to parenting was representative throughout their class of society. Mothers of this era implied they felt they had no reason to be concerned about the racial identities of their children. As my own mother explained, the war was over, everyone was supposedly free, employed, healthy and anticipated infinite prospects for a successful future. They believed that all of their children would grow up to be happy, educated and successful and they did not realize until their children headed into the tumultuous '60s, that they might have overlooked some vital lessons in their children's lives. Perhaps this is one of the reasons why my grandfather decided not to burst the bubble at that time.

The study suggested that today's young mothers tend to have a different perspective as they feel a profound sense of responsibility for their children's physical, mental and spiritual welfare and education. They are often actively involved in perpetuating a new version of their children's racial and cultural heritage. Examples of this behaviour can be readily observed in many family rituals and practices, which may or may not

180

The unveiling of a commemorative portrait of Dr. Anderson
Ruffin at the Toronto General Hospital in 2000. *From left to right*:
Barbara (Abbott) Fraser, Marion (Abbott) Young, Christine
(Young) Genovese and Catherine (Young) Slaney.

reflect traditional values. They tend to participate in diverse community
activities and events and actively promote a multiracial/cultural school
policy and curriculum. All of the mothers, regardless of their generation,
voiced great pride in their own and their children's racial and cultural
ancestry. However, the younger mothers, like myself and my sister,
reported that they actively engaged their children in conversations about
their multiracial/cultural heritage and encouraged them to recognize the
advantages of their uniqueness. These mothers saw such awareness as a
passport to cultural enhancement.

With respect to multicultural experiences at school, it would seem once
again that the generation gap is the defining factor in the findings of this
study. My mother raised us when a multicultural policy was not a part
of the curriculum, nor even a part of the community. Teachers, texts and
learning materials are now considered to have been poor promoters of
the present-day aspirations of tolerance, acceptance and respect. The
mothers of the earlier generation were more concerned that their children
learn to read and write properly, so that they would be accepted into
university or land a good job. In general, these mothers attributed their
limited involvement to naivety rather than to racism.

Mothers today are much more involved in their children's education
and participate whenever possible. We try to be alert and sensitive to the
challenges that the school system faces at this time. We are relatively

satisfied with our children's schools and teachers, despite the fact that they have not yet addressed the multi or mixed aspects of racial identification. However, we feel that if teachers were made aware of this omission most of them would probably be receptive to constructive suggestions. For the most part, our children look forward to sharing their family stories and traditions with the class and school projects are often directed towards this goal. Overall, we believe that our children, because of their multiracial/cultural identities, will more easily find a place for themselves within a racially and culturally diverse society than we did. Although none of the mothers denied that racism exists in Canada today, they all felt that their children's future prospects were better here than anywhere else. Furthermore, they were proud to be Canadians first and foremost and hoped that their children would also cherish their nationality. They all believed it to be vital that Canadian children are made aware of the significant contributions of all minority cultures to the development of Canada and its policies.

It would seem that we are beginning to move forward into an era of increased awareness of racial and cultural diversity and our social dimensions are expanding beyond the former boundaries that once incited feelings of divisiveness, exclusion and segregation. It is the children who will reap the benefits of our labours, and it is also our children who will suffer the most if we do not cultivate and nurture new and innovative notions of peace, tolerance and understanding.

CHAPTER 23

THE REUNIFICATION

We search for the meaning of life in the realities of our experiences, in the realities of our dreams, our hopes, our memories.[1]

ONE DAY, UPON RETURNING home from work, and idly perusing the day's messages, I came upon a curious letter in the pile of mail that typically landed in scattered disarray across the kitchen table. The return address indicated that it was from a group called Smile Theatre. Just another solicitation, I thought, but curiosity got the better of me and I opened the envelope to reveal an intriguing request. As it turned out, Smile Theatre is a unique group of dedicated artists who regularly create musical plays that are presented in hospitals and nursing homes for seniors, schools and the occasional public performance. It provides a much appreciated form of entertainment for those who are shut-in and who would find it impossible to attend such performances in the public theatre. Most of the subjects of the plays are historically based on nostalgic and memorable Canadian themes. The result is that many young and blossoming actors and singers are able to make their mark on the stage under the very knowledgeable tutelage of professional directors.

Tom Kneebone, the Artistic Director, and Dinah Christie, singer and song-writer, had teamed up to write a musical drama about, would you believe, Anderson Ruffin Abbott. They wondered if I would be able to provide some background. This proved to be a wonderful time for me as I was thoroughly entranced by the whole remarkable process of re-creating the story of "Doc Ruffin." The cast was composed of Gavin Hope, Saidah Baba Talibah and Heather Cherron, all of whom were tremendously gifted and will certainly be seen and heard frequently over the coming years.

The play received such a great response, that we decided that we should take advantage of its popularity and so we organized a Gala Affair as the

Left, The playbill for the production of *Doc Ruffin* produced by Smile Theatre and ultimately part of the first Abbott family reunion in 1993.
Above, The cast for *Doc Ruffin* From left to right: Heather Cherron, Gavin Hope and Saidah Baba Talibah in 1993.

Annual Fundraiser for Smile Theatre. Along with that, we began to plan a "Gala Family Reunion" around the event and sent out invitations to the entire Abbott clan, right across the continent.

It was at this stage that I had one last duty to perform. I still had to inform the last branch of the family who had resisted the revelation. Cousin Gus had not yet relented, and his children still did not know about their Black ancestors. I felt that I just could not let this whole affair go by without informing them. So, with a great deal of trepidation, I wrote and then apprehensively waited for the response. What a relief when they responded with an explosion of surprise and joy and gratitude!

The excitement escalated and I became involved with details outside the actual play itself. It occurred to me that perhaps we might be able to locate the famous Lincoln Shawl that had been presented to Anderson by Mary Todd Lincoln, for our occasion. A number of problems became evident as I began to look for a secure and qualified venue for exhibiting the Shawl, for it was not simply a matter of shipping it over. In the first

The showing of Lincoln's Shawl and Anderson Abbott's sword, flanked by a colour guard from local Civil War Re-enactment members.

place, I had to establish my own credibility and "ownership" of the shawl. This involved getting the formerly recalcitrant Gus, who had donated the shawl in the first place, to convince the Historical Society that the Toronto Textile Museum would take good care of the artifact. After a great number of telephone calls, I finally connected directly with the Curators of the State Historical Society of Wisconsin, William Crowley and Leslie Bellais, who were able to facilitate the transfer of the shawl to the care of John Vollmer, the Curator of the Museum for Textiles in Toronto. The shawl was booked to be left on display for several weeks, whereupon it would be returned to Wisconsin.

It was then decided that we should take advantage of this opportunity to make the general public aware of a bit of Canadian Black history, including the significance of the "Shawl" and the up-coming Gala performance, by holding a Press Conference. Thus, on the morning of February 17th, 1993, the Toronto press was greeted by a number of Abbott family members, the cast of *Doc Ruffin* and a contingent of local Civil War Re-enactment members, dressed in full Union and Confederate uniforms, who acted as escorts and guards for the exhibit.[2]

It proved to be quite an affair. My Uncle Bob produced Dr. Abbott's dress sword and the medical officer's green sash that had always held a place of honour over the mantle in his home. At precisely 11 o'clock, the great black and white houndstooth Shawl[3] was unveiled. The cast of *Doc Ruffin* gave a rousing chorus to the song, "Lincoln's Shawl," which was written and composed by Dinah Christie. After my "speech," providing some historical background and thanking the press and the public for their presence, I was even interviewed for the evening news!

Then it was back to the various hotels to gather the family members together for a little sightseeing. Despite the February chill, all went over to the Necropolis Cemetery to view the Abbott plot and there, arm in arm, both black and white, we stood together as a true family. It was a moving experience, for it is not often that one takes time these days to even visit the cemetery plot of antecedents, but this was a special moment and it united us in body and in spirit.

Several days later, the rest of the Abbott clan rallied in Toronto for the grand performance at the Jane Mallet Theatre. Cousins from all over Canada and the United States had enthusiastically responded to our invitation to attend the event. On Saturday, February 19, we gathered with great excitement in the lobby of the theatre. We all wore colour-coded name tags to indicate the various family branches and scrolls of family trees cascaded over tables erected around the outside of the foyer. The Civil War Re-enactment Band, the boys of company 'C,' lent the final touch to the festivities and played renditions of Civil War musical selections throughout the evening. Just as the curtain was about to rise, a drummer boy and flutist gave note to those splendid chords that normally accompany such occasions and as chills ran down our spines, the Colour Parade proceeded to stream down the aisles of the theatre like some ghostly scene from historic moments of long ago. It was a truly awesome moment!

After the performance, the family was able to really get down to the business of getting re-acquainted. Together we moved over to the Royal York Hotel for dinner, where our cast members, Heather and Gavin, worked part-time as singing waiters. Although they were not scheduled to wait on tables that night, they did join us, along with Saidah, Tom and Dinah and regaled us throughout the evening with much song and laughter.

It proved to be a very special night for all of us and we felt privileged to be there. It's a funny thing when something like this pulls total strangers together, but all of us sensed a tremendous spiritual connection. I can truly speak for all when I say that race and colour were the least of out concerns that evening; we were just so happy to finally reunite. My mother, Marion, recalls the evening with deep pleasure:

I guess my most vivid memory is the wonderful feeling of "coming home" that I had that night. I can remember going around from table to table visiting with all the branches of the family and thinking how enormously alike we all were. Certainly not in looks, in fact we were just about every shade imaginable, but there was some indefinable spark that seemed to bind us. It was like looking at the same person in a

186

At dinner at the Royal York Hotel in Toronto following the production of "Doc Ruffin." *Seated from left to right*: Irene Hubbard, Carlton Watson and his wife Lorraine Hubbard.

dozen different guises! Especially the women…it was almost like seeing yourself over and over again, in a variety of colours. I couldn't get over how much alike we all were in personality; all the women talking with their hands and all obviously excited and delighted with the evening and in meeting each other. I remember thinking how pleased my grandfather would have been to see us all together again. It's hard to describe that evening; one of those things you really have to experience…I can just recall a true sense of FAMILY! I might add, I am eternally thankful that you have brought us all to this, dear.[4]

I just had to include that last part, but although this was my own mother speaking, I received dozens of similar responses in the mail from other members of the family:

Until last winter's performance in Toronto of the play *Doc Ruffin* and the family gathered afterward, I did not even know that most of you existed! Almost everyone there I had either never met before or had not seen in close to twenty years. It was really quite a wonderful experience to discover my "new" extended family. I would like to thank you again for everything you've done. This has all been a truly wonderful experience for me.[5]

I don't know how to begin to thank you for all you did on top of all your other activities. It is truly appreciated.[6]

I know Mama and Aunt Lydia would have been so thrilled about all of this.[7]

I'm so sorry that it has taken almost a year to contact you, but my life and family have been so moved by what happened in Canada that it's been hard to put all of the emotions down on paper. First let me start by saying that the weekend we spent in Toronto, the Play, meeting all of my new-found family, was all very exciting. We came back to Texas with such a sense of pride. There had always been such a big feeling of void because I didn't know why my family was so small. Also I always knew that my family was in Canada but we never knew why there was never any association with the rest of our family or who they were.... Well now that feeling has gone away and has been replaced with such a feeling of joy and pride—it's just wonderful.... This was like finding missing pieces to a puzzle!

Members of the extended family and descendants of the Abbotts on that 1993 occasion. Family reunions are now much anticipated regular events. *Top, left to right*: Kathleen (Sayre) Curry, Wilson (Bill) Abbott, __, __, Frank Sayre, Lori (Stubenvoll) Brewer, __, Kim Stubenvoll, Lorelle Curry. *Botton, left to right*: Pianna Curry, Wynn (Abbott) Stubenvoll, Bonnie (Abbott) Grosnik, Marlo Curry (with hat), Cherie (Stubenvoll) Barnett, __.

I think I've been in somewhat a state of astonishment over this whole story. It feels good to have a lot of questions answered that I could never quite put my finger on...I wish my father could have lived to see that reunion. It would be great to know exactly how much he knew about his Uncle Wilson Ruffin.... It has been so great that we have found the other half of our family. We're so glad that your side of the family is reaching out to get to know our side of the family. I realize the implication of being identified as a Black person in America— from what I hear it's not quite as bad in Canada. As sad as it may be, racism hasn't indeed changed very much in America since Dr. Wilson Abbott made the decision not to reveal his Black heritage. I hope that circumstances are such that your family isn't too threatened by the revelation of their heritage. I'm especially glad that we have had a chance to get to know more about our whole family.[8]

Since that time the family has enjoyed several reunions, where we were able to bring our own children into a gathering that encompassed everyone. Often various branches of the family now make a point of calling, writing, emailing or stopping by if they happen to be travelling through a city where a cousin resides. Sometimes I think it is rather peculiar that I have spent so much time and effort tracking down distant relatives and yet rarely find time to socialize with those that live nearby. In future, I do hope to make more time for all of my family as they have consistently brought so much deeper meaning to my life.

Thus it is that, in spite of the efforts over the years to wash away the past, the Abbott descendants re-discovered their own form of assimilation. In the words of my cousin Bonnie Grosnick, "We are all parts of each other and in a way we are all one."[9]

CHAPTER 24

MY RECONCILIATION

Before we as a society can liberate ourselves from the grip of racism, we have to acknowledge that it exists, and that it is not something which has been blown out of proportion; neither is it the figment of some people's imagination.[1]

SO WHERE DOES THIS all lead me in my quest to validate my own ancestry? Well, obviously I began my search from a state of confusion. I was raised thinking I was a dark-skinned, white person of Anglo-Saxon ancestry, with a "touch" of Spanish. I never questioned this and took some pride and interest in that identity. However, as I learned more about my Black ancestry later on in life, I began to experience difficulty holding the image together. The story that my own mother had told me while I was growing up did not reflect the reality I faced as an adult. I had to reconfigure my identity so that it not only accurately reflected my ancestry, but also the values with which I had been raised. Although this was disconcerting, I did not perceive it in a negative way. Rather, I was eager to open the shutters that had previously filtered out what I felt to be my rightful inheritance.

It is difficult to explain the actions of those who have now passed on. And indeed, I do not want to speak for them, but I can assuage a part of my conflict and resolve some of my own misconceptions for I see that social, economic and political pressures affected their lives in so many different ways. Just before my grandparents were married in 1915, they were faced with a growing public conception that Blacks were superstitious, slow, lazy and salacious. Increasingly it was believed that miscegenation would lead to a deterioration of the white race that dominated Canadian society.

In their day, the population of Toronto[2] was not very racially or culturally mixed, and minorities were certainly not able to integrate as they do

190

today. Indeed Hill notes that many "old-liners" intermarried across racial boundaries and did not tend to become involved in Black organizations but rather avoided any form of race consciousness. Tolerance and acceptance of others generally meant making room for others, but it did not mean equality. Canadian historians have finally revealed that, contrary to popular belief, those who were different were usually relegated to the lower rungs of the social ladder. When I first heard of my Black ancestors, I had no idea that so much racism had been such a definite part of our Canadian history.

Somehow, my grandfather's "passing" does not seem so mysterious to me anymore. My grandparents raised their children with different priorities than many of us do today, and they demonstrated their values in ways that not only vary from current but also past mainstream norms. As a granddaughter, I am trying to understand. As a mother, I understand completely, for I, too want the best for my children and every day I must choose which opportunities might best embrace their multiracial/cultural diversity and offer a high quality of life for them and those they will come to love.

My academic studies offered me an opportunity to explore my personal sense of self as an individual and my roles as a daughter, a mother, a wife, a teacher and a student. My life has become entwined with my research as I adjust my level of awareness and find a new place for myself within the world of inquiry and academia. I am presently quite happily immersed in my roles as a mother and a teacher, but I know that only by continuing to develop my Self will I be able to model new possibilities for my children, grandchildren and students.

Has the revelation of a Black ancestry affected my life? I suppose I must admit it has, for I have been propelled into realms I never before envisioned. Over the last ten years, I have written a family history, recorded seven generations of my family's genealogy, reunited a family separated for almost a century, rekindled and generated dozens of new friendships, collaborated on a musical play about my family ancestors, redirected my academic studies to new and exciting fields of discovery, completed a thesis and started yet another. My quest to understand my past has truly evoked a new future of further investigations as I explore the meaning of my own whiteness and how it has affected the way I live my life today. As I continue my studies, I will attempt to break down some of my misunderstandings and replace them with a new perspective and appreciation of where I come from and how I came to be.

In 1904, an Abbott, Hubbard and Lightfoot family reunion was held in Dundas, Ontario. This would have occurred after Dr. Anderson Abbott and his family returned from Chicago to resume living in Toronto. It was not until 1993, when Catherine Slaney, his great-grand-daughter, made contact with family members living across the United States and Canada that the family was reunited. Those in attendance were:

Back row (l-r): Emma (McIlroy) Lightfoot; man in light suit behind her, ___; Jenny Robinson; Lizzie Robinson; young boy with L. Robinson's hand on his shoulder, Gordon Watts Robinson, son of John Alexander and Nancy Etta Lightfoot; behind Gordon, with striped tie, Will Hubbard; woman, ___; woman, ___; woman, ___; young man directly in front of tree trunk, Gordon Anderson Abbott; woman clasping her hands, Ida (Abbott) Stevenson: man behind Ida Stevenson, Benjamin Sayre; woman beside B. Sayre, his wife, Helene (Abbott) Sayre; woman immediately in front of Helene Sayre, ___; woman, ___; man with dark suit, Kenneth Seth; man behind K. Seth, ___; woman with dark bow on left shoulder, "Bird" Bryant; man immediately behind, ___; woman Grace (Abbott) Hubbard; man behind G. Abbott, ___; woman Florence Lightfoot, wife of Walter Lightfoot; man immediately behind, Walter Clifford Lightfoot, son of Levi and Hannah (Casey) Light-foot; woman in white dress, Etta Isobel Lightfoot, daughter of Levi and Hannah (Casey) Lightfoot.

Middle row (l-r): young lad, James Edward "Eddie" Lightfoot; young girl seated, Adah May Lightfoot, daughter of John Alexander and Nancy Etta Lightfoot; woman, ___; young man in suit jacket, Raymond Wilson Lightfoot, son of Levi and Hannah (Casey) Lightfoot; young woman behind; Anna Louise Lightfoot; woman, ___; man holding bowler hat, Arthur H. Lightfoot, son of Lewis Cresswell Lightfoot; woman with hands on shoulder of A.H. Lightfoot, his sister, Mary Amelia Lightfoot; woman, Lillian Hubbard; man with bow tie, Fred Hubbard, son of William P. Hubbard; woman, Mabel Ann Ellen Lightfoot; woman turned to her left, Kitty Lightfoot; woman with dark collar, ___; young boy, Clarence Victor Lightfoot; girl with ringlets, Myrtle Alice Lightfoot, daughter of Emma Lightfoot.

Front row (l-r): woman standing, Mrs. Judah; man with light trousers, kneeling, William P. Hubbard; man with dark trousers, kneeling, Levi Wilson Lightfoot; man standing behind, holding child, John Alexander Lightfoot, holding his son, Edwin C. Lightfoot; his wife, Nancy Etta (Watts) Lightfoot; woman with hands sheltering a young boy almost hidden from view, Mary Ann (Casey) Abbott, wife of Dr. Anderson R. Abbott; young boy, head hidden, Cecil Lightfoot, son of John A. and Nancy Etta Lightfoot; woman in white dress, Alice Barbara (Smithers) Lightfoot; woman holding hat, Amelia Loguen Douglass, daughter of Reverend Jermain Wesley Loguen, standing beside her husband, Lewis H. Douglass, son of Frederick Douglass; woman, ___; man sitting on ground in front, Lewis Cresswell Lightfoot; woman seated on ground, Hannah Elizabeth (Casey) Lightfoot. *Courtesy of Laurie (Lightfoot) Sexton. For input into the ongoing process of identification of people in this group photograph, see http://freepages.genealogy.rootsweb.com/~lightfoot/page3.html or contact the author.*

The Past and Present here unite
Beneath Time's flowing tide,
Like footprints hidden by a brook,
But seen on either side.[3]

APPENDIX I

Abbott Family Tree

from Wilson Ruffin Abbott to Catherine Young Slaney

A

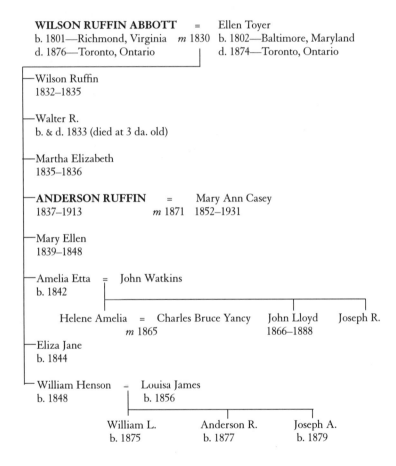

WILSON RUFFIN ABBOTT　=　Ellen Toyer
b. 1801—Richmond, Virginia　*m* 1830　b. 1802—Baltimore, Maryland
d. 1876—Toronto, Ontario　　　　　d. 1874—Toronto, Ontario

Wilson Ruffin
1832–1835

Walter R.
b. & d. 1833 (died at 3 da. old)

Martha Elizabeth
1835–1836

ANDERSON RUFFIN　=　Mary Ann Casey
1837–1913　　*m* 1871　1852–1931

Mary Ellen
1839–1848

Amelia Etta　=　John Watkins
b. 1842

　　Helene Amelia　=　Charles Bruce Yancy　　John Lloyd　　Joseph R.
　　　　　　m 1865　　　　　　　　　　1866–1888

Eliza Jane
b. 1844

William Henson　–　Louisa James
b. 1848　　　　　　b. 1856

　　　William L.　　　Anderson R.　　　Joseph A.
　　　b. 1875　　　　b. 1877　　　　　b. 1879

195

B

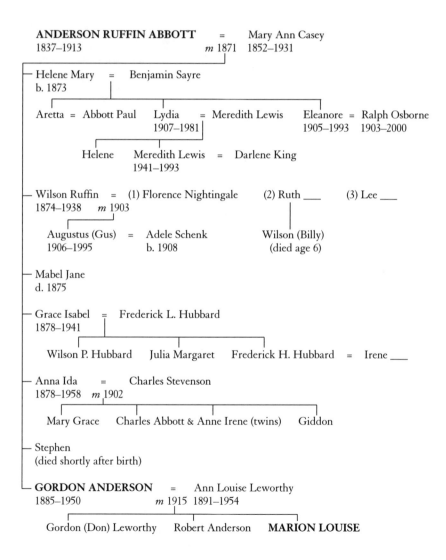

ANDERSON RUFFIN ABBOTT = Mary Ann Casey
1837–1913 *m* 1871 1852–1931

Helene Mary = Benjamin Sayre
b. 1873

Aretta = Abbott Paul   Lydia = Meredith Lewis   Eleanore = Ralph Osborne
1907–1981   1905–1993 1903–2000

Helene   Meredith Lewis = Darlene King
1941–1993

Wilson Ruffin = (1) Florence Nightingale   (2) Ruth ___   (3) Lee ___
1874–1938   *m* 1903

Augustus (Gus) = Adele Schenk   Wilson (Billy)
1906–1995   b. 1908   (died age 6)

Mabel Jane
d. 1875

Grace Isabel = Frederick L. Hubbard
1878–1941

Wilson P. Hubbard   Julia Margaret   Frederick H. Hubbard = Irene ___

Anna Ida = Charles Stevenson
1878–1958 *m* 1902

Mary Grace   Charles Abbott & Anne Irene (twins)   Giddon

Stephen
(died shortly after birth)

GORDON ANDERSON = Ann Louise Leworthy
1885–1950   *m* 1915 1891–1954

Gordon (Don) Leworthy   Robert Anderson   **MARION LOUISE**

196

C

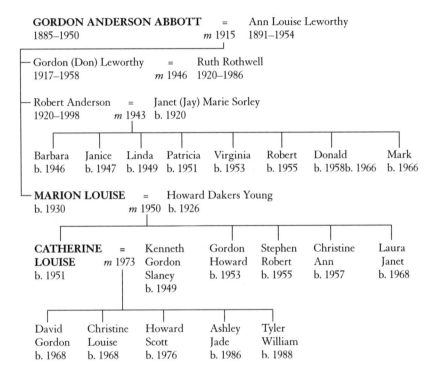

GORDON ANDERSON ABBOTT   =   Ann Louise Leworthy
1885–1950   *m* 1915   1891–1954

── Gordon (Don) Leworthy   =   Ruth Rothwell
   1917–1958   *m* 1946   1920–1986

── Robert Anderson   =   Janet (Jay) Marie Sorley
   1920–1998   *m* 1943   b. 1920

Barbara	Janice	Linda	Patricia	Virginia	Robert	Donald	Mark
b. 1946	b. 1947	b. 1949	b. 1951	b. 1953	b. 1955	b. 1958 b. 1966	b. 1966

── **MARION LOUISE**   =   Howard Dakers Young
   b. 1930   *m* 1950   b. 1926

CATHERINE =	Kenneth	Gordon	Stephen	Christine	Laura
LOUISE *m* 1973	Gordon	Howard	Robert	Ann	Janet
b. 1951	Slaney	b. 1953	b. 1955	b. 1957	b. 1968
	b. 1949				

David	Christine	Howard	Ashley	Tyler
Gordon	Louise	Scott	Jade	William
b. 1968	b. 1968	b. 1976	b. 1986	b. 1988

APPENDIX II

Last Will and Testament of W.R. Abbott, 1876

Last Will and Testament of Wilson Ruffin Abbott
Late of the City of Toronto
Esquire deceased
Dated 21 Nov. 1876
Enregistered   76/11/21
No. 199/59 W   C.J. Weiler   Fee $8.50

I Wilson Ruffin Abbott of the City of Toronto in the Province of Ontario Esquire hereby declare this to be my last will and testament. Thereby give unto my dear wife Ellen Abbott all my personal Estate whatever and wheresoever to hold unto her, her heirs, executors and administrators absolutely and forever. I also give unto my wife during the term of her natural life the sum of four hundred dollars per annum payable in equal monthly installments by my children, hereafter named as devisees of this my will. The first payment to be made one month after my decease.

WILLIAM

I give unto my son William H. Abbott of the City of Boston in the state of Massachusetts, clergyman during the term of his natural life and after his decease to the heirs of his body all the property, lands and tenements hereafter described that is to say.

One brick house situated on the North west corner of Adelaide and York Streets occupied by James Patterson being number 130.

One two-story frame house situated on the south side of Melinda Street, occupied by one John Neville and being number 21.

One rough cast house, situated on Terauly Street occupied by James Mills or Myles and numbered 6.

One frame house on Terauly Street aforesaid, known as "Big house" numbered 8 and 10 occupied by Stephen Moore and Charles Stewart.

One frame house on the south side of Albert Street at present occupied by David Storey and numbered 73.

Two frame houses situated on Albert Street aforesaid occupied respectively by Thomas Clark and William Rams and numbered 24 and 81 respectively.

One frame house on Adelaide Street opposite the courthouse occupied by Mr. James Adams as a saloon and as offices.

One brick house on the south side of Carlton Street, numbered 23 occupied by testator (initialled ARA) (subject to the life estate hereby devised to my wife therein.)

198

Three frame houses situated on Ann Street numbered 40, 42, respectively and occupied by William Anderson, Thomas Gamble and Samuel Perkins respectively.

One vacant lot on the west side of Jordan Street having a frontage of thirty feet on Jordan Street, and a depth of seventy feet and being the lot lately purchased from Alister M. Clark on which I propose erecting a warehouse all of which said property is situated in the said City of Toronto.

Also five frame houses situated on the east side of Sheaffe Street in the City of Hamilton in the said Province occupied by Nicholas Rock, Alexander Dingwall, William Fox or Hox, William Forsythe and John Gabjoy.

Also to him, his heirs, executors and administrators absolutely and forever lot number 19 on the east side of the Scrope Street and 19 on the west side of Murdoch Street in the town of Owen Sound.

ANDERSON

I give to my son Anderson Ruffin Abbott, of the City of Toronto, aforesaid, physician all the lands and tenements hereinafter described during the term of his natural life and after his decease to the heirs of his body to wit.

The wholesale warehouse on the north side of Wellington Street between Scot Street and Change Alley occupied by Walls and Walsh and numbered 28.

Two frame houses and three rough cast houses on the east side of Chestnut (late Sayer) Street numbered 15,1 7, 19, 21 and 23 respectively and occupied by Henry Meredith, William H. Middleton, William Whitcourt, William H. Williams and James Harrison respectively.

One frame house situated on the west side of Elizabeth Street being number 18 and occupied by Samuel Thornton.

One frame house situated on the south side of Melinda Street number 27 occupied by John Ryan.

One frame house on the south side of Albert Street numbered 69 occupied by Francis Clark all of which said property is situated in the City of Toronto aforesaid.

Also five houses situated on the west side of Sheaffe Street in the said City of Hamilton occupied respectively by Michael Morgan, Elizabeth Blainey, Michael Syron, Duncan Murray and Thomas? Trauy also to hold unto him, his heirs, executors and administrators absolutely and forever lots 7 and 8 on the south side of Union Street in the Town of Owen Sound.

AMELIA

I give unto my daughter Amelia Watkins wife of John Watkins of the City of Toronto, Merchants Clerk, during the term of her natural life and after her decease to the heirs of her body for her sole and separate use and free from her husband's control the following property to wit.

Two brick houses on the north side of Adelaide Street opposite the Court house occupied by Columbus H. Greene, Wadsworth and Unnivise? Respectively and numbered respectively 40 and 44.

One frame house on the south side of Albert Street occupied by John Forsythe number 83.

One rough cast house on the south side of Melinda Street numbered 25 lately occupied by Richard Hill.

Two frame houses on the south side of Albert Street numbered 67 and 77 and occupied respectively by Mary Dempsey and Mary Daley.

One frame house situated on the west side of Elizabeth Street number 20 occupied by J. B. Lewis as a carpenter shop.

Two frame houses on the south side of Richmond Street off Yonge Street number 99 and 101 occupied respectively by John O'Connor and John Bevans and Ann Shields with the houses situated in the rear of the said lot.

One house on the south side of Albert Street number 79 occupied by John Kennedy.

And two houses on the north side of Albert Street numbered 96 and 96 and a half occupied by Thomas Halgrove and Thomas Davis all in the said City of Toronto.

Also all of the houses I own on Park Street in the City of Hamilton occupied by Charles J. Towers(?), William Larkin, Joseph Rowen and James M. Huliffe.

Also a vacant lot on Park Street having a frontage of sixty feet.

Also to hold unto her and her heirs, executors and administrators absolutely and forever lots number 10 and on the south west side of Garafraxa Street and 10 on the north east side of Garafraxa Street in the town of Owen Sound.

ELLEN

I give to my wife during the term of her natural life the house I now live in being number 23 on the south side of Carlton Street.

MARY TOYER

I give to my housekeeper Mary Toyer during the term of her natural life an annuity of $72 per ? to be paid to her by my children heretofore names a devisees in equal shares of two dollars each monthly first payment to be made one month after my decease.

I charge all the property devised to my children situated in Toronto aforesaid with the payment of the annuity of four hundred dollars to my wife.

In case any of my said children die leaving a wife or husband surviving, it is my will and desire that such wife or husband should receive an annuity of $120 dollars during the term of her or his natural life and only while they remain the widows of my said children and unmarried and only while my said daughter's husband remains her widower payable out of the income to be derived from her or his husband or wife's property.

And I hereby appoint my said sons William H. Abbott and Anderson Ruffin Abbott and my friend Adolphus H. Judah of Toronto, Carpenter, executors of this my will at the same time revoking all wills, codicils, testamentary dispositions and appointments by me at any time heretofore made.

Signed W.R. Abbott

Signed by the said testator as his last will and testament in presence of us present at the same time who at his request in his presence and in the presence of each other have subscribed our names as witnesses this thirty first day of March A.D. 1871.

Signed R.H. Semple
J. E. Robertson

APPENDIX III

CIVIL WAR MEMOIRS FROM DR. ANDERSON ABBOTT

A. THE WHITE HOUSE LEVEE

When Dr. Abbott was appointed as Dr. Augusta's Assistant Surgeon-in-chief in Washington, they enjoyed many adventures together and even managed to crash a levee at the White House, much to the surprise of the guests, Robert Lincoln, son of the President and possibly even the President himself. However, one has to wonder at the audacity of the two doctors engaging in such a bold endeavour. Perhaps Mrs. Lincoln's Lady-in-waiting, Mrs. Keckley, a coloured woman and good friend of Mrs. Augusta and Dr. Abbott was able to procure the invitation.

Elizabeth Keckley, a talented dressmaker acted as Mrs. Lincoln's Lady-in-waiting. She had been a slave for thirty years in Virginia and had endured her share of good and bad times. As a skilful dressmaker, she was eventually able to save enough money to purchase the freedom of herself and her son, George, in 1855. Shortly afterwards he enlisted in the Union Army but was killed in action. Elizabeth was deeply concerned about the welfare of the thousands of Negro refugees that flocked to Washington, under the impression that they were heading for a haven. In response to the critical need for the necessities of life, including food, clothing, shelter and medical services, she founded the Contraband Relief Society.[1] This endeavour would likely have brought her into close contact with Dr. Abbott's hospital and contraband camp.

I suspect she may well have provided the doctors with a unique opportunity to attend one of the Presidential soirees. Since Mrs. Augusta was also a dressmaker and designer she may have had a professional as well as a social acquaintance with Mrs Keckley. At any rate, the two coloured doctors made a name for themselves and a point for their race one night. Here is Anderson's account of their dramatic ascent into the upper echelons of Washington society:

> Dr. Augusta and I determined to visit the President at the next Levee that he held in the White House. One evening we appeared at the White House in full uniform. As we entered the porch, we were conducted to a room and relieved of our wraps, for it was in the winter. The White House was a blaze of light. Soldiers were guarding the entrance. Carriages containing handsomely-dressed ladies, citizens and soldiers were continually depositing the elite of Washington at the entrance to the porch. Music was wafted to our ears from the Marine band, which was stationed in the Conservatory. Ushers, lackeys, waiters and messengers were scurrying here and there attending the guests.
>
> After leaving the vestibule we were led along a wide hall to a door. There we were

201

met by Mr. B.B. French, a Commissioner of the Treasury Department, who conducted us with all the urbanity imaginable, to the President, who was standing just inside the door. Mr. French introduced Dr. Augusta first. We had previously given him our cards. Mr. Lincoln, on seeing Augusta, advanced eagerly a few paces forward, grasped his hand and as he held the Doctor's hand, Robert Lincoln, who had been standing beside his mother about six paces off, came up to the President and asked a question very hastily, the purport of which I took to be, "Are you going to allow this invasion?" referring, doubtless, to our presence there! The President replied, "Why not?" Nothing more was said and Robert Lincoln returned to his mother's side. Then the President turned again to Augusta and gave his hand a hearty shake and then I was introduced and the President shook hands with me also. Then we passed on to a position in front of Mrs. Lincoln and were introduced to that lady.

We then passed out into a room on the opposite side from where we had entered, called the East Room. Next, we were destined to undergo an ordeal with which, in comparison to what we had experienced thus far, was only a dream. The moment we entered the room, which was crowded and brilliantly lit up, we became the cynosure of all eyes. I had never experienced such a sensation as I did when I entered the room. We could not have been more surprised ourselves nor could we have created more surprise if we had been dropped down upon them through the skylight.

I suppose it was because it was the first time in the history of the United States that a colored man had appeared at one of these Levees. What made us more conspicuous, of course, were our uniforms. Colored men in the uniforms of the United States, military officers of high rank had never been seen here before. I felt as though I should have liked to crawl into a hole. But as we had decided to break the record, we held our ground. I bit my lips, took Augusta's arm and sauntered around the room endeavoring to or pretending to, view the very fine pictures which adorned the wall. I tried also to become interested in the beautiful music discoursed by the Marine band, but it was the first time that music had failed to absorb my attention. Wherever we went, a space was cleared for us and we became the centre of a new circle of interest. Some stared at us merely from curiosity, others with an expression of friendly interest, while others again scowled at us in such a significant way, that left no doubt as to what views they held the Negro question. We remained in the room and faced monocles and lorgnettes. Stares and fascinating eyes levelled at us for half of an hour or so and then we passed out of the room and secured our wraps. Just as we were leaving, we were besieged by an ubiquitous reporter who wanted to interview us, but I handed him our cards and so ended our first visit to the White House.

I do not know whether we were really the first colored guests to visit the President of the United States at one of his levees but I am inclined to think we were. I asked an attaché of the Haitian Embassy whom I met in Washington if he had visited any of those levees and he replied that he had done so frequently, without any embarrassment. But I can understand that in his case, as he was so light complexioned, that he would pass unnoticed in a throng like that. However, we had broken the ice.

The following morning there appeared in the Washington Star the following item among the news from the White House, "During the evening Dr. Augusta, the Colored Surgeon of the District of Columbia Colored Regiment, dressed in his Major's uniform and also Dr. Abbott, Assistant Surgeon of the Colored Regiment called upon the President and was kindly received by him. "The Honorable Fred Douglass shortly afterwards visited one of the President's Levees and was received very cordially.[2]

Frederick Douglass[3] was formerly a slave. His eloquent speeches and descriptions of slavery made him a powerful member of the Anti-Slavery Society, fighting for civil rights and racial equality while recruiting troops for coloured regiments.

B. ON THE EVE OF THE NEW YORK DRAFT RIOT

The Union Army instituted Conscription in March 1863, mainly because it was suffering massive desertion among the ranks. Each area of the nation was required to produce a certain number of recruits, but individuals with sufficient means were could be exempt from conscription if they could pay a stipend or provide a stand-in. Agencies were set up to seek out naïve candidates, often targeting young farm boys from the rural outback states. But many of the agents were only profit-seekers and, in the end, their recruits proved to be temporary and unreliable. Some men even presented themselves repeatedly to a number of different recruiting stations.

New York City was one of the last areas to be targeted for conscription. Fatefully the event occurred just as Dr. Abbott was escorting Mrs. Augusta to Washington. In the early evening of July 10, 1863, Dr. Abbott and Mrs. Augusta arrived in New York City only to discover that their connection would be delayed for several hours. While they were waiting in the station, a white man pretending to be inebriated began to harass them:

> We looked around for a policeman to protect us but there was not a soul to be seen about the place, except these two drunken toughs and a man who appeared to be a watchman, employed by the ferry company. When we asked him if there was no means by which we could receive protection, he did not deign to answer us or notice us in any way.
>
> At this juncture several soldiers came in the room. They seemed to have previously consorted with these two men because they addressed them by name and proceeded to endeavour to coax these partners to go out with them. Mrs. Augusta and I thought it a good opportunity to escape. There was quite a stretch of dark street before us that we would have to traverse, with not even the glimmer of a light. There was some danger that friends of these men might way lay us in the darkness, however we decided to risk it. Starting on the walk and then on the run we succeeded, at length, in reaching a well-lit and busy street and took refuge in an oyster saloon, where we remained until it was time for our train departure. When we returned to the depot all was life and bustle within, so we had no further trouble.[4]

It must have been a frightening realization for the two travellers when they arrived in Washington for they later realized that they must have suffered some preliminary effects of the impending riots. On the next Monday morning it was reported that coloured people in particular were being hunted down and even murdered in the streets of New York City during the ensuing riots.[5]

C. A NIGHT OF HORRORS

The night that President Lincoln was assassinated, the city of Washington was in the midst of great celebration, for the Confederates had conceded to some brutal blows on the battlefield and a true end to the Civil War appeared imminent. Dr. Abbott has captured a first-hand impression of the turmoil experienced within the city during the crisis. He wrote the following article that appeared in the *Anglo-American Magazine* in May of 1901, under the title, "Some Recollections of Lincoln's Assassination." Like many others, he was profoundly affected by the event and never gave way as so many others did to express harsh criticism of Mr. Lincoln's policies:

> The days previous to the assassination of President Lincoln were devoted to festivities exceeding in brilliancy and grandeur anything I had before witnessed. Washington was brilliantly illuminated and decorated and the enthusiasm of the people ran up to the white heat of felicitation on the downfall of Richmond and the surrender of Lee's army. All the resources of science and art were brought into requisition to give appropriate expression to the intense feeling of joy which thrilled the heart of the nation. People who thronged Pennsylvania Avenue that memorable morning had no thought that a plot was brewing which would turn all that joy and splendor into sorrow's darkest night.
>
> I wended my way homeward in the evening feeling somewhat hungry, for I had participated so freely in the general enthusiasm that I had neglected to eat anything since morning. After supper, in company with a friend, I again set forth, this time to see a torch light procession which was to take place in honor of Mr.Stanton, the Secretary of War. The light of the torches and the music of the bands told that the procession was approaching from the direction of the Capitol. As far as the eye could reach from the elevated position which we occupied, it appeared like a fiery serpent winding its sinuous course through the streets and avenues of the city. When it reached the Secretary's residence, the people sent up a shout that made the welkin ring. Mr. Stanton came out and addressed the crowd, calmly and earnestly, congratulating them upon the speedy restoration of peace.
>
> It was nine o'clock when he had finished speaking, after which my friend and I repaired to another friend's, intending to spend the remainder of the evening in a social way. We were about to begin singing and a young lady had but struck the first chords of the piano when at that instant a fierce ringing of the doorbell arrested our attention. After opening the door and ascertaining the cause of the interruption, our host returned with slow, hesitating steps and with an expression on his countenance that I shall never forget and said in a tremulous voice, "I have sad news to tell you. President Lincoln was shot at Ford Theatre to-night and Secretary Seward's throat has been cut and both are dying." The effect of this announcement can be better imagined than described. "Oh horrible!" exclaimed the ladies. "The Lord have mercy on us!" was the pious ejaculation of the hostess.
>
> As soon as we had recovered from the shock I proposed that we should go around to Secretary Seward's, whose residence was but a short distance away and learn the particulars of so tragic an event.
>
> For the first time during my stay in Washington I was troubled with a feeling of uncertainty regarding my safety. I had been in the city on two other occasions when it had been greatly disturbed, but suffered no such apprehension at either of those

times as I experienced on this occasion. To what extent does this infamous plot extend? Is Sumner safe? Is Chase alive? These were some of the thoughts that followed one another through my brain as we walked along. By this time it was half-past eleven o'clock. The night had become very dark and Washington streets at that time were proverbially dark because of their width, they being but dimly lighted with gas and the dark shadows of alleys and porches affording convenient lurking places for garroters, murderers, assassins and thieves.

As we passed Secretary Stanton's house, we observed a cavalryman's horse at the door. We supposed it belonged to the courier who had been sent to warn the Secretary of his danger. Lights appeared in houses where all was darkness before and, as the inmates received the startling intelligence, the illumination became more general.

In the neighbourhood of Lafayette Square and Secretary Seward's house we found an excited crowd of soldiers and citizens By this time the sad news had been very widely circulated. Senators, Congressmen, clerks in the departments, citizens, soldiers all rushed by in a frenzy of excitement. The soldiers seemed to be arresting anyone who looked or acted at all suspicious. An unfortunate man had been found in Lafayette Park, opposite the Secretary's house. As the gates are locked at 9:00 p.m., the fact of his being in the park at so late an hour was regarded with suspicion. It required the strenuous efforts of the soldiers to prevent the crowd from lynching him. Two men, who had been dragged from their beds in adjoining houses, clothed in their *robe de chambres*, were pleading for their freedom and lives.

We thought it prudent to keep at a safe distance from the mob. I was left in charge of the ladies, while my companion went forward to obtain further information. The latter soon returned with news, which too painfully confirmed all that we had previously learned.

Everything seemed tranquil in the Secretary's house. In only one room could a light be seen and only at long intervals did anyone pass in or out of the house. A deep gloom hung over it and the ominous silence within indicated that something serious was transpiring.

The crowd had grown much larger while we waited and, fearing that our egress would be entirely blocked, we thought it prudent to retire. After escorting the ladies to their homes we returned to our respective places of abode and were soon asleep.

But my experience of tragedy had not ended. About two o'clock in the morning, a messenger came to the door with a request from Mrs. Lincoln that Mrs. Elizabeth Keckley, who usually dressed Mrs. Lincoln for her receptions, should come to her. I volunteered to accompany Mrs. Keckley, but it was with much difficulty that we reached the White House, owing to the crowd that thronged the streets. A further barrier to our progress proved to be a cordon of troops that were drawn up in front of the White House and so strict were the orders excluding everyone that we found great difficulty in getting someone to take in Mrs. Keckley's card.

However, after some persistence we succeeded, only to find that Mrs. Lincoln was with the President at No. 453 Tenth Street. We had therefore to make our way to that point. A cordon of military was drawn up there also, but a card to Mrs. Lincoln furnished an open sesame for us. It was a three-story brick house opposite the theatre, in one room of which was the dying President, while his companion was lying in an adjoining room prostrate with anguish.

205

Then I returned to my lodgings, thoroughly exhausted and not long after had again succumbed to nature's sweet restorer. In fact, I was not conscious of anything more until aroused by the first strike of the bell at twenty minutes past seven the next morning (Friday, April 15th), which announced the painful intelligence that our beloved President was no more.

A widespread apprehension existed next morning that the water in the city reservoir had been poisoned, so that the use of tea and coffee had to be abandoned. The report, however, turned out to be false, but it was an indication of the feeling of anxiety which prevailed.

The city rapidly assumed a funeral aspect, in striking contrast to the gay and festive appearance presented the days previous to the assassination. The draping of the public buildings, business houses and residences was quite general. As I rode around the outskirts of the city, I noticed that even the cabins of the freedmen bore some emblem of mourning, even if, as in one case, it was nothing more appropriate than a Black skirt hung over the door.

There was an ill-disguised expression of anxiety on the faces of everyone as to the extent of the conspiracy. The lives of Cabinet ministers and other prominent government officials were not considered safe and special detectives were detailed to accompany them wherever they went.

At that time I was shown a cardboard box containing the index finger of a Negro and a pen-picture of a coffin surmounted by a drawing of a skull and crossbones, with the word "Beware" inscribed upon it, that had been sent to Senator Sumner. A colored man armed with a loaded revolver slept at the door of the Senator's sleeping chamber for several weeks.

The surroundings of the White House were sombre in the extreme. The heavy mourning drapery, the deep gloom of the interior, the hushed voices and muffled footsteps, all gave painful evidence of the presence of the remains of the illustrious dead. As I looked upon the pale, cold face of the President as he lay in state in the Guest room, a great sorrow weighed heavily upon my heart, for I thought of the loss to the Negro race in the recent life of freedom, of the great guiding hand that now lay paralysed in death.

It would be ungracious to pursue this description into the circle of the afflicted family. Suffice it to say that the anguish of the widow in the privacy of her apartments, surrounded by her children and with Mrs. Keckley as her sole companion, was pitiable in the extreme. It was so intense, I think Mrs. Lincoln's mind never recovered its equilibrium after the shock of that awful tragedy at Ford's Theatre.[6]

Dr. Abbott returned to Toronto from Washington in 1865. Deeply sorrowed over the assassination of President Lincoln, he would forever praise the honourable intentions of his deceased hero and the supreme success in securing the Emancipation Proclamation. He truly believed Abraham Lincoln was a good man, caught in a dreadful dilemma and anxious to do the right thing.

APPENDIX IV

On William Peyton Hubbard

Dr. Abbott was a regular contributor to the *New York Age* and the following essay was published in the January 27, 1898 issue.

A Canadian Councilman
Alderman W.P. Hubbard Re-elected for the Fifth Time
Toronto, January 11th, 1898

An Afro-Briton has forced his way to the front of this community in such a rapid manner that he is likely to make history before his career is ended. A community whose institutions are founded upon a monarchical system and whose sentiments are moulded, to some extent, by the mildew relics of an obsolete feudal system involving considerations of caste and accidents of birth, would in the reasonableness of things, be least expected to raise a colored man from the humble walks of life and place him in one of the highest positions of trust and responsibility in its civic affairs.

This distinguished honor has been conferred upon Alderman W.P. Hubbard, who has been re-elected for the fifth time as a representative from the fourth ward of the Toronto City Council. This ward is one of the largest and most populous and contains the residences of the wealthiest and most influential citizens such as Sir Oliver Mowat, Sir William P. Howland, Mr. Goldwyn Smith and many professional and businessmen. Last year Mr. Hubbard was returned at the head of the polls. This year notwithstanding there were eleven candidates in the field, he came within sixty votes of the same result. Among the successful aldermanic candidates for re-election he stands in the first rank and the confidence and enthusiasm manifested by his supporters at his first election have in no way abated. Such a marked recognition of his ability is very gratifying to his friends and must be regarded by him as an unqualified expression of the esteem and regard in which he is held by his fellow citizens of all classes.

Mr. Hubbard is one to whom the term self-made will apply without any qualification. He was born in this city of parents who removed here in 1840 from Richmond, Virginia. The family was poor and consisted of six sons and three daughters. They settled in the suburbs of Toronto on what was then known as the Baldwin property. They occupied a log house with ten acres attached which they cultivated as a market garden. When young Hubbard was twelve years old he was adopted by the late Col. Wells with whom he remained for five years and who sent him to the Model School for two years. After that he secured with difficulty, owing to his color, a place as an apprentice with Mr. Kerr, a baker, with whom he set up business for himself.

In 1875 he discontinued the baking business and opened a livery stable in partner-

207

ship with his brother. He was married about his time to Miss Julia Luckett, a teacher in the public schools of Washington, DC by whom he has had three children, a girl and two boys. By thrift and industry he had accumulated some means, which enabled him to build a comfortable home for his family, also several neat cottages which bring him revenue. He is now 50 years of age and enjoys excellent health. He is possessed of more than an ordinary fluency of speech, a gift he has inherited from his mother. His services were in much demand during political campaigns and in this way he drifted into politics and became an eloquent and forcible exponent of the principles of the Conservative party with which he has always been allied.

But it is not in respect of Mr. Hubbard's political career that I think it worthwhile to express congratulations at his re-election because in the municipal contest just past there was no political significance attached to the result. He received support from both parties and the issues involved were of purely civic character. In municipal elections in Toronto the party lines are entirely obliterated and Mr. Hubbard was re-elected solely because of the honesty and faithfulness with which he had served the citizens for the past four years. In a letter that I received from him in answer to my congratulations he says:

"I have always felt that I am the representative of a race, hitherto despised, but if given a fair opportunity, would be able to command the esteem and respect of my fellow citizens; that opportunity has been given to me." After serving three years on the council he was elected Chairman of the Fire and Light Committee and as an indication of the manner in which he had discharged his duties, the committee decided to name the new steam fire engine, recently purchased, after him. Brass tablets were engraved with his name and on Friday last, his worship, the Mayor, (who is also a Toronto boy) named the engine "The W.P. Hubbard."

The inaugural ceremonies of the City Council took place yesterday at the Pavilion, a building surrounded by beautiful landscape gardens and capable of seating 3,000 people. The building was beautifully decorated for the occasion with flowers, ferns and streamers. A dais, richly carpeted, had been built in front of the platform and furnished in a manner, similar to the council chamber, with the aldermen arranged in a circle. Admission was by ticket. The building was filled to its utmost capacity. On the platform were seated the wives and daughters of the aldermen, among whom were a sprinkling of clergymen. Seats were reserved for the members of the legislature, which is now in session.

As the aldermen filed in and took their seats, the favorites were easily recognized by the applause that greeted their appearance. Alderman Hubbard deported himself with becoming dignity and to the complete satisfaction of the dozen or so Afro-Canadians in the audience, who take a just pride in his achievement. After calling the roll, the Mayor proceeded to read his inaugural address, upon the conclusion of which Alderman Hallam arose and presented the names of the ten aldermen as candidates for election to the Board of Control. This board consists of three members elected from the council. And exercises the most important function of the city government. It controls the expenditures and has supervision over all the other departments. To be a member of this board is considered an honor only secondary in importance to the Mayority. When the Mayor announced the result of the balloting the votes stood: Leslie, 11; Hubbard, 11; Burns, 10; and they were declared elected. This announcement was received with tumultuous applause. The council was then adjourned.

I am quite conscious of the fact that election of an Afro-American to the City Council is not now regarded as an extraordinary event. It has become a matter of common occurrence for Afro-Americans to be elected to such positions in the United States and others of equal trust and responsibility and far more remunerative. But while it is a fact that many colored men have attained marked distinction in the United States, it has been in most instances through the influence and patronage of political parties who have found it necessary to cater to the colored vote. No such contingent fortified Mr. Hubbard's appeal to the electorate. He was elected by a purely white constituency, with the exception of fourteen colored votes in that ward. The ten candidates who were running in opposition to him were white men. Some of them had previously been honored with seats at the council, others were men of undoubted probity and ability and two men were substantial citizens who were his colleagues last year in the council. It is obvious therefore that his color did not enter into the contest as a factor in the remotest degree and that racial prejudice was entirely ignored when pitted against recognized personal merit.

There are two other lessons in this connection which play in the moral and adopt a tale. Mr. Hubbard labored under the same social van as other colored young men. He had no influential friends at court. In fact, his experience in early life must have been an unusually bitter one, because he was not only poor, but did not enjoy even the meretricious advantage of being able to 'pass for white' and thus escape as so many are doing the 'slings and arrows of outrageous fortune.' Yet he succeeded in exemplifying the possibilities of the Afro-American and to that extent has become a benefactor of his race.

Another lesson it teaches us is that it is not necessary for the Afro-American to serve his affiliation with is own race in order to keep in touch with the white race and succeed in life. How many youth have started out with a noble ambition to forge to the front by virtue of their personal merit and in spite of race proscription, have been unable to withstand the buffetings of adverse fate and finally yielded to the more facile method and shorter cut to success by crossing the color line? No one can estimate the difficulties encountered in the effort to maintain an attitude of self-respect under such circumstances. The rupture of family ties, the estrangement of social relations, the dissembling, the constant harassing fear of betrayal form one of the most pathetic phases of our history on this continent.

In conclusion I would say that Mr. Hubbard's success is an indication of the revolution that is taking place in public sentiment towards the colored man and of the rapid progress the race is making all along the line. Conditions were such ten years ago that would have rendered such an event as transpired yesterday, utterly impossible, even in Canada where color prejudice is supposed to be mild and innocuous.

NOTES

INTRODUCTION

1. A. Walker, *The Temple of My Familiar* (New York: Simon and Schuster, 1990) 354.

2. The inevitable challenge of using "correct" terminology persistently invokes some spatial and temporal considerations throughout the text when referring to racial designations. Abbott used the terms Negro, Afro-American, Afro-Canadian, Afri-Canadian and Black freely, and did not appear to restrict his references to depict any particular type of individual. I have also used all of these terms to fall in line with their usage during those years or because they originally appeared in that form in the supporting historical documents. Such usage does not imply any specific correlation between these terms and anyone's degree of Black ancestry. The term "Negro" was commonly used until the middle of the 20th century, as can be seen in the numerous historical references. The term "colored" was prevalent prior to the 1960s. More recently, the names African American and African Canadian are preferred by many people of African descent, and have been in use over the course of the last century. The term Black became popular during the Civil Rights movements of the 1960s and the phrase, "people of colour" has been used interchangeably for decades to refer to any combination thereof, in various references. For purposes of this project, I have attempted to adopt the modern terms of reference, but in some instances have retained the original words when I felt they furthered an appreciation of the context of the time and place of the incident.

3. The term "old-line Black families" refers to the early (Canadian) Black settlers and their descendants. Daniel Hill, in his 1960 doctoral dissertation entitled "Negroes in Toronto: A Sociological Study of a Minority Group," noted that "a solid core of Negro families remained, the majority apparently in-marrying. They were accustomed to the integrated nature of the institutions and social life of the city; many were financially secure property holders. Their descendants—the contemporary "old-line" families—inherited a middle-class standing in the white community in whose organizations and social life they had shared." See Daniel Hill (1960) 340.

4. The influx of immigrant Black refugees and free Blacks saw an advent of several new communities, some of which were designated Black settlements. Most of them ranged across southwestern and central Ontario, such as Dresden, Buxton, Amherstberg, and Sandwich; some established healthy populations within larger urban centers such as Toronto, St. Catharines, Owen Sound and Hamilton.

5. It should be noted that Ontario was referred to as Upper Canada until 1841, then Canada West from 1841 to 1867; not until Confederation was it known by its present-day name of Ontario.

6. Daniel G. Hill, "Negroes in Toronto, 1793–1865," *Ontario History*, LV. 2, 1963— referring to an article written by Anderson Ruffin Abbott in 1912, found in the Abbott Collection, Baldwin Room, Toronto Reference Library.

7. A.R. Abbott, The Abbott Collection, Toronto Public Library (TRL): S-90. Hereafter referred to as The Abbott Collection.

8. The Town of York became the City of Toronto in 1834. A wonderful stroll through the pages of Toronto's history can be found in *Yesterday's Toronto: 1870–1910*, edited by Linda Shapiro, Toronto: Coles, 1978. According to Diane Beasley, "Lieutenant-Governor John Graves Simcoe changed the aboriginal name of Toronto to York in honour of the Duke of York, but in 1834 the name was reinstated upon incorporation of the City of Toronto. Throughout the last two centuries it has been known as the meeting place, where there are trees in the water, Muddy York, Queen City of the West and most recently, Toronto the Good." "From Toronto to York and Back Again," *Explore Historic Toronto*, December 1993, 6.

9. In North America miscegenation can be traced back through the period of colonialism in New England in the 1600 and 1700s, when such mixing occurred between white indentured servants and enslaved or free Blacks. In the 1800s those of mixed ancestry gradually lost their privileged status as it became important to whites to distance themselves from people of colour. Thus they were accorded the same legal status as Blacks, according to the "one-drop rule." It should be noted that miscegenation during the slavery era was often a result of sexual assault and rape between white male slave owners and their female African slaves.

10. "Passing" refers to the deliberate attempt of people of colour to pass as white, often under particular circumstances in the presence of certain people. Some individuals chose to pass on a permanent basis and completely abandoned any association with their former family and friends of colour.

11. Numerous archives and libraries house untold volumes of Canadian history that do not see the light of day. The Abbott Collection was left in the hands of the Hubbard family after the death of Mary Ann Abbott (wife of Anderson Ruffin Abbott). Upon the urging of Dr. Daniel Hill, they were donated in the name of Grace Hubbard in 1963, to the Toronto Reference Library and now are housed at the Baldwin Room of the Toronto Reference Library.

12. Dr. Hill (1960) noted that in 1951 the Toronto Census only recorded about 1,000 Blacks, although a 1941 survey had already enumerated 4,000 to 5,000 persons. He explains that this discrepancy in numbers was due to the unreliable methods of enumeration as well as the variation in the ways people interpreted the definition of "Negro."

13. This in itself was a revelation to me as I became more aware of the sheltered and privileged life I had led. Race was something that applied to the "other," not to white people. One day, as a child, I asked my mother what my race was and was told I was Caucasian. I had never heard of the term and I remember thinking, what a strange word to describe a person! I had no idea where Caucasus was or why I should be related to people of that region. (Caucasus is the general name of the high mountain range that lies between the Black Sea and the Caspian Sea.)

14. Blauner's (1990) study, published in *Black Lives, White Lives: Three Decades of Race Relations in America*, notes that from a mainstream perspective, whites do not consider race or racism to be pressing realities in their everyday lives. For the most part, they view themselves as equity-minded and do not readily acknowledge that they live a life of privilege. Judy Scales-Trent, a light-skinned African-American considers, in her book, the fact that "her position does not allow [her] the luxury of thinking that the notion of race makes any sense." See Judy Scales-Trent, *Notes of a White Black Woman: Race, Color, Community* (University Park, PA: Pennsylvania State University Press, 1995) 7.

15. Avery Gordon, *Ghostly Matters: Haunting and the Sociological Imagination* (Minneapolis: University of Minnesota Press, 1997) 63.

16. G.R. Daniel, "Passers and Pluralists: Subverting the Racial Divide," in M.R. Root, ed., *Racially Mixed People in America* (Newbury Park, CA: Sage, 1992) 91–107.

17. Examples of passing can be found in: Nella Larson's *Passing and Quicksand* (11th ed.) (New Brunswick, NJ: Rutgers University Press, 1998); George Schuyler's *Black No More* (London, NI: The X Press, 1998); Harriet E. Wilson's *Our Nig: Or Sketches from the Life of a Free Black* (New York: Random House, 1983); William Wells Brown's *Clotel: Or the President's Daughter* (Toronto: Random House of Canada, 2000); and Jessie Redman Faust's *Plum Bun: A Novel Without a Moral* (Boston: Beacon Press, 1990).

18. E. Imber-Black, *The Secret Life of Families* (New York: Bantam-Dell-Doubleday, 1999) 6.

19. *Ibid*, xiv.

1. ON A QUEST

1. A. Walker, *The Temple of My Familiar* (New York: Simon and Schuster, 1990) 351.

2. Marconigrams were early radio messages that could be conducted from one location to another without the need for wires between the towers, much like the early telegraph system. It became a prominent form of communication during World War I.

3. No offence is intended in this reference to the Barbour family as the name was commonly used within the community during that period of time.

4. This was the beginning of a whole new phase for the family, as we became immersed in the world of horses. We bred, trained and showed our horses, Dad became a Master of the Eglinton and Caledon Hunt Club, my children all joined the Caledon Pony Club and my sister and I began competing in the Eventing and Dressage arenas. I even became a certified judge. It was lots of fun, expensive, labour-intensive and time-consuming and consequently involved the entire family for many years.

5. Dan Hill became a great friend and mentor for me when I began my quest. However, he did not press us during this initial period, as he obviously sensed that various members of the family needed time to sort out the implications. It seemed ironic that he was supposed to be the one seeking information for his book, *The Freedom-Seekers: Blacks in Early Canada*, and we were, in fact, the beneficiaries of his research.

6. Anderson Ruffin Abbott is recognized as the first Canadian-born Black doctor, graduating from the University of Toronto in 1861.

7. I have taken the liberty of correcting obvious grammatical or spelling errors and have reworded some phrases to enhance the reading process, while maintaining the meaning.

8. Unfortunately, many of the newspaper clippings lack a heading, date and author so that it is sometimes impossible to determine which ones were actually penned by Abbott and which ones were simply articles that he collected. Any clarification or corrections of errors or omissions found in this book would be greatly appreciated by the author and publisher.

9. Personal interview by author, May 2001.

10. My Auntie Jay (Sorley) says that her grandparents, the Seons, were "befriended" by the Abbotts when they first immigrated to Toronto. This in itself is significant, because even my own mother, as a child, remembers her parents looking after "newcomers."

11. Indeed Bob Abbott and Jay Sorley were in kindergarten together! My aunt told me that although they attended Northern Secondary together, she did not remember him until the day he delivered a shoe repair to her house. From then on, an irreversible chain of events led to their union.

12. This Wilson Ruffin Abbott was named after his own grandfather, Wilson Ruffin Abbott. It was a common practice to use the same name over and over again. In fact, if a child died in infancy, his name might well be bestowed on the next male child born, making it particularly difficult to decipher the genealogy of the family.

13. You can imagine my surprise when I encountered this name in the archives—as if one celebrity were not enough! But it turned out not to be the famous nurse. However, Anderson Abbott demonstrated his admiration of Florence Nightingale's innovative philosophy and skills that quite literally turned around the state of nursing and hospital administration during the Crimean War.

14. The Nightingales were a prominent white family, well-placed within the upper social strata of Chicago society during the 1800s.

15. Letter to the author from Gus Abbott, December 4, 1990.

16. I had never met Lorraine Hubbard until this day, but her grandmother was Grace Abbott (Anderson's daughter and my great-aunt) and her grandfather was William Peyton Hubbard.

2. IN THE BEGINNING

1. Frederick Douglass, "The Effort of His Life"—speech made before the National Convention of Colored Men, cited in newspaper clippings in Abbott Collection, not dated.

2. Obituary of Ellen Toyer Abbott, October 14, 1874. Abbott Collection.

3. Black Codes were instituted by both American federal and state legislations during the antebellum period, as a means of regulating segregation and ensuring the accountability of free Blacks. In order to procure employment, a free Black man (women of any race were not given legal acknowledgement) must wear a sign such as an armband prominently displayed and post a monetary bond with one or more white men of upstanding reputation, who would vouch for them in the case of a charge of indiscretion or unlawfulness against said Black man. Although

213

Canada did not institute such a law, the French Regime in 1705 ordained the "Code Noir," which declared that "Negroes were movable property and therefore provided for their humane treatment." Cited in D. Hill, 1960, 10.

4. Such a lack of reliable fact does tend to spur one on to fanciful speculation, and upon further investigation, I did discover a possible ancestor in a Josiah Bartlett Abbott, who married Anne Wilson in Salem, New Jersey. The coincidence of names and events has led me to consider the possibility that Josiah and Anne might have been Wilson Abbott's parents. According to the records of a Salem Quaker Meeting, this marriage was "contrary to discipline." This term usually refers to the fact that one of the partners is not of the Quaker faith but perhaps it indicated a difference in race in this case. Upon being turned away from their church, the newlyweds sold their farm for $6,400, a substantial sum at the time, and moved to Richmond, Virginia, where Josiah became a Hatter. Apparently Anne died soon after the birth of her two children and they were sent away and fostered by a Colonel Edward Carrington. Census records show that Josiah then came into possession of a female Black slave. Based on the dates and names, it is conceivable that this woman may have been Wilson's mother, but to date it has not been possible to substantiate this possibility. John Hale Stutesman, *Some Watkin Family and Some of their Kin*. Richmond, Virginia State Archives (0170876).

5. Ordinance of April 14, 1830, in Mobile County, AB, Alabama Archives, researched by Chris Nordmann, 1998.

6. The 1830 consensus indicates that about 550 free persons of colour resided in Mobile County, according to Chris Nordmann, 1998. In Charleston, South Carolina, and in New Orleans, during the 1700s and early 1800s, people of mixed race were often viewed as allies by the white communities and served as a buffer group between the two communities. This relationship dissolved as racial unrest swept across the South in the 1800s.

7. Chris Nordmann. Ordinance of April 14, 1830 in Mobile County, Alabama.

8. Elizabeth Fox-Genovese, *Within the Plantation Household: Black and White Women of the Old South* (Chapel Hill: University of North Carolina Press, 1988) 52.

9. Papers in the Abbott Collection indicate that the legal firm employed was Cleveland and Hazzard, but their location has not been determined.

3. THE CANADIAN ALTERNATIVE

1. Allen P. Stouffer, *The Light of Nature and the Law of God: Anti-slavery in Ontario 1833–1877* (Montreal & Kingston: McGill-Queen's University Press, 1992) 47.

2. Stouffer notes that by 1759 "just before the British seized New France, there were 3604 slaves in the colony." Stouffer, 9.

3. Ironically, while "Canadians" were devising new anti-slavery laws, the Americans were passing another Fugitive Slave Act (the first one of which was instituted in 1793), authorizing any Federal court or State magistrate to determine the legal status of a Negro fugitive, without the benefit of a trial by jury. Since it was a federal law, all of the states were implicated. In retaliation, some states proposed the abolition of slavery, and passed Personal Liberty laws, with the intent to restrict the power of these acts. However, the Southern states were adamant, and continued to lobby the federal government for stronger enforcement of the Fugitive Slave Act.

4. Bronte would later be known as Oakville.

5. Daniel G. Hill, *The Freedom-Seekers: Blacks in Early Canada* (Toronto: Book Society of Canada, 1981) 32.

6. For an interesting account of the original Black settlers of Priceville, Ontario, refer to the National Film Board (NFB) documentary, *Speakers for the Dead* by Jennifer Holness and David Sutherland and released for broadcast in 2001. The video reveals the mystery that, to this day, lies behind the disappearance of a Grey County Black community named after a Black officer. At one time the area was home to a number of Black Loyalists. The film indicates that these settlers were forced off the land granted to their families by the British government, squeezed out of the town of Priceville and off their nearby settlements along the Old Durham Road in Artemesia township, Grey County, through deliberate and subversive expressions of racism. The film traces the efforts of a small group of concerned descendants who are working to confirm and acknowledge the presence and contributions of their ancestors. For more information on the Old Durham Road Black Pioneer Cemetery see *Broken Shackles: Old Man Henson from Slavery to Freedom* (Toronto: Natural Heritage Books, 2001).

7. E.C. Kyte, *Old Toronto: A Selection of Excerpts from Landmarks of Toronto by John Ross Robertson* (Toronto: Macmillan of Canada, 1954) 42. For more information on early Black settlement in Toronto see *The Underground Railroad: Next Stop Toronto!* (Toronto: Natural Heritage Books, 2002).

8. J.E. Jones, *Crimes and Punishments in Toronto and the Home District* (Toronto: George N. Morang, 1924) 11–14.

9. A.R. Abbott, as cited in Abbott Collection.

10. M. La Terreur, *Dictionary of Canadian Biography*, Vol. 1, 1871–1880 (Toronto: University of Toronto Press, 1972). Also in D. Newby, *Anderson Ruffin Abbott, First Afro-Canadian Doctor* (Markham, Ont.: Fitzhenry & Whiteside, 1998) 18.

11. Indenture Papers, "Abbott Collection," Baldwin Room, Toronto Reference Library. For more detail on Wilson's properties, see Appendix II, "Last Will and Testament of Wilson Ruffin Abbott—Nov. 21, 1876."

12. On Monday, October 9, 1837, William Lyon Mackenzie received word that rebels in Lower Canada were about to strike and that it would propitious for him to align his own rebellion with theirs. After several false starts and much disarray, Mackenzie and his followers finally made their move, only to be thwarted by a rather unprepared but able group of British supporters.

13. Headly Tullock, *Black Canadians: A Long Line of Fighters* (Toronto: NC Press, 1975) 107–108.

14. A.R. Abbott, as cited in the Abbott Collection.

15. The diary also contained the following information: Ellen Toyer 60 Vyet [Fayette?], Baltimore, to the care of Mr. Walter Toyer, Ellen's brother. Walter migrated (his tombstone says he came from Maryland in 1852) to Canada where he became a farmer and BME minisher in Buxton and Chatham. Kent County Land Registry listings indicate that he transferred some land to Anderson Abbott, who, in turn, gave Toyer a life lease. Walter's brother, and neighbour, Hanson Toyer, also sold land to Anderson. Wilson Ruffin Abbott purchased, from Samuel Shepley, two farms in Buxton, one of which was 100 acres in 1/2 of Lot 10, Concession 11. This information on Walter Toyer is courtesy of Bryan Prince, Raleigh Township Centennial Museum.

Further on the diary notes some items listed as "Ship Linen" on May 1, 1843—sheets 78, counterpins 23, towels 65, blanket 16, pillow slips 46, sofa covers 15 and table cloths 15.

She also shares a recipe for a cough syrup as follows: 2 oz of cinnamon, 1 oz of cloves, 1/4 lb of longwood, 2 qts of water, then boil it down to one quart and add 1 quantity of best brandy and a 1/4 lb loaf sugar.

On another page we find that the diary was bequeathed to Ellen from her brother-in-law, Joseph G. Miller, Toronto, June 22, 1843.

Then we discover a page that notes her loans or gifts: Mrs. Abbott to Mrs. Judah £10, Gave Mary Toyer 3 yds cotton (bleached) also £8.2 1/2.

The next item of interest records an Indenture of Mortgage, David Hollin to W.R. Abbott; As memorial here of us Rue...died in thy county of York this 23 day of February A.D. 1839 at 10 o'clock A.M. in Lib V fol 39...Memorial No. 15869, Robert Austin D.Reg.

Then she makes a note of the deaths of her children: Wilson Abbott who died 13th February, 1835; Martha Elizabeth died 5th September 1838; Walter R. Abbott died January 18th, 1833; Mary Ellen Abbott died October 11th 1840; Josephine Elizabeth Miller died May 18th 1843. Then she records the marriage of Amelia E. Abbott to Mr. Jon. [John] L. Watkins, married June 1st 1865 by Rev. Mr. Stronghall; Progency Jon L. Watkins born February 27th, 1866 1/2 past one A.M. Later a note appears denoting Edward A. Strong, Curate in Charge, St. James Church, Dundas.

Another address appears on a separate page: 17 Thomas Street, care of Washington Parker.

Another list of gifts is recorded: Toronto, November 19, 1848, 1 present to Jane Judah, 1 mahogany sideboard, 6 warnet [walnut] chairs, flug bottoms...1 walnut dinner table, 1 feather bed, 1 maple bedstead, the property of Miss Jane Judh.

Then we have another list of children's births: William R. Abbott born Jan 18th, 1832; Walter R. Abbot born Jan 13th 1833; Martha Elizabeth Abbott born December 3rd 1835, Anderson R. Abbott born April 7th 1837; Mary Ellen Abbott born October 1st 1839; Amealyetta [Amelia] Abbott was born April 3rd 1842; Eliza Jane Abbott was born February 14th 1844, 15 minutes past six evening; Wilson Ruffin Abbott Miller was born 22nd November 1843 at 1/2 past eleven o'clock morning; Josephine Elizabeth Miller was born May the 4th 1842.

16. Records at the Raleigh Museum in Buxton indicate the following births and deaths of Abbott family members: Wilson R.—b. Jan 18, 1832, d. Feb. 13, 1835; Walter R.—b. Jan 1833, d. Jan 18, 1833; Martha Elizabeth—b. Dec. 5, 1835, d. Sept. 5, 1836; Anderson Ruffin—b. Apr. 7, 1837, d. Dec. 29, 1913; Mary Ellen—b. Oct. 1, 1839, d. Oct. 11, 1840; Amealyeta (Amelia Etta)—b. April 3, 1842; Eliza Jane—b. Feb. 12, 1844.

17. Amelia Etta is found in a variety of spellings including "Amealyeta" and "Amealyetta."

18. A.R. Abbott, cited in the Abbott Collection.

19. In this role William Henson Abbott was responsible for a number of tasks at the Annual Conferences held in various centres such as Windsor, Chatham and Buxton and served on the Letters and Petitions Committee, the Temperance and Tobacco Committee and the Education and Sabbath Schools Committee. He often

acted in the capacity of Reporter to the Press. Sometimes he was assigned legal tasks that would make him responsible for the defence or prosecution of ministers that were "on trial" for misdemeanours. In addition, he was also assigned a major role in the evaluation and selection of ministerial candidates who were applying for their Holy Orders. As a member of the Literary Shareholders Association, he was instrumental in raising finances to support the *Missionary Messenger*, a newspaper for the British Methodist Episcopal (BME) Church.

20. The Judah and Lightfoot families apparently originated in Kentucky, but in the early 1800s their fathers and masters, as enlightened slave owners, sent their coloured male offspring to Canada to prosper as freed men.

21. The Elgin Association was an organization created by the residents of the self-sufficient Black settlement in Buxton.

22. C. Peter Ripley, ed., *The Black Abolitionist Papers, Vol. 2: Canada 1830–1865* (Chapel Hill: University of North Carolina Press, 1985) 304.

23. Interview with Alberta Judah Price, May 1989.

24. Apparently, public appearances were important. Alberta related with pride, "Dad helped a lot of the people that weren't too well off. I know of a couple of homes that he just wrote off. He loaned people money to get a start—white people as well as coloured people. He was a real humanitarian. Before the A & P came in, he was a big businessman but he just couldn't compete with that big store and he ended up moving out west to Alberta. Interview with Alberta Judah Price, 1989.

4. EARLY BLACK CHURCHES IN TORONTO

1. Dorothy Shreve, *The AfriCanadian Church: A Stabilizer* (Jordon Station, Ont.: Paideia, 1983) 13.

2. For more details pertaining to the role of the early Black churches, refer to Dorothy Shreve, *The AfriCanadian Church: A Stabilizer*. She gives an interesting explanation regarding the use of the term AfriCanadian, which she proposes as a unique Canadian term.

3. Daniel G. Hill, "Negroes in Toronto: A Sociological Study of a Minority Group." Unpublished Doctoral Thesis, University of Toronto, 1960.

4. Abbott family records indicate that, in 1838, the property of the Colored Wesleyan Church in Toronto, located near the corner of Richmond and York, was purchased from John Cawthra and James Leslie for 125 pounds, by Wilson Abbott and two other co-founders of the church. The intent was that the property was to be made available for the coloured people of Toronto.

5. Dorothy Shreve, *The AfriCanadian Church*, 44.

6. A.R. Abbott, as cited in the Abbott Collection.

7. *Ibid*.

8. *Ibid*.

5. THE ELGIN SETTLEMENT

1. Henry Williamson cited in Benjamin Drew, *Narratives of Fugitive Slaves*, Boston: John P. Jewett & Co., 1856; republished in (Toronto: Coles, 1981) 133–134.

2. Dorothy Shreve, *The AfriCanadian Church*, 30.

3. Presented here is a concise, very condensed chronicle of William King and the Elgin Settlement. For a complete description of the life of William King and the Elgin Settlement, refer to Victor Ullman, *Look to the North Star: A Life of William King* (Toronto: Umbrella Press, 1994).

4. King as cited in Ullman, 64.

5. Ullman, 79.

6. King as cited in Ullman, 72.

7. King as cited in Ullman, 72.

8. The fugitives who settled in the Dawn Settlement, were led by Reverend Josiah Henson. His intention was to develop the "'Education, Mental, Moral and Physical of the Colored Inhabitants of Canada, not excluding white persons and Indians' had been founded four years earlier by British Abolitionists. It was known as the British-American Institute and taught Negro crafts and trades perceived as being urgently needed in Canada, and particularly in Chatham." (Ullman, 67.)

9. *Ibid*, 84.

10. C. Peter Ripley, ed., *The Black Abolitionist Papers, Vol. 2: Canada 1830–1865* (Chapel Hill: University of North Carolina Press, 1985) 304. King believed in the intent, and indeed, the implementation of Canadian law with respect to Black immigrants. "In Upper Canada, he [King] explained, the Negro had every right accorded to white citizens. They had all the protection of the laws of the Province. They could hire layers and go to court with the assurance of equal judicial treatment. They had the right of petition to all branches of government for redress of injustices. The laws of the Province, and more important, the enforcement of those laws, was colorblind." (Ullman, 141.)

11. Attributed to William King, as cited in Ullman, 148. "The bounty hunters did not dare go 'too far into Canada, for fear of being arrested.'" Attributed to a Montreal Sheriff in response to a slave catcher's ploy.

12. Letter from A.R. Abbott to Mrs. Annie Straith Jamieson, grandniece of William King. She was collecting information for a biography entitled *William King: Friend and Champion of Slaves*, by F.A. Robinson of Toronto and published in Canada in 1925.

13. Ullman, 109.

14. Howe, 33.

15. For an excellent rendition of the history of the common and separate schools in Canada refer to Lois Sweet, *God in the Classroom: The Controversial Issue of Religion in Canada's Schools* (Toronto: McClelland & Stewart, 1997).

16. Ullman, 121.

17. The Tuskegee Institute was established in Alabama in 1881 as a high school and vocational school for Blacks. Booker T. Washington, the first President, was appointed to "take charge of what was to be a normal school for the coloured people in the little town of Tuskegee." Booker T. Washington, *Up From Slavery* (Toronto: Ryerson Press, 1967) 72.

18. As cited in the Abbott Collection. Booker T. Washington asserted that Negro interests could be best served through the acquisition of an industrial education rather than political agitation. He was strongly opposed by many Negro intellectuals for his belief that the best interests of the Negro were gained through industrial education rather than political agitation.

19. Arnold Adoff, ed., *Black on Black* (Toronto: Macmillan of Canada, 1969) 229. William Edward Burghardt DuBois (1868–1963) was a Professor of sociology, economics, history and an expert on Negro American history. He wrote many books, was the founder of the NAACP in 1909, and initiated the Pan-African Congresses of African and American Negroes to focus on social and economic problems for Black people. As a controversial spokesman, he made militant and radical attacks on all forms of economic exploitation and racial discrimination. DuBois left the United States in 1961 and died in Ghana in 1963.

20. Ullman, 120

21. *Ibid*, 124–125.

22. *Ibid*, 125

23. Dalyce Newby, *Anderson Ruffin Abbott: First Afro-Canadian Doctor* (Markham, Ont.: Fitzhenry & Whiteside, 1998) 28.

24. A.R. Abbott, as cited in the Abbott Collection.

6. BACK IN TORONTO

1. Charles Dickens, *A Tale of Two Cities*, 1859, cited in Linda Shapiro (ed.) *Yesterday's Toronto: 1870–1910* (Toronto: Coles, 1978) 2.

2. *The Globe*, December 11, 1847.

3. This corner is the site of the present day Toronto City Hall.

4. St. Patrick's Ward in 1861 was the third largest municipal riding in the city and encompassed the area of Toronto between Queen and Bloor streets, and Park Lane and Dufferin Street.

5. Daniel G. Hill, *The Freedom-Seekers: Blacks in Early Canada* (Agincourt, Ont.: The Book Society of Canada, 1981) 226.

6. Cited in the Abbott Collection. More information can be found in the Toronto City Council minutes located in the Ontario Archives.

7. *Ibid*.

8. *Ibid*.

9. Daniel G. Hill, "Negroes in Toronto: A Sociological Study of a Minority Group." Unpublished Doctoral Thesis, University of Toronto, 1960, 14.

10. George Brown was an ardent abolitionist and became the owner and editor of the *Globe* newspaper. The George Brown House on the corner of Beverley and Baldwin streets is a heritage site in Toronto.

11. Hill (1981) notes that Thomas F. Cary was an enterprising businessman who owned four ice-houses, several barbershops (one of which was located at 88 King Street West) and a bathhouse on Front Street, east of Church. He went on to co-publish the *Provincial Freeman* newspaper with his brother-in-law, Isaac S. Shadd.

12. There were fourteen women on the Ladies Committee of the Provincial Union Association.

13. Hill (1981) 187.

14. Geoffrey Blodgett, *Oberlin College: A Historical Sketch*—a pamphlet published by Oberlin College in 1988.

15. A perpetual ticket was issued for each course and served as a pass that the student would have to show and have certified each time they attended a lecture.

16. Dr. A.T. Augusta was the first Black non-Canadian to graduate in Medicine from the University of Toronto in 1860.

7. OFF TO WAR

1. Victor Ullman, *Look to the North Star* (Toronto: Umbrella Press, 1994) 116.
2. C. Peter Ripley, *The Black Abolitionist Papers, Vol. 2: Canada, 1830–1965* (Chapel Hill: University of North Carolina Press, 1985) 514.
3. Herbert M. Morris, *International Library of Negro Life and History: The History of the Negro in Medicine,* (New York: Publishers Company Inc., 1967) 36.
4. The government of the day considered poorhouses to be an efficient and inexpensive way of caring for the poor. The intention was to discourage people from seeking public assistance by forcing them to use an unpleasant mode of dwelling. The poorhouse was also known as the House of Refuge.
5. *The Provincial Freeman*, April 14, 1855.
6. Lyceum lectures were popular during the mid-nineteenth century for the purpose of providing education and entertainment to the general public in the form of lectures, debates and dramatic readings.
7. A.R. Abbott, as cited in the Abbott Collection.
8. Mike Filey, *Toronto Sun*, Saturday, February 5, 1994.
9. Mary Ann Shadd was born in Delaware, but lived in Windsor and then Chatham while publishing and editing the *Provincial Freeman*.
10. Martin R. Delany was a free Black, born in West Virginia, who became the first Black graduate in medicine from Howard University. He established a medical practice in Chatham in 1856.
11. Josiah Henson, with the support of Hiram Wilson, a Congregationalist missionary from Boston, and the Society of Friends (Quakers) in England, founded a temporary settlement and school for Black refugees near Amherstburg. Eventually the land was sold and the money sued to set up the Wilberforce Educational Institute in Chatham.
12. Dorothy Sterlying, *The Making of an Afro-American: Martin Delany, 1812–1885* (New York: Doubleday, 1971) 245.
13. A.R. Abbott, cited in the Abbott Collection.
14. W. Montague Cobb, M.D., "A Short History of Freedmen's Hospital," *Journal of the National Medical Association*, May 1962, Vol. 54, No. 3, 279.
15. A.R. Abbott, Abbott Collection.
16. The Freedmen's Hospital and Asylum was first established in 1862, the forerunner to the Howard University Hospital in the District of Columbia, and served the Black community, caring for freed, disabled, and aged Blacks. In 1863, Dr. Alexander Augusta was appointed Surgeon-in Chief and hence became the first African-American to head a hospital. In 1868 it was considered the teaching hospital of Howard University Medical School.
17. Howard University, intended for African Americans, was established in November of 1866 by Major General Oliver Otis Howard, shortly after the end of the Civil War. It opened as a theological seminary and a normal school, but later expanded to include the College of Liberal Arts, Medicine and Pharmacy, as well as the School of Law and Religion. The University charter was enacted by Congress in 1867. Initially it was funded by the Freedman's Bureau but later resorted to private and government support.
18. Abbott Collection.

19. *Ibid.*
20. *Ibid.*
21. *Ibid.*

8. DR. ABBOTT AND THE CIVIL WAR

1. Wendell Phillips, cited in G.C. Ward, R. Burns, & K. Burns, *The Civil War* (New York: Knopf, 1990) 249.
2. Steven F. Miller worked on the Freedmen and Southern Society Project at the University of Maryland and was able to provide further details regarding Camp Barker and suggested referring to a volume that he co-edited, *The Wartime Genesis of Free Labor: The Upper South*, Cambridge, 1993, series 1, volume 2 of *Freedom: A Documentary History of Emancipation.* The American Missionary Association papers, copies of which are located in Robarts Library at the University of Toronto, offer considerable correspondence from and about the Washington, DC, and northern Virginia contraband camps. (Personal correspondence with Steven F. Miller, Monday, April 19, 1994.)
3. Dr. R.O. Abbott was white and no relation to Dr. Anderson Ruffin Abbott.
4. Cobb, W. Montague. "A Short History of Freedmen's Hospital." *Journal of the National Medical Association,* Vol. 54, No. 3, May 1962, 271–287.
5. Washington F. Cursor, M.D., as cited in Charles B. Purvis, M.D. *Medical Department, Howard University* on October 30, 1899, 12. Dr. Washington was one of the eight students of the first session of the Howard Medical School. From a compilation by Hollis Gentry of the National Archives of the United States for Dalyce Newby.
6. A.R. Abbott, as cited in the Abbott Collection.
7. Leech, 253.
8. A.R. Abbott, as cited in the Abbott Collection.
9. *Ibid.*
10. *Ibid.*
11. *Ibid.*
12. Ibid
13. Ibid
14. Although Abbott describes the Shawl as "plaid," it is, in reality, a shawl with a houndstooth pattern.
15. A.R. Abbott, as cited in Abbott Collection. It is interesting that a very similar quote can be found in Elizabeth Keckley's book, *Behind the Scenes: Or, Thirty Years a Slave and Four Years in the White House* (London, UK: Oxford University Press, 1989) in which the third cane is allocated to Mr. WM. Slade, the steward of the White House, who in Mr. Lincoln's lifetime, was his messenger. This gentleman also received some of Mr. Lincoln's apparel, among which was his heavy gray shawl." (*Behind the Scenes,* 308–309.) She describes Dr. Abbott as "one of his warmest friends." See page 309.

9. THE GRAND ARMY OF THE REPUBLIC

1. A.R. Abbott, as cited in the Abbott Collection. "Grand Army Address" on May 22, 1907.

2. Memorial Day
3. Stuart McConnell, *The Grand Army of the Republic 1865–1900* (Chapel Hill: University of North Carolina Press, 1992) xiv.
4. *Ibid,* xiii.
5. *Ibid.*
6. A.R. Abbott, as cited in the Abbott Collection.
7. McConnell, 71.
8. A.R. Abbott, as cited in the Abbott Collection
9. *Ibid.*
10. *Ibid.*
11. "Lines of Canada's 64,000 Boys in Blue Fast Withering," *Toronto Sunday World*, May 31, 1914.

10. EARLY MEDICAL PRACTICE IN THE NINETEENTH CENTURY

1. From "A Young Physician" by John Greenleaf Whittier (1807–1992), an outspoken Quaker abolitionist among the poets of his generation. Cited in the Abbott Collection.
2. Thomsonian Physiomedicalism of Eclecticism became popular during the mid-1800s as an alternative method to orthodox medicine. Samuel Thompson, the founder of the movement, believed that the purpose of medicine should be to help the body heal itself. His practice of using hot baths to induce sweating and herbal regiments to purge the body of toxins was strongly opposed by the medical establishment at that time. Today, the use of naturopathy thrives as people continue to seek viable healing alternatives.
3. H.E. MacDermot, *One Hundred Years of Medicine in Canada* (Toronto: McClelland & Stewart Ltd., 1967) 208.
4. Charles M. Godfrey, M.D., *Medicine for Ontario: A History*, (Belleville, Ont.: Mika Publishing Company, 1979) 60.
5. One of the major grievances revolved around the process of licensing doctors, which of course was a necessary requirement to legally establishing a medical practice.
6. This lot, Lot 4, was located on the north side of Newgate Street (Adelaide Street). Indenture Papers, Abbott Collection.
7. Letter to the *Globe*, cited in the Abbott Collection. Not dated.

11. SETTLING DOWN

1. A.R. Abbott, "The Declaration," The Abbott Collection. A poem written to his betrothed, Mary Ann Casey.
2. Robin Winks, *The Blacks in Canada: A History* (Montreal: McGill-Queen's University Press, 1971) 288.
3. A.R. Abbott, as cited in Abbott Collection.
4. A.R. Abbott, as cited in the Abbott Collection—The first sentence of this tribute is to Mary Ann Casey.

"The Rover's Bride"
The sunset lingers in the West,
The sea-bird's gone to rest,
The evening shadows gather fast
Upon the ocean's breast...
Anderson Ruffin Abbott, Chatham, May 12, 1875.

5. A.R. Abbott, "The Declaration," in the Abbott Collection.

Oh Mary dear, I come not here
With blandishment to woo thee,
I know the secret of your heart,
I know full well you love me.
I see in your soft bright eye
What your lips concealeth
I hear it in that smothered sigh
Your chaste breath upheaveth.
With courage then I've come at last,
To tell you how I love thee,
Knowing full well you'll not refuse,
You cannot do without me.
This death to me, my Mary dear,
If you reject my love plea;
You know that love, and knowing it
You would not long survive me.
Oh! Then my darling do not pout
That coldness is all put on.
Just say the word—yes sweetest,
Go and fetch the parson.

Toronto *Globe*, November 1869, Abbott Collection.

6. "Jim Crow" refers to racial discrimination and segregation practices requiring Blacks to use separate facilities, transportation cars, seats in theatres, beaches and resorts, etc.

7. *Provincial Freeman*, 1854.

8. From personal communication with Nellie Lightfoot, 1994. Unfortunately, since the Bishop Strachan School archives do not have any records of this time period, they will have to remain part of the mystery.

9. Abbott Collection—a newspaper clipping, not dated.

10. From the Abbott Collection.

11. *Ibid.*

12. *Ibid.*

12. THE COUNTRY LIFE

1. Frederick Douglass, "West Indies Emancipation Speech of August 1857," cited in *Black on Black: Commentaries by Negro Americans*, edited by Arnold Adoff (New York: Macmillan, 1968) 1.

2. *Chatham Tri-weekly Planet*, March 8, 1860.

3. Gwen Robinson, *Seek the Truth: A Story of Chatham's Black Community* (Chatham: privately published, 1989) 4.

4. S.G. Howe, *The Refugees from Slavery in Canada West. Report to the Freedmen's Inquiry Commission* (Boston: Wright & Potter, 1864) 25. Library of Congress call number E450H5.

5. *Ibid*, 26. This was the case when Thomas Powers Casey, a coloured man, married Mary Ann Adams, a white woman and daughter of the mayor to boot!

6. *Ibid*, 26.

7. *Ibid*, 37.

8. *Ibid*, 33.

9. A.R. Abbott, as cited in the Abbott Collection.

10. *Ibid*.

11. *Ibid.* The Cow By-law.

12. *Ibid*.

13. *Ibid*.

14. At the time of publication, it was not possible to obtain names of individuals in this photo in front of the BME Church. If you are able to identify any of the individuals by name, please inform the publisher.

15. Abbott Collection.

16. A.R. Abbott, as cited in the Abbott Collection.

17. The *Voice of the Fugitive* was published by Henry Bibb from 1851 to 1853 for the benefit of the Black fugitives from the United States. Mary Ann Shadd and her brother Isaac, with early support from Samuel Ringgold Ward, published the *Provincial Freeman* from 1853 to 1858. It reiterated its motto, "Self reliance is the true road to independence" by promoting the concerns and interests of Blacks across Ontario.

18. A.R. Abbott, as cited in the Abbott Collection.

19. *Ibid*.

20. *Ibid*.

21. *Ibid*.

22. *Ibid*.

23. *Ibid*.

24. *Ibid*.

13. EDUCATION—SEPARATE BUT EQUAL?

1. Afua P. Cooper, "Black Woman Teacher Mary Bibb, " in *We're Rooted Here and They Can't Pull Us Up: Essays in African Canadian Women's History*, P. Bristow, *et al*, eds. (Toronto: University of Toronto Press, 1994) 148.

2. Lois Sweet, *God in the Classroom: The Controversial Issue of Religion in Canada's Schools* (Toronto: McClelland & Stewart, 1997) 25.

3. Robin Winks, *The Blacks in Canada: A History* (Montreal: McGill-Queen's University Press, 1971) 375.

4. A.R. Abbott, as cited in Abbott Collection.

5. Abbott Collection. Letter from Chatham published in *Missionary Messenger*, not dated.

6. A.R. Abbott, Abbott Collection.

7. Abbott Collection, "Election of public school trustees," news clipping, not dated.
8. A.R. Abbott, Abbott Collection.

14. THE POLITICAL ARENA

1. Cited in Stephen L. Hubbard, *Against All Odds* (Toronto, Dundurn Press, 1987) 38.
2. A.R. Abbott, as cited in the Abbott Collection.
3. *Ibid.*
4. *Ibid.*
5. C. Peter Ripley, (ed.), *The Black Abolitionist Papers, Canada, 1830–1965*, Vol. 2, 323.
6. In February 1901, still an ardent fan of the British monarchy, Anderson lamented the death of Queen Victoria with a poem written in her honour, part of the Abbott Collection.

　　　"'Neath the Crown and Maple Leaf"
　　　(Afro-Canadian Elegy)
　　　(first and last stanzas)
　　　A sigh is breathed from a million hearts,
　　　From Slavery's chains set free:
　　　A million tongues now sadly cry;
　　　Great Queen, we weep for thee!
　　　While Afric's sons, wherever found,
　　　In free and blest manhood,
　　　Revere the name of England's Queen,
　　　Victoria the Good.

7. A.R. Abbott, as cited in the Abbott Collection.
8. Robin Winks, *The Blacks in Canada: A History*, 212–213.
9. A.R. Abbott, as cited in the Abbott Collection.
10. George Brown was the publisher of the *Globe*, a Toronto newspaper. An abolitionist, he used his influence and financial resources to further the interests and rights of the Black community.
11. A.R. Abbott, as cited in the Abbott Collection.
12. Adam Beck, born in Baden, Ontario, became Mayor of London, Ontario, in the mid-1800s. Known as the "Father of Hydro" in Ontario, he became the first Chairman of the Hydro Commission.
13. Stephen Hubbard, "Who was William Peyton Hubbard?" *Hydroscope,* June 3, 1988, Vol. 25, No. 11.
14. Dr. Abbott was a regular contributor to the *New York Age* newspaper in New York City.
15. By A.R. Abbott, a newspaper clipping from *New York Age*, January 27, 1898.
16. The Tuskegee Black Flyers were recruited into a segregated Black contingent of U.S. Air Force pilots. They successfully completed some of the most challenging assignments during World War II.
17. A movie was made about the Tuskegee Airmen, produced by Price Enertainment Productions, Frank Price, producer.

15. THE DUNDAS YEARS

1. From the poem entitled "When All is Done," by Paul Laurence Dunbar (1872–1906).
2. Home Circle was a social gathering of fellow church members, often including a meal and musical entertainment or speaking debates. Frequently it served the purpose of introducing young people to each other as propsective spouses.
3. From a newspaper clipping in the Abbott Collection. Often A.R. Abbott penned these notices for the local newspaper, in this case, the *Dundas Banner*, not dated.
4. The Dundas Mechanics Institute, originally an English organization, was considered to be the precursor of the modern library and, in 1841, represented an early attempt to provide educational resources and opportunities for the purposes of the general public. The Mechanics Institute offered the use of books to all classes of people at a time when most would have found it impossible to afford the luxury of a personal library. Intensive debates provided a stimulating alternative to otherwise long dreary evenings, with little entertainment available. Dr. Abbott became intimately involved within the administration of the Institute, as well as on a personal level, for he was undoubtedly an addicted debater and would have revelled in the sport. The Dundas Mechanics Institute/Library was incorporated under the Ontario Public Libraries Act in 1882 and the Mechanics Institutes were gradually phased out by 1895. For a more detailed description of the Dundas Mechanics Institute refer to Dundas Public Library Archives, "Local Public Libraries had Curious Beginning," *Dundas Star*, September 20, 1941.

16. THE CHICAGO YEARS

1. St. Clair Drake, "Churches and Voluntary Associations in the Chicago Negro Community, Report of Official Project 465-54-386," conducted under the auspices of the Work Projects Administration, Horace R. Clayton, Superintendent, December, 1940, 46.
2. Since the 1850s, the city's Black population had increased thirty times, with most of the new arrivals migrating from the southern states. Although many Blacks had settled in the south end of the city, no Black ghetto was established, and the Black leaders did their best to oppose segregation.
3. St. Clair Drake, "Churches and Voluntary Associations in the Chicago Negro Community," Report of Official Project 465-54-386," 49.
4. Dalyce Newby, *Anderson Ruffin Abbott: First Afro-Canadian Doctor* (Markham, Ont: Fitzhenry & Whiteside, 1998) 110.
5. From a Chicago newspaper clipping "Successful Musical," not dated—cited in the Abbott Collection.
6. From "Plan of Organization," cited in the Abbott Collection.
7. Cook Country Hospital in Chicago remained segregated for whites only for a number of years afterwards.
8. Drake, 102.
9. R.C. Hayden, *11 African American Doctors* (Frederick, MD: Twenty-first Century Books, 1992) 194–195.
10. A man who had been involved in a barroom brawl was brought into the hospital on a gurney with a stab wound in the chest. Doctors who first saw George Cotton's injury gave him one chance in a million to live. They sent him to Williams in the

operating room. Cotton spent the next six hours in the operating room. A nurse fainted as Williams opened up his chest, sawed through his ribs and exposed the heart. In between Cotton's heartbeats, Williams sewed up the slit in the heart and closed his chest with more than 70 stitches. Daily Southtown newspaper, not dated, in the Abbott Collection.

11. Hayden, 195–196.

12. "Change at Provident." *Conservatore Chicago*, December 1894.

17. DR. ABBOTT'S PHILOSOPHY:
AN AFRICAN-CANADIAN PERSPECTIVE

1. W.E. DuBois, *The Souls of Black Folk* (New York: Simon and Schuster, 1970) 11.

2. A.R. Abbott, as cited in the Abbott Collection.

3. Abbott attended lectures on Biology given at the University of Toronto by Professor Ramsay Wright.

4. The Canadian Institute later became the Royal Canadian Institute. It had its own building, including a library and museum and it edited the *Canadian Journal*. Correspondence with Louise Herzberg, May 27, 1994

5. Louise Herzberg, while doing research for her book on William Brodie, showed me a photograph that depicts Abbott with Brodie and other members of the Natural History Society, which later became affiliated with the Canadian Institute. Correspondence, May 27, 1994.

6. A.R. Abbott on the "Amalgamation of the Races," as cited in the Abbott Collection.

7. Daniel G. Hill, 1960, 341.

8. A.R. Abbott, "Prejudice in Canada," in the Abbott Collection.

9. N. Adams, T. Causey, M. Jacobs, P. Munro, M. Quinn & Trousdale, "Womentalkin': A Reader's Theatre Performance of Teachers' Stories," *Qualitative Studies in Education*, 11 (3), 383–395, 1998: the quote is on page 395.

18. THE SEPARATION BEGINS

1. Lawrence Hill, *Black Berry, Sweet Juice: On Being Black and White in Canada* (Toronto: HarperCollins, 2001) 41.

2. Interview with Eleanore Sayre Osborne (Helene Abbott's daughter), May 24, 1991.

3. Fanny Barner, "The Colored Woman of Today" in *Godey's Magazine*, Lady's Book, Anniversary Number, Vol. 11897, The Godey Company of New York , July 1897, 29–30.

4. Compiled by Julia Davis, retired teacher from St. Louis Public School Board, not dated. Obtained from Helene's daughter, Lydia Sayre.

5. Interview with Eleanore Sayre Osborne, May 1991.

6. *Ibid.*

7. *Ibid.*

8. The Veterans Service was part of the United States Public Health Service at that time.

9. Interview with Eleanore Sayre Osborne, May 24, 1991.

10. Letter from Augustus Abbott, December 4, 1990.

11. Interview with Eleanore Sayre Osborne, May 24, 1991.

12. *Ibid.*

13. *Ibid.*

14. From the *Chicago Defender*, December 12, 1896.
15. Interview with Robert Abbott, March 22, 1995.
16. Ibid.
17. Interview with Marion Abbott Young, May 3, 2001.
18. Interview with Robert Abbott, March 22, 1995.
19. Interview with Marion Abbott Young, December 11, 1994.
20. Interview with Robert Abbott, March 22, 1995.
21. Hill, (1960), 255.

19. FADE TO BLACK

1. First verse of a poem entitled "Things to Forget," (author unknown) the author found copied in her mother's diary. She had noted this when she was a teenager and was taken by the message. The poem is shown here in its entirety. Attempts to determine its origin were unsuccessful. Author and publisher would appreciate knowing the background to this work.

    "Things to Forget"
    If you see a tall fellow ahead of a crowd,
    A leader of men, marching fearless and proud,
    And you know of a tale whose mere telling aloud
    Would cause his proud head to in anguish to bowed,
    It's a pretty good plan
    to forget it!

    If you know of a skeleton hidden away
    In a closet and guarded and kept from the day,
    In the dark; and whose showing, whose sudden display
    Would cause grief and sorrow and lifelong dismay.
    It's a pretty good plan
    to forget it!

    If you know of a thing that will darken the joy
    Of a man or a woman, a girl or a boy.
    That will wipe out a smile or the least way annoy
    A fellow, or cause any gladness to cloy.
    It's a pretty good plan
    to forget it!
    —Author Unknown
2. Letter from Abbott Sayre to Catherine Slaney, January 21, 1993.
3. Letter from Bonnie Grosnick to Catherine Slaney, March 19, 1995.
4. Lisa Roads as cited in letter from Bonnie Grosnick to Catherine Slaney, March 19. 1995.
5. Letter from Bonnie Grosnick to Catherine Slaney, March 19, 1995.
6. Letter from Kathleen Curry to Catherine Slaney, February 2, 1997.
7. Letter from Augustus Abbott to Catherine Slaney, December 4, 1990.
8. Letter from Bonnie Grosnick to Catherine Slaney, March 19, 1999.
9. Letter from Meredith Lewis to Catherine Slaney, December 14, 1992.
10. Paul Laurence Dunbar, "When All is Done," cited in the Abbott Collection and recited at the end of the eulogy for Meredith Lewis, December 31, 1993.

20. CROSSING THE COLOUR LINE

1. I.M. Young, "The Scaling of Bodies and the Politics of Identity," in I.M. Young (ed.), *Justice and the Politics of Difference* (Princeton, NJ: Princeton University Press, 1990) 99.
2. Interview with Ralph Osborne, May 24, 1991.
3. Later I realized that he must have been stationed in a segregated base and therefore it would have been obvious that he was Black, whether he looked it or not!

21. THE PASSING YEARS

1. R. McTair (ed.), *The Black Experience in the White Mind: Meditations on a Persistent Discourse* (Toronto: Coach House Books, 1995) 34.
2. Judy Scales-Trent, *Notes of a White Black Woman: Race, Color, Community* (University Park, PA: Penn State Press, 1995) 6.
3. Interview with Robert Abbott, March 22, 1995.
4. Lewis Walker and Ben C. Wilson have compiled a comprehensive history of Idlewild which includes many superb photographs in *The Idlewild Community: Black Eden* (East Lansing, MI: Michigan State University Press, 2002).
5. Interview with Eleanore Osborne, May 24, 1991.
6. Interview with Robert Abbott, March 22, 1995.
7. *Ibid.*
8. *Ibid.*
9. Letter from Bonnie Grosnick, March 19, 1995.
10. Interview with Eleanore Osborne, May 24, 1991.
11. Conversation with Marion Abbott Young and Jay Abbott, March 22, 1995.
12. Calvin W. Ruck offers detailed insight into the formation of this battalion in *The Black Battalion: 1916–1920, Canada's Best Kept Military Secret* (Halifax: Nimbus Publishing, 1987).
13. Interview with Marion Abbott Young, March 22, 1995.
14. *Ibid.*
15. *Ibid.*
16. *Ibid.*
17. *Ibid.*
18. *Ibid.*
19. A.R. Abbott, as cited in the Abbott Collection.

22. LOCATING MYSELF ON THE COLOUR LINE

1. Alice Walker, *The Temple of My Familiar* (New York: Simon and Schuster, 1990) 287.
2. Catherine Slaney, "Exploring Multiracial/cultural Identities through Mothers' Voices," M.Ed. Thesis, Brock University, 2001.

23. THE REUNIFICATION

1. Chester Himes, "Beyond the Angry Black," 1966. Cited in Dorothy Winbush Riley (ed.), *My Soul Looks Back, 'Less I Forget: A Collection of Quotations by People of Color* (New York: HarperCollins, 1993) 243.

2. The American Civil War Historical Re-enactment Society (ACWHRS) offers membership to those who enjoy reliving the past and, in particular, the Civil War. It has been claimed that an estimated 50,000 Canadians took part in the American Civil War and consequently pride and kinship prevails in their camaraderie. Such groups promote a valuable service in the form of public education and awareness of historical events. Their uniformed re-enactment events involve the acting out of various military campaigns and provide an activity in which the whole family can participate.

   Members of the 10th Louisiana Company "C" and the musical band known as Hardtack and Harmony, escorted us and played period music to honour our celebration. The inside cover of their CD notes the importance of music to the soldier as "an escape, a stress release, a form of entertainment, and a reminder of home and loved ones far away who were themselves in great danger. Many of the songs spoke about camp life, their feelings and fears, their hopes and aspirations, and the battles lost and won. It was a way of recording history in musical form." Hardtack and Harmony, 1995.

3. The original article was published in the *New York Weekly News* on October 19, 1867 (Huntington Library, San Marino, CA.) The Shawl is now housed permanently in the Textile Department of the State Historical Society of Wisconsin, in Madison, Wisconsin. My mother, not aware of the historical value of the shawl to Canadian history, had sent it to her cousin, Augustus Abbott who lived in Wisconsin, thinking that it would hold greater significance to her American relatives. Augustus did not want to acknowledge his racial identity at the time and hence donated the shawl to the museum, where it is highly prized as a Civil War momento to this day.

4. Letter from Marion Young to Catherine Slaney, December 6, 2002.
5. Letter from Wilson Abbott to Catherine Slaney, June 8, 1994.
6. Letter from Wynn Stubenvoll to Catherine Slaney, July 6, 1994.
7. Letter from Karen Rucker to Catherine Slaney, February 22, 1995.
8. Letter from Kathleen Curry to Catherine Slaney, February 2, 1997.
9. Letter from Bonnie Grosnik to Catherine Slaney, March 19, 1995.

24. MY RECONCILIATION

1. Adrienne Shadd, originally from Ormond McKague's, *Racism in Canada* (Saskatoon: Fifth House, 1991). Citation taken from www.crr.ca.
2. In 1911, only 468 Negroes were recorded in the Toronto census. By 1951 there were 1,000 Blacks enumerated in Toronto, but in 1941, a social welfare agency had reported that 4,000 to 5,000 Blacks lived in the City of Toronto. This discrepancy highlights deficiencies in the criteria of race definitions, and thus Dr. Daniel Hill concludes that varying methods of enumeration plus the divergent definitions of "Negroid" heritage contribute to the vast differences in numbers. Hill, 1960, 2.
   In 2000, the minority population of Toronto was 52% of the total. T. Rees & A. Shelton, "Anti-racist Community Based Activism: Lesson from the Past, Directions for the Future." Paper presented at the era21 conference held in Vancouver, B.C. in November 2000.
3. Henry Wadsworth Longfellow from "A Gleam of Sunshine." Taken from www.americanpoems.com/poets/longfellow/agleamof.shtml, December 2, 2002.

APPENDIX IV:
CIVIL WAR MEMOIRS FROM DR. ANDERSON ABBOTT

A. The White House Levee

1. During the early part of the Civil War, runaway slaves who sought sanctuary in the Northern encampments were regularly returned to their masters. On May 24, 1861, General Benjamin F. Butler of the Union Army refused to continue this practice and detained the refugees, designating them as "contraband." The subsequent Confiscation Act of August 6, 1861, reiterated the decision that former slaves would not be returned to masters who were at war with the United States of America. As a result, great numbers of fugitive slaves made their way to Union encampments, including the District of Columbia. Abbott and Augusta would eventually be placed in charge of such encampments. Benevolent efforts were made on the part of the citizens of Columbia, particularly amongst the women, to institute a system of social assistance for "contraband" individuals until they could settle themselves elsewhere. For further details on this topic, refer to Bruce Catton, *Reflection on the Civil War*, edited by John Leekley (Garden City, NY: Doubleday, 1981) 13.

2. From a "Personality" article in America's Civil War publication by Pasco E. First, as found in the Abbott Collection.

3. Frederick Douglass, a powerful Black orator, gained great popularity as a speaker for the slaves and regularly delivered admonishments to those who engaged in the enslavement of others. He was bent on "voicing" the experiences, thoughts and feelings of the slaves and imparting what he believed to be the truth—something that was not often possible, as slaves did not have the opportunity to do this for themselves. Even when freed, they rarely offered public narratives, as they were often illiterate or unable to articulate the true essence of their experiences.

B. On the Eve of the New York Draft Riot

4. A.R. Abbott, as cited in the Abbott Collection.

5. The New York Draft Riot occurred in response to the call to arms of all able-bodied (white) men to the Union cause. It was not well-received by the numerous poor and indigent Irish immigrants who did not want to fight for the cause of slavery. Upon reflection, some years later, Abbott notes the irony between the time when President Lincoln turned down a request to accept two Negro regiments and, a year later, faced fierce opposition to conscription.

C. A Night of Horrors

6. "Some Recollections of Lincoln's Assassination," *The Anglo-American Magazine*, May 1901. Found in the Abbott Collection.

BIBLIOGRAPHY

Abbott, Anderson Ruffin. The Abbott Collection. Toronto Public Library, (TRL) S-90.

Adoff, A., ed. *Black Out Loud*. New York: Dell, 1970.

_____. *Black on Black: Commentaries by Negro Americans*. New York: Macmillan, 1969.

Angle, P.M. *The Lincoln Reader*. Scranton, PA: Rutgers, 1947.

Balsiger, D., & C.E. Sellier, Jr. *The Lincoln Conspiracy*. Los Angeles: Schick Sunn Classic Books, 1977.

Berlin, I., J.R. Reidy & L.S. Rowland. *Freedom: Series II. The Black Military Experience*. Toronto: University of Toronto Press.

Bernard, J. *Journey Toward Freedom: The Story of Sojourner Truth*. New York: Grosset & Dunlap, 1967.

Billingsley, A. *Climbing Jacob's Ladder: The Enduring Legacy of African-American Families*. New York: Simon & Schuster, 1992.

Bishop, J. *The Day Lincon was Shot*. New York: Harper, 1955.

Blauner, B. *Black Lives, White Lives: Three Decades of Race Relations in America*. Los Angeles: University of California Press, 1989.

Blodgett, G. "Oberlin College: A Historical Sketch." Oberlin College, Ohio, 1988.

Brooks, T. & R. Trueman. *Anxious for a Little War: The Involvement of Canadians in the Civil War of the United States*. North York: WWEC, 1993.

"A Toronto Chronology in Outline." Toronto: The Society of Heritage Associates, February 1994.

Cobb, W. M. "A Short History of Freedmen's Hospital." *Journal of the National Medical Association*, Vol. 54, No. 3, May 1962.

Coles, R. *The South Goes North*. Boston: Little, Brown & Co., 1971.

Crook, B. & C.R. Crook. *Famous Firsts in Medicine*. New York: G.P. Putnam & Sons, 1974.

Degler, C.N. *Out of Our Past: Forces That Shaped Modern America*. New York: Harper & Row, 1959.

Doane, G. & J.B. Bell. *Searching for Your Ancestors: The How and Why of Genealogy*. 5th edition revised. Toronto: Bantam Books, 1982.

Douglass, F. *The Life and Times of Frederick Douglass*. New York: Collier Books, 1962. (Reprinted from revised edition of 1892.)

Drake, S.C. "Churches and Boundary Associations in the Chicago Negro Community," Report of Official Project 465-54-3-386 under the Work Projects Administration, 1940.

Dubois, W.E.B. *The Souls of Black Folk*. New York: Avon Books, 1965.

_____. *Black Folk Then and Now*. New York: Holt, Rinehart & Winston, 1939.

_____, *Black Reconstruction in America, 1860–1880*. (1935). Reprint, Cleveland: Meridian, 1962.

Elliott, L., ed. *The Bibliography of Literary Writings by Blacks in Canada*. Toronto: Williams-Wallace, 1986.

Fanon, F. *The Wretched of the Earth*. New York: Grove Press, 1968.

Farrell, J.K.A. "History of the Negro Community in Chatham, Ont. 1787–1885." Unpublished Ph.D.thesis, Univeristy of Ottawa.

Filey, M. *Toronto Sun*, February 5, 1994.

Foner, E. *Reconstruction: America's Unfinished Revolution, 1863–1877. New York: Harper & Row, 1988*.

Foster, C. *A Place Called Heaven. The Meaning of Being Black in Canada*. Toronto: Harper-Collins, 1996.

Fox-Genovese, E. *Within the Plantation Household.Black and White Women of the Old South*. Chapel Hill: University of North Carolina Press, 1988.

Furnas, J.C. *Goodbye to Uncle Tom*. New York: William Sloane, 1956.

Godfrey, C. *Medicine for Ontario*. Belleville, ON: Mika, 1979.

Graham, S. *The Story of Phillis Wheatley: A Poetess of the American Revolution*. New York: Washington Square Press, 1970.

Green, E. "Upper Canada's Black Defenders." Ontario Historical Society, 27.

Greenwood, V. *The Researcher's Guide to American Genealogy*. Baltimore: Genealogical Publishing, 1976.

Hare, N. *The Black Anglo-Saxons*. Chicago: Third World Press, 1991.

Hayden, R.C. *11 African American Doctors*. New York: Twenty-First Century Books, 1992.

Hayman, L. *The Death of Lincoln*. Richmond Hill, ON: Scholastic, 1968.

Henry, K. *Black Politics in Toronto since World War I*. Toronto: Multicultural History Society of Ontario, 1981.

Hill, Daniel G. *The Freedom-Seekers: Blacks in Early Canada*. Agincourt, ON: The Book Society of Canada, 1981.

_____. "Black History Research Collection," Toronto "A" file, Archives of Ontario, July 1940.

_____. "Negroes in Toronto: A Sociological Study of a Minority Group." Unpublished Doctoral Thesis, University of Toronto, 1960.

Hill, L. *Trials and Triumphs: The Story of African-Canadians*. Toronto: Umbrella Press, 1993.

Hopkins, L.B. *Important Dates in Afro-American History*. New York: Franklin Watts, 1969.

Howe, S.G. *The Refugees from Slavery in Canada West: Freedmen's Inquiry Commission Report*. Boston: Wright & Porter, 1864.

Hubbard, S. "Who was William Peyton Hubbard?" *Hydroscope*, Vol 24, No.II. June 3, 1988.

Hubbard, S. *Against All Odds*. Toronto: Dundurn Press, 1987.

Hughes, L., M. Meltzer, C.E. Lincoln & J.M. Spencer. *A Pictorial History of African Americans, Black Americans, Wherever in America, From 1619 to the Present*. New York: Crown Publishers, 1995.

James, C.L.R. *The Black Jacobins: Toussaint L'Ouverture and the San Domingo Revolution*. New York: Random House, 1963.

Johnson, J.W. *The Autobiography of an Ex-Colored Man: From Three Negro Classics*. New York: Avon, 1965.

July, R.W. *A History of the African People*. New York: Charles Scribner's Sons, 1970.

Kent County Land Records (Raleigh Township). Raleigh Township Centennial Museum, North Buxton, ON.

Kyte, E.C., ed. *Old Toronto. A Selection of Excerpts from Landmarks of Toronto by John Ross Robertson*. Toronto: Macmillan, 1954.

Landon, F. "Manuscripts and Notes." Private Collection. London, Ontario.

Leech, M. *Reveille in Washington 1860–1865*. New York: Garden City, 1945.

Litwack, L.F. *Been in the Storm So Long*. New York: Knopf, 1979.

Lower, A.R.M. *Colony to Nation*. Toronto: Longmans, Green & Co., 1946.

MacDermot, H.E. *One Hundred Years of Medicine in Canada*. Toronto: McClelland & Stewart, 1967.

McConnell, S. *The Grand Army of the Republic 1865–1900*. Chapel Hill: University of North Carolina Press, 1992.

Marciniak, E. "Speech Program for Integrating Negro Physicians on Hospital Staffs in Chicago." Copy of speech, Chicago, October 19, 1965.

Medley, K.W. "The Sad Story of How 'Separate But Equal' Was Born." *Smithsonian Magazine*, February, 1994.

Miller, S.R. "Freedmen and Southern Society Project." College Park: University of Maryland, Correspondence papers.

Milton, G.F. *Abraham Lincoln and the Fifth Column*. New York: Collier, 1962.

National Archives, Washington. Compiled Military Service Records, Pension File, letterbooks and order books from the regiment, Personal Papers, Surgeons and Medical Officers.

Ortiz, V. *Sojourner Truth: A Self-Made Woman*. Philadelphia and New York: J.B. Lippincott, 1974.

Petry, A. *Harriet Tubman, Conductor on the Underground Railroad*. New York: Washington Square Press, 1971.

Pine, L.G. *Trace Your Family History*. Teach Yourself Books. Sevenoaks: Hodder and Stoughton, 1984.

Power, M. & N. Butler. "Slavery and Freedom in Niagara." Niagara-on-the-Lake: The Niagara Historical Society, 1993.

Randall, R.P. *Mary Lincoln: Biography of a Marriage*. Boston: Little, Brown & Co., 1953.

Ripley, C. Peter, ed. *The Black Abolitionist Papers. Vol 2: Canada, 1830–1965*. Chapel Hill: University of North Carolina Press, 1985.

Robinson, G. *Seek the Truth*. Chatham, ON: privately published, 1989.

Ruck, C.W. *The Black Battalion, 1916–1920: Canada's Best Kept Military Secret*. Halifax: Nimbus, 1987.

Sadlier, Rosemary. *Tubman: Harriet Tubman and the Underground Railroad*. Toronto: Umbrella Press, 1997.

Spear, A.H. *Black Chicago: The Making of a Negro Ghetto*. Chicago: University of Chicago Press, 1967.

Sterling, D. *The Making of an Afro-American: Martin Robinson Delany, 1812–1885*. New York: Doubleday, 1971.

Stowe, Harriet Beecher. *Uncle Tom's Cabin*. Boston: Houghton, Mifflin and Company, 1883.

Styron, W. *The Confessions of Nat Turner*. New York: Random House, 1968.

Streve, D.S. *The AfriCanadian Church: A Stabilizer*. Jordan Station: Paideia, 1983.

Stutesman, J.H. *Some Watkin Family Members and Some of Their Kin*. Baltimore: Gateway Press, 1989.

Scales-Trent, Judy. *Notes of a White Black Woman: Race, Color, Community*. University Park, PA: Pennsylvania State University Press, 1995.

Scott, J.A. *Hard Trials on my Way*. New York: New American Library, 1974.

Sweet, Lois. *God in the Classroom*. Toronto: McClelland & Stewart, 1997.

Talbot, C. *Growing up Black in Canada*. Toronto: Williams-Wallace, 1984.

Tanser, H.A. "Settlement of Negroes in Kent County, Ontario." Report published in Chatham, Ontario, 1939.

Tullock, H. *Black Canadians: A Long Line of Fighters*. Toronto: NC Press, 1975.

Ullman, V. *Look to the North Star*. Toronto: Umbrella Press, 1994.

Walker, A. *The Temple of My Familiar*. New York: Simon & Schuster, 1990.

Walker, J.W. *Racial Discrimination in Canada: The Black Experience*. Ottawa: Canadian Historical Association, 1985.

_____. *The West Indians in Canada*. Ottawa: Canadian Historical Association and Multiculturalism Program, Government of Canada, 1984.

Ward, G.C., R. Burns & K. Burns. *The Civil War*. New York: Knopf, 1990.

Washington, Booker T. *Up From Slavery*. New York: Airmont, 1967.

Winks, Robin W. *The Blacks in Canada: A History*. Montreal: McGill-Queen's University Press, 1971.

INDEX

236

ABOUT THE AUTHOR

CATHERINE SLANEY WAS BORN in Toronto, Ontario, in 1951 to "white" parents. She presently lives in Georgetown, Ontario, with her family and, so far, has been blessed with five children and ten grandchildren. Her life is very full as she has been a full-time professor at Sheridan College for twenty-five years, teaching in the field of Animal Science and Ethics and, in her spare time, judging horse shows and grooming dogs.

Catherine developed an interest in Black history quite by accident when, in 1990, she decided to investigate a little family genealogy and came across the stories of her Black ancestors. Her curiosity led her across the continent as she contacted distant cousins in an effort to seek the truth, for it quickly became apparent that certain family secrets had slipped out of reach. It became a personal quest for her to find a means to explain why some of her ancestors found it necessary pass as white.

Today she is able to share the many experiences of a very special family that now includes all shades of colour and yet are all related in blood. Although they are scattered across North America, they appear to retain some indefinable quality that connects them as family and thus their initial reunion became the first step in breaking down the barriers and revealing the family secrets.

Currently Catherine is pursuing a Doctorate Degree in Sociology and Equity Studies in Education at the Ontario Institute for Educational Studies at the University of Toronto (OISE/UT), where her current study focuses on racial/cultural identity, assimilation and the practice of passing.